The Be.

The Best Book of

ANIMAL STORIES

including

THE NATURAL HISTORY

OF THE TEN COMMANDMENTS

by

Ernest Seton Thompson

Ashgrove Publishing
London

To the Preservation of Our Wild Creatures

Ernest Seton Thompson

Contents

LOBO
The King of Currumpaw
– 7 –

RAGGYLUG
The Story of a Cottontail Rabbit
– 23 –

THE SPRINGFIELD FOX
– 45 –

THE BIOGRAPHY OF A GRIZZLY
– 61 –

A STREET TROUBADOUR
Being the Adventures of a Cock Sparrow
– 99 –

WULLY
The Story of a Yaller Dog
– 111 –

TITO:
The Story of the Coyote that Learned How
– 123 –

JOHNNY BEAR
– 159 –

THE PACING MUSTANG
– 177 –

THE WINNIPEG WOLF
– 197 –

BINGO
The Story of My Dog
– 211 –

THE NATURAL HISTORY
OF THE TEN COMMANDMENTS
– 227 –

LOBO

The King of Currumpaw

I

Currumpaw is a vast cattle range in northern New Mexico. It is a land of rich pastures and teeming flocks and herds, a land of rolling mesas and precious running waters that at length unite in the Currumpaw River, from which the whole region is named. And the king whose despotic power was felt over its entire extent was an old grey wolf.

Old Lobo, or the king, as the Mexicans called him, was the gigantic leader of a remarkable pack of grey wolves, that had ravaged the Currumpaw Valley for a number of years. All the shepherds and ranchmen knew him well, and, wherever he appeared with his trusty band, terror reigned supreme among the cattle, and wrath and despair among their owners. Old Lobo was a giant among wolves, and was cunning and strong in proportion to his size. His voice at night was well-known and easily distinguished from that of any of his fellows. An ordinary wolf might howl half the night about the herdsman's bivouac without attracting more than a passing notice, but when the deep roar of the old king came booming down the canyon, the watcher bestirred himself and prepared to learn in the morning that fresh and serious inroads had been made among the herds.

Old Lobo's band was but a small one. This I never quite understood, for usually, when a wolf rises to the position and power that he had, he attracts a numerous following. It may be that he had as many as he desired, or perhaps his ferocious temper prevented the increase of his pack. Certain is it that Lobo had only five followers during the latter part of his reign. Each of these, however, was a wolf of renown, most of them were above the ordinary size, one in particular, the second in command, was a veritable giant, but even he was far below the leader in size and prowess. Several of the band, besides the two leaders, were especially noted. One of those was a beautiful white wolf, that the Mexicans called Blanca; this was supposed to be a female, possibly Lobo's mate. Another was a yellow wolf of remarkable swiftness, which, according to current stories, had, on several occasions, captured an antelope for the pack.

It will be seen, then, that these wolves were thoroughly well-known to the cowboys and shepherds. They were frequently seen and oftener heard, and their lives were intimately associated with those of the cattlemen, who would so gladly have destroyed them. There was not a stockman on the Currumpaw who would not readily have given the value of many steers for the scalp of any one of Lobo's band, but they seemed to possess charmed lives, and defied all manner of devices to kill them. They scorned all hunters, derided all poisons, and continued, for at least five years, to exact their tribute from the Currumpaw ranchers to the extent, many said, of a cow each day. According to this estimate, therefore, the band had killed more than two thousand of the finest stock, for, as was only too well-known, they selected the best in every instance.

The old idea that a wolf was constantly in a starving state, and therefore ready to eat anything, was as far as possible from the truth in this case, for these freebooters were always sleek and well-conditioned, and were in fact most fastidious about what they ate. Any animal that had died from natural causes, or that was diseased or tainted, they would not touch, and they even rejected anything that had been killed by the stockmen. Their choice and daily food was the tenderer part of a freshly killed yearling heifer. An old bull or cow they disdained, and though they occasionally took a young calf or colt, it was quite clear that veal or horseflesh was not their favourite diet. It was also known that they were not fond of mutton, although they often amused themselves by killing sheep. One night in November, 1893, Blanca and the yellow wolf killed two hundred and fifty sheep, apparently for the fun of it, and did not eat an ounce of their flesh.

These are examples of many stories which I might repeat, to show the ravages of this destructive band. Many new devices for their extinction were tried each year, but still they lived and throve in spite of all the efforts of their foes. A great price was set on Lobo's head, and in consequence poison in a score of subtle forms was put out for him, but he never failed to detect and avoid it. One thing only he feared – that was firearms, and knowing full well that all men in this region carried them, he never was known to attack or face a human being. Indeed, the set policy of his band was to take refuge in flight whenever, in the daytime, a man was descried, no matter at what distance. Lobo's habit of permitting the pack to eat only that which they themselves had killed, was in numerous cases their salvation, and the keenness of his scent to detect the taint of human hands or the poison itself, completed their immunity.

On one occasion, one of the cowboys heard the too familiar rallying-cry of Old Lobo, and stealthily approaching, he found the Currumpaw pack in a hollow, where they had 'rounded up' a small herd of cattle. Lobo sat apart on a knoll, while Blanca with the rest was endeavouring to 'cut out' a young cow, which they had selected; but the cattle were standing in a compact mass with their heads outward, and presented to the foe a line of horns, unbroken save when some cow, frightened by a fresh onset of the wolves, tried to retreat into the middle of the herd. It was only by taking advantage of these breaks that the wolves had succeeded at all in wounding the selected cow, but she was far from being disabled, and it seemed that Lobo at length lost patience with his followers, for he left his position on the hill, and, uttering a deep roar, dashed toward the herd. The terrified rank broke at his charge, and he sprang in among them. Then the cattle scattered like the pieces of a bursting bomb. Away went the chosen victim, but ere she had gone twenty-five yards Lobo was upon her. Seizing her by the neck he suddenly held back with all his force and so threw her heavily to the ground. The shock must have been tremendous, for the heifer was thrown heels over head. Lobo also turned a somersault, but immediately recovered himself, and his followers falling on the poor cow, killed her in a few seconds. Lobo took no part in the killing – after having thrown the victim, he seemed to say, 'Now, why could not some of you have done that at once without wasting so much time?'

The man now rode up shouting, the wolves as usual retired, and he, having a bottle of strychnine, quickly poisoned the carcass in three places, then went away, knowing they would return to feed, as they had killed the animals themselves. But next morning, on going to look for his expected victims, he found that, although the wolves had eaten the heifer, they had carefully cut out and thrown aside all those parts that had been poisoned.

The dread of this great wolf spread yearly among the ranchmen, and each year a larger price was set on his head, until at last it reached $1,000, an unparalleled wolf-bounty, surely; many a good man has been hunted down for less. Tempted by the promised reward, a Texan ranger named Tannerey came one day galloping up the canyon of the Currumpaw. He had a superb outfit for wolf-hunting – the best of guns and horses, and a pack of enormous wolf-hounds. Far out on the plains of the Panhandle, he and his dogs had killed many a wolf, and now he never doubted that, within a few days, old Lobo's scalp would dangle at his saddle-bow.

Away they went bravely on their hunt in the grey dawn of a summer morning, and soon the great dogs gave joyous tongue to say that they were already on the track of their quarry. Within two miles, the grizzly band of Currumpaw leaped into view, and the chase grew fast and furious. The part of the wolf-hounds was merely to hold the wolves at bay till the hunter could ride up and shoot them, and this usually was easy on the open plains of Texas; but here a new feature of the country came into play, and showed how well Lobo had chosen his range; for the rocky canyons of the Currumpaw and its tributaries intersect the prairies in every direction. The old wolf at once made for the nearest of these and by crossing it got rid of the horsemen. His band then scattered and thereby scattered the dogs, and when they reunited at a distant point of course all of the dogs did not turn up, and the wolves, no longer outnumbered, turned on their pursuers and killed or desperately wounded them all. That night when Tannerey mustered his dogs, only six of them returned, and of these, two were terribly lacerated. This hunter made two other attempts to capture the royal scalp, but neither of them was more successful than the first, and on the last occasion his best horse met its death by a fall; so he gave up the chase in disgust and went back to Texas, leaving Lobo more than ever the despot of the region.

Next year, two other hunters appeared, determined to win the promised bounty. Each believed he could destroy this noted wolf, the first by means of a newly devised poison, which was to be laid out in an entirely new manner; the other a French Canadian, by poison assisted with certain spells and charms, for he firmly believed that Lobo was a veritable 'loup-garou', and could not be killed by ordinary means. But cunningly compounded poisons, charms, and incantations were all of no avail against this grizzly devastator. He made his weekly rounds and daily banquets as aforetime, and before many weeks had passed, Calone and Laloche gave up in despair and went elsewhere to hunt.

In the spring of 1893, after his unsuccessful attempt to capture Lobo, Joe Calone had a humiliating experience, which seems to show that the big wolf simply scorned his enemies, and had absolute confidence in himself. Calone's farm was on a small tributary of the Currumpaw, in a picturesque canyon, and among the rocks of this very canyon, within a thousand yards of the house, old Lobo and his mate selected their den and raised their family that season. There they lived all summer, and killed Joe's cattle, sheep, and dogs, but laughed at all his poisons and traps, and rested securely among the recesses of the cavernous cliffs, while Joe vainly racked his brain for some method of smoking them out, or of reaching them with dynamite. But they escaped entirely unscathed, and continued their ravages as before. 'There's where he lived all last summer,' said Joe, pointing to the face of the cliff, 'and I couldn't do a thing with him. I was like a fool to him.'

II

This history, gathered so far from the cowboys, I found hard to believe until, in the fall of 1893, I made the acquaintance of the wily marauder, and at length came to know him more thoroughly than anyone else. Some years before, in the Bingo days, I had been a wolf-hunter, but my occupations since then had been of another sort, chaining me to stool and desk. I was much in need of a change, and when a friend, who was also a ranch-owner on the Currumpaw, asked me to come to New Mexico and try if I could do anything with this predatory pack, I accepted the invitation and, eager to make the acquaintance of its king, was as soon as possible among the mesas of that region. I spent some time riding about to learn the country, and at intervals, my guide would point to the skeleton of a cow to which the hide still adhered, and remark, 'That's some of his work.'

It became quite clear to me that, in this rough country, it was useless to think of pursuing Lobo with hounds and horses, so that poison or traps were the only available expedients.

At present we had no traps large enough, so I set to work with poison.

I need not enter into the details of a hundred devices that I employed to circumvent this 'loup-garou'; there was no combination of strychnine, arsenic, cyanide, or prussic acid, that I did not essay; there was no manner of flesh that I did not try as bait; but morning after morning, as I rode forth to learn the result, I found that all my efforts had been useless. The old king was too cunning for me. A single instance will show his wonderful sagacity. Acting on the hint of an old trapper, I melted some cheese together with the kidney fat of a freshly killed heifer, stewing it in a china dish, and cutting it with a bone knife to avoid the taint of metal. When the mixture was cool, I cut it into lumps, and making a hole in one side of each lump, I inserted a large dose of strychnine and cyanide, contained in a capsule that was impermeable by any odour; finally I sealed the holes up with pieces of the cheese itself. During the whole process, I wore a pair of gloves steeped in the hot blood of the heifer, and even avoided breathing on the baits. When all was ready, I put them in a raw-hide bag rubbed all over with blood, and rode forth dragging the liver and kidneys of the beef at the end of a rope. With this I made a ten-mile circuit, dropping a bait at each quarter of a mile, and taking the utmost care, always, not to touch any with my hands.

Lobo, generally, came into this part of the range in the early part of each week, and passed the latter part, it was supposed, around the base of Sierra Grande. This was Monday, and that same evening, as we were about to retire, I heard the deep bass howl of his majesty. On hearing it one of the boys briefly remarked, 'There he is, we'll see.'

The next morning I went forth, eager to know the result. I soon came on the fresh trail of the robbers, with Lobo in the lead – his track was always easily distinguished. An ordinary wolf's forefoot is 4 1/2 inches long, that of a large wolf 4 3/4 inches, but Lobo's, as measured a number of times, was 5 1/2 inches from claw to heel; I afterward found that his other proportions were commensurate, for he stood three feet high at the shoulder, and weighed 150 pounds. His trail, therefore, though obscured by those of his followers, was never difficult to trace. The pack had soon found the track of my drag, and as usual followed it. I could see that Lobo had come to the first bait, sniffed about it, and had finally picked it up.

Then I could not conceal my delight. 'I've got him at last,' I exclaimed; 'I shall find him stark within a mile,' and I galloped on with eager eyes fixed on the great broad track in the dust. It led me to the second bait and that also was gone. How I exulted – I surely have him now and perhaps several of his band. But there was the broad paw-mark still on the drag; and though I stood in the stirrup and scanned the plain I saw nothing that looked like a dead wolf. Again I followed – to find now that the third bait was gone – and the king-wolf's track led on to the fourth, there to learn that he had not really taken a bait at all, but had merely carried them in his mouth. Then having piled the three on the fourth, he scattered filth over them to express his utter contempt for my devices. After this he left my drag and went about his business with the pack he guarded so effectively.

This is only one of many similar experiences which convinced me that poison would never avail to destroy this robber, and though I continued to use it while awaiting the arrival of the traps, it was only because it was meanwhile a sure means of killing many prairie wolves and other destructive vermin.

About this time there came under my observation an incident that will illustrate Lobo's diabolic cunning. These wolves had at least one pursuit which was merely an amusement, it was stampeding and killing sheep, though they rarely ate them. The sheep are usually kept in flocks of from one thousand to three thousand under one or more shepherds. At night they are gathered in the most sheltered place available, and a herdsman sleeps on each side of the flock to give additional protection. Sheep are such senseless creatures that they are liable to be stampeded by the veriest trifle, but they have deeply ingrained in their nature one, and perhaps only one, strong weakness, namely, to follow their leader. And this the shepherds turn to good account by putting half a dozen goats in the flock of sheep. The latter recognize the superior intelligence of their bearded cousins, and when a night alarm occurs they crowd around them, and usually, are thus saved from a stampede and are easily protected. But it was not always so. One night late in last November, two Perico shepherds were aroused by an onset of wolves. Their flocks huddled around the goats, which being neither fools nor cowards, stood their ground and were bravely defiant; but alas for them, no common wolf was heading this attack. Old Lobo, the weir-wolf, knew as well as the shepherds that the goats were the moral force of the flock, so hastily running over the backs of the densely packed sheep, he fell on these leaders, slew them all in a few minutes, and soon had the luckless sheep stampeding in a thousand different directions. For weeks afterward I was almost daily accosted by some anxious shepherd, who asked, 'Have you seen any stray OTO sheep lately?' and usually I was obliged to say I had; one day it was, 'Yes, I came on some five or six carcasses by Diamond Springs;'

or another, it was to the effect that I had seen a small 'bunch' running on the Malpai Mesa; or again, 'No, but Juan Meira saw about twenty, freshly killed, on the Cedra Monte two days ago.'

At length the wolf traps arrived, and with two men I worked a whole week to get them properly set out. We spared no labour or pains, I adopted every device I could think of that might help to insure success. The second day after the traps arrived, I rode around to inspect, and soon came upon Lobo's trail running from trap to trap. In the dust I could read the whole story of his doings that night. He had trotted along in the darkness, and although the traps were so carefully concealed, he had instantly detected the first one. Stopping the onward march of the pack, he had cautiously scratched around it until he had disclosed the trap, the chain, and the log, then left them wholly exposed to view with the trap still unsprung, and passing on he treated over a dozen traps in the same fashion. Very soon I noticed that he stopped and turned aside as soon as he detected suspicious signs on the trail, and a new plan to outwit him at once suggested itself. I set the traps in the form of an H; that is, with a row of traps on each side of the trail, and one on the trail for the cross-bar of the H. Before long, I had an opportunity to count another failure. Lobo came trotting along the trail, and was fairly between the parallel lines before he detected the single trap in the trail, but he stopped in time, and why and how he knew enough I cannot tell; the Angel of the wild things must have been with him, but without turning an inch to the right or left, he slowly and cautiously backed on his own tracks, putting each paw exactly in its old track until he was off the dangerous ground. Then returning at one side he scratched clods and stones with his hind feet till he had sprung every trap. This he did on many other occasions, and although I varied my methods and redoubled my precautions, he was never deceived, his sagacity seemed never at fault, and he might have been pursuing his career of rapine today, but for an unfortunate alliance that proved his ruin and added his name to the long list of heroes who, unassailable when alone, have fallen through the indiscretion of a trusted ally.

III

Once or twice, I had found indications that everything was not quite right in the Currumpaw pack. There were signs of irregularity, I thought; for instance there was clearly the trail of a smaller wolf running ahead of the leader, at times, and this I could not understand until a cowboy made a remark which explained the matter.

'I saw them today,' he said, 'and the wild one that breaks away is Blanca.' Then the truth dawned upon me, and I added, 'Now, I know that Blanca is a she-wolf, because were a he-wolf to act thus, Lobo would kill him at once.'

This suggested a new plan. I killed a heifer, and set one or two rather obvious traps about the carcass. Then cutting off the head, which is considered useless offal, and quite beneath the notice of a wolf, I set it a little apart and around it placed six powerful steel traps properly deodourized and concealed with the utmost care.

During my operations I kept my hands, boots, and implements smeared with fresh blood, and afterward sprinkled the ground with the same, as though it had flowed from the head; and when the traps were buried in the dust I brushed the place over with the skin of a coyote, and with a foot of the same animal made a number of tracks over the traps. The head was so placed that there was a narrow passage between it and some tussocks, and in this passage I buried two of my best traps, fastening them to the head itself.

Wolves have the habit of approaching every carcass they get the wind of, in order to examine it, even when they have no intention of eating it, and I hoped that this habit would bring the Currumpaw pack within reach of my latest stratagem. I did not doubt that Lobo would detect my handiwork about the meat, and prevent the pack approaching it, but I did build some hopes on the head, for it looked as though it had been thrown aside as useless.

Next morning, I sallied forth to inspect the traps, and there, oh, joy! were the tracks of the pack, and the place where the beef-head and its traps had been was empty. A hasty study of the trail showed that Lobo had kept the pack from approaching the meat, but one, a small wolf, had evidently gone on to examine the head as it lay apart and had walked right into one of the traps.

We set out on the trail, and within a mile discovered that the hapless wolf was Blanca. Away she went, however, at a gallop, and although encumbered by the beef-head, which weighed over fifty pounds, she speedily distanced my companion who was on foot. But we overtook her when she reached the rocks, for the horns of the cow's head became caught and held her fast. She was the handsomest wolf I had ever seen. Her coat was in perfect condition and nearly white.

She turned to fight, and raising her voice in the rallying cry of her race, sent a long howl rolling over the canyon. From far away upon the mesa came a deep response, the cry of Old Lobo. That was her last call, for now we had closed in on her, and all her energy and breath were devoted to combat.

Then followed the inevitable tragedy, the idea of which I shrank from afterward more than at the time. We each threw a lasso over the neck of the doomed wolf, and strained our horses in opposite directions until the blood burst from her mouth, her eyes glazed, her limbs stiffened and then fell limp. Homeward then we rode, carrying the dead wolf, and exulting over this, the first death-blow we had been able to inflict on the Currumpaw pack.

At intervals during the tragedy, and afterward as we rode homeward, we heard the roar of Lobo as he wandered about on the distant mesas, where he seemed to be searching for

Blanca. He had never really deserted her, but knowing that he could not save her, his deep-rooted dread of firearms had been too much for him when he saw us approaching. All that day we heard him wailing as he roamed in his quest, and I remarked at length to one of the boys, 'Now, indeed, I truly know that Blanca was his mate.'

As evening fell he seemed to be coming toward the home canyon, for his voice sounded continually nearer. There was an unmistakable note of sorrow in it now. It was no longer the loud, defiant howl, but a long, plaintive wail: 'Blanca! Blanca!' he seemed to call. And as night came down, I noticed that he was not far from the place where we had overtaken her. At length he seemed to find the trail, and when he came to the spot where we had killed her, his heart-broken wailing was piteous to hear. It was sadder than I could possibly have believed. Even the stolid cowboys noticed it, and said they had 'never heard a wolf carry on like that before'. He seemed to know exactly what had taken place, for her blood had stained the place of her death.

Then he took up the trail of the horses and followed it to the ranch-house. Whether in hopes of finding her there, or in quest of revenge, I know not, but the latter was what he found, for he surprised our un-fortunate watchdog outside and tore him to little bits within fifty yards of the door. He evidently came alone this time, for I found but one trail next morning, and he had galloped about in a reckless manner that was very unusual with him. I had half expected this, and had set a number of additional traps about the pasture. Afterward I found that he had in-deed fallen into one of these, but such was his strength, he had torn himself loose and cast it aside.

I believed that he would continue in the neighbourhood until he found her body at least, so I concentrated all my energies on this one enterprise of catching him before he left the region, and while yet in this reckless mood. Then I realized what a mistake I had made in killing Blanca, for by using her as a decoy I might have secured him the next night.

I gathered in all the traps I could command, one hundred and thirty strong steel wolf-traps, and set them in fours in every trail that led into the canyon; each trap was separately fastened to a log, and each log was separately buried. In burying them, I carefully removed the sod and every particle of earth that was lifted we put in blankets, so that after the sod was replaced and all was finished the eye could detect no trace of human handiwork. When the traps were concealed I trailed the body of poor Blanca over each place, and made of it a drag that circled all about the ranch, and finally I took off one of her paws and made with it a line of tracks over each trap. Every precaution and device known to me I used, and retired at a late hour to await the result.

Once during the night I thought I heard Old Lobo, but was not sure of it. Next day I rode around, but darkness came on before I completed the circuit of the north canyon, and I had nothing to report. At supper one of the cowboys said, 'There was a great row among the cattle in the north canyon this morning, maybe there is something in the traps there.' It was afternoon of the next day before I got to the place referred to, and as I drew near a great grizzly form arose from the ground, vainly endeavouring to escape, and there revealed before me stood Lobo, King of the Currumpaw, firmly held in the traps. Poor old hero, he had never ceased to search for his darling, and when he found the trail her body had made he followed it recklessly, and so fell into the snare prepared for him. There he lay in the iron grasp of all four traps, perfectly helpless, and all around him were numerous tracks showing how the cattle had gathered about him to insult the fallen despot, without daring to approach within his reach. For two days and two nights he had lain there, and now was worn out with struggling. Yet, when I went near him, he rose up with bristling mane and raised his voice, and for the last time made the canyon reverberate with his deep bass roar, a call for help, the muster call of his band. But there was none to answer him, and, left alone in his extremity, he whirled about with all his strength and made a desperate effort to get at me. All in vain, each trap was a dead drag of over three hundred pounds, and in their relentless fourfold grasp, with great steel jaws on every foot, and the heavy logs and chains all entangled together, he was absolutely powerless. How his huge ivory tusks did grind on those cruel chains, and when I ventured to touch him with my rifle-barrel he left grooves on it which are there to this day. His eyes glared green with hate and fury, and his jaws snapped with a hollow 'chop,' as he vainly endeavoured to reach me and my trembling horse. But he was worn out with hunger and struggling and loss of blood, and he soon sank exhausted to the ground.

Something like compunction came over me, as I prepared to deal out to him that which so many had suffered at his hands.

'Grand old outlaw, hero of a thousand lawless raids, in a few minutes you will be but a great load of carrion. It cannot be otherwise.'

Then I swung my lasso and sent it whistling over his head. But not so fast; he was yet far from being subdued, and, before the supple coils had fallen on his neck he seized the noose and, with one fierce chop, cut through its hard thick strands, and dropped it in two pieces at his feet.

Of course I had my rifle as a last resource, but I did not wish to spoil his royal hide, so I galloped back to the camp and returned with a cowboy and a fresh lasso. We threw to our victim a stick of wood which he seized in his teeth, and before he could relinquish it our lassoes whistled through the air and tightened on his neck.

Yet before the light had died from his fierce eyes, I cried, 'Stay, we will not kill him; let us take him alive to the camp.' He was so completely powerless now that it was easy to put a stout stick through his mouth, behind his tusks, and then lash his jaws with a heavy cord which was also fastened to the stick. The stick kept the cord in, and the cord kept the stick in, so he was harmless. As soon as he felt his jaws were tied he made no further resistance, and uttered no sound, but looked calmly at us and seemed to say, 'Well, you have got me at last, do as you please with me.' And from that time he took no more notice of us.

We tied his feet securely, but he never groaned, nor growled, nor turned his head. Then with our united strength we were just able to put him on my horse. His breath came evenly as though sleeping, and his eyes were bright and clear again, but did not rest on us. Afar on the great rolling mesas they were fixed, his passing kingdom, where his famous band was now scattered. And he gazed till the pony descended the pathway into the canyon, and the rocks cut off the view.

By travelling slowly we reached the ranch in safety, and after securing him with a collar and a strong chain, we staked him out in the pasture and removed the cords. Then for the first time I could examine him closely, and proved how unreliable is vulgar report where a living hero or tyrant is concerned. He had *not* a collar of gold about his neck, nor was there on his shoulders an inverted cross to denote that he had leagued himself with Satan. But I did find on one haunch a great broad scar, that tradition says was the fang-mark of Juno, the leader of Tannerey's wolf-hounds – a mark which she gave him the moment before he stretched her lifeless on the sand of the canyon.

I set meat and water beside him, but he paid no heed. He lay calmly on his breast, and gazed with those steadfast yellow eyes away past me down through the gateway of the canyon, over the open plains – his plains – nor moved a muscle when I touched him. When the sun went down he was still gazing fixedly across the prairie. I expected he would call up his band when night came, and prepared for them, but he had called once in his extremity, and none had come; he would never call again.

A lion shorn of his strength, an eagle robbed of his freedom, or a dove bereft of his mate, all die, it is said, of a broken heart; and who will aver that this grim bandit could bear the threefold brunt, heartwhole? This only I know, that when the morning dawned, he was lying there still in his position of calm repose, but his spirit was gone – the old king-wolf was dead.

I took the chain from his neck, a cowboy helped me to carry him to the shed where lay the remains of Blanca, and as we laid him beside her, the cattleman exclaimed: 'There, you *would* come to her, now you are together again.'

RAGGYLUG

The Story of a Cottontail Rabbit

Raggylug, or Rag, was the name of a young cottontail rabbit. It was given him from his torn and ragged ear, a life-mark that he got in his first adventure. He lived with his mother in Olifant's swamp, where I made their acquaintance and gathered, in a hundred different ways, the little bits of proof and scraps of truth that at length enabled me to write this history.

Those who do not know the animals well may think I have humanized them, but those who have lived so near them as to know somewhat of their ways and their minds will not think so.

Truly rabbits have no speech as we understand it, but they have a way of conveying ideas by a system of sounds, signs, scents, whisker-touches, movements, and example that answers the purpose of speech; and it must be remembered that though in telling this story I freely translate from rabbit into English, *I repeat nothing that they did not say*.

I

The rank swamp grass bent over and concealed the snug nest where Raggylug's mother had hidden him. She had partly covered him with some of the bedding, and, as always, her last warning was to 'lay low and say nothing, whatever happens!'

Though tucked in bed, he was wide awake and his bright eyes were taking in that part of his little green world that was straight above. A bluejay and a red-squirrel, two notorious thieves, were loudly berating each other for stealing, and at one time Rag's home bush was the centre of their fight; a yellow warbler caught a blue butterfly but six inches from his nose, and a scarlet and black ladybug, serenely waving her knobbed feelers, took a long walk up one grassblade, down another, and across the nest and over Rag's face – and yet he never moved nor even winked.

After awhile he heard a strange rustling of the leaves in the near thicket. It was an odd, continuous sound, and through it went this way and that way and came even nearer, there was no patter of feet with it. Rag had lived his whole life in the Swamp (he was three weeks old) and yet had never heard anything like this. Of course his curiosity was greatly aroused. His mother had cautioned him to lay low, but that was understood to be in case of danger, and this strange sound without footfalls could not be anything to fear.

The low rasping went past close at hand, then to the right, then back, and seemed going away. Rag felt he knew what he was about, he wasn't a baby; it was his duty to learn what it was. He slowly raised his roly-poly body on his short, fluffy legs, lifted his little round head above the covering of his nest and peeped out into the woods. The sound had ceased as soon as he moved. He saw nothing, so took one step forward to a clear view, and instantly found himself face to face with an enormous Black Serpent.

'Mammy,' he screamed in mortal terror as the monster darted at him. With all the strength of his tiny limbs he tried to run. But in a flash the Snake had him by one ear and whipped around him with his coils to gloat over the helpless little baby bunny he had secured for dinner.

'Mam-my–Mam-my,' gasped poor little Raggylug as the cruel monster began slowly choking him to death. Very soon the little one's cry would have ceased, but bounding through the woods straight as an arrow came Mammy. No longer a shy, helpless little Molly Cottontail, ready to fly from a shadow: the mother's love was strong in her. The cry of her baby had filled her with the courage of a hero, and-hop, she went over that horrible reptile. Whack, she struck down at him with her sharp hind claws as she passed, giving him such a stinging blow that he squirmed with pain and hissed with anger.

'M-a-m-m-y,' came feebly from the little one. And Mammy came leaping again and again and struck harder and fiercer until the loathsome reptile let go the little one's ear and tried to bite the old one as she leaped over. But all he got was a mouthful of wool each time, and Molly's fierce blows began to tell, as long bloody rips were torn in the Black Snake's scaly armour.

Things were now looking bad for the Snake; and bracing himself for the next charge, he lost his tight hold on Baby Bunny, who at once wriggled out of the coils and away into the underbrush, breathless and terribly frightened, but unhurt save that his left ear was much torn by the teeth of that dreadful Serpent.

Molly had now gained all she wanted. She had no notion of fighting for glory or revenge. Away she went into the woods and the little one followed the shining beacon of her snow-white tail until she led him to a safe corner of the Swamp.

II

Old Olifant's Swamp was a rough, brambly tract of second-growth woods, with a marshy pond and a stream through the middle. A few ragged remnants of the old forest still stood in it and a few of the still older trunks were lying about as dead logs in the brushwood. The land about the pond was of that willow-grown, sedgy kind that cats and horses avoid, but that cattle do not fear. The drier zones were overgrown with briars and young trees. The outermost belt of all, that next the fields, was of thrifty, gummy-trunked young pines whose living needles in air and dead ones on earth offer so delicious an odour to the nostrils of the passer-by, and so deadly a breath to those seedlings that would compete with them for the worthless waste they grow on.

All around for a long way were smooth fields, and the only wild tracks that ever crossed these fields were those of a thoroughly bad and unscrupulous fox that lived only too near.

The chief indwellers of the swamp were Molly and Rag. Their nearest neighbours were far away, and their nearest kin were dead. This was their home, and here they lived together, and here Rag received the training that made his success in life.

Molly was a good little mother and gave him a careful bringing up. The first thing he learned was 'to lay low and say nothing'. His adventure with the snake taught him the wisdom of this. Rag never forgot that lesson; afterward he did as he was told, and it made the other things come more easily.

The second lesson he learned was 'freeze'. It grows out of the first, and Rag was taught it as soon as he could run.

'Freezing' is simply doing nothing, turning into a statue. As soon as he finds a foe near, no matter what he is doing, a well-trained Cottontail keeps just as he is and stops all movement, for the creatures of the woods are of the same colour as the things in the woods and catch the eye only while moving. So when enemies chance together, the one who first sees the other can keep himself unseen by 'freezing' and thus have all the advantage of choosing the time for attack or escape. Only those who live in the woods know the importance of this; every wild creature and every hunter must learn it; all learn to do it well, but not one of them can beat Molly Cottontail in the doing. Rag's mother taught him this trick by example. When the white cotton cushion that she always carried to sit on went bobbing away through the woods, of course Rag ran his hardest to keep up. But when Molly stopped and 'froze', the natural wish to copy made him do the same.

But the best lesson of all that Rag learned from his mother was the secret of the Brierbrush. It is a very old secret now, and to make it plain you must first hear why the Brierbrush quarrelled with the beasts.

•

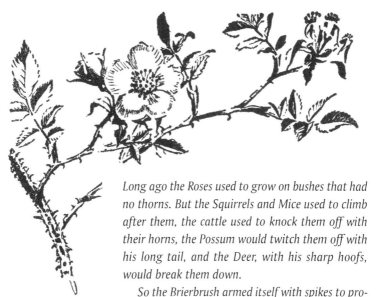

Long ago the Roses used to grow on bushes that had no thorns. But the Squirrels and Mice used to climb after them, the cattle used to knock them off with their horns, the Possum would twitch them off with his long tail, and the Deer, with his sharp hoofs, would break them down.

So the Brierbrush armed itself with spikes to protect its roses and declared eternal war on all creatures that climbed trees, or had horns, or hoofs, or long tails. This left the Brierbrush at peace with none but Molly Cottontail, who could not climb, was hornless, hoof-less and had scarcely any tail at all.

In truth the Cottontail had never harmed a Brierrose, and having now so many enemies the Rose took the Rabbit into especial friendship, and when dangers are threatening poor Bunny he flies to the nearest Brierbrush, certain that it is ready, with a million keen and poisoned daggers, to defend him.

So the secret that Rag learned from his mother was, 'The Brierbrush is your best friend'.

Much of the time that season was spent in learning the lay of the land, and the bramble and brier mazes. And Rag learned them so well that he could go all around the swamp by two different ways and never leave the friendly briers at any place for more than five hops.

It is not long since the foes of the Cottontails were disgusted to find that man had brought a new kind of bramble and planted it in long lines throughout the country. It was so strong that no creatures could break it down, and so sharp that the toughest skin was torn by it. Each year there was more of it and each year it became a more serious matter to the wild creatures. But Molly Cottontail had no fear of it. She was not brought up in the briers for nothing. Dogs and foxes, cattle and sheep, and even man himself might be torn by those fearful spikes: but Molly understands it and lives and thrives under it. And the further it spreads the more safe country there is for the Cottontail. And the name of this new and dreaded bramble is – *the barbed-wire fence.*

III

Molly had no other children to look after now, so Rag had all her care. He was unusually quick and bright as well as strong, and he had uncommonly good chances; so he got on remarkably well.

All the season she kept him busy learning the tricks of the trail, and what to eat and drink and what not to touch. Day by day she worked to train him; little by little she taught him, putting into his mind hundreds of ideas that her own life or early training had stored in hers, and so equipped him with the knowledge that makes life possible to their kind.

Close by her side in the clover-field or the thicket he would sit and copy her when she wobbled her nose 'to keep her smeller clear,' and pull the bite from her mouth or taste her lips to make sure he was getting the same kind of fodder. Still copying her, he learned to comb his ears with his claws and to dress his coat and to bite the burrs out of his vest and socks. He learned, too, that nothing but clear dewdrops from the briers were fit for a rabbit to drink, as water which has once touched the earth must surely bear some taint. Thus he began the study of woodcraft, the oldest of all sciences.

As soon as Rag was big enough to go out alone, his mother taught him the signal code. Rabbits telegraph each other by thumping on the ground with their hind feet. Along the ground sound carries far; a thump that at six feet from the earth is not heard at twenty yards will, near the ground, be heard at least one hundred yards. Rabbits have very keen hearing, and so might hear this same thump at two hundred yards, and that would reach from end to end of Olifant's Swamp. A single *thump* means 'look out' or 'freeze'. A slow *thump thump* means 'come'. A fast *thump thump* means 'danger'; and a very fast *thump thump thump* means 'run for dear life'.

At another time, when the weather was fine and the bluejays were quarrelling among themselves, a sure sign that no dangerous foe was about, Rag began a new study. Molly, by flattening her ears, gave the sign to squat. Then she ran far away in the thicket and gave the thumping signal for 'come'. Rag set out at a run to the place but could not find Molly. He thumped, but got no reply. Setting carefully about his search he found her foot-scent, and following this strange guide, that the beasts all know so well and man does not know at all, he worked out the trail and found her where she was hidden. Thus he got his first lesson in trailing, and thus it was that the games of hide and seek they played became the schooling for the serious chase of which there was so much in his after life.

Before that first season of schooling was over he had learnt all the principal tricks by which a rabbit lives, and in not a few problems showed himself a veritable genius.

He was an adept at 'tree', 'dodge' and 'squat'; he could play 'log-lump' with 'wind', and 'baulk' with 'back-track' so well that he scarcely needed any other tricks. He had not yet tried it, but he knew just how to play 'barb-wire', which is a new trick of the brilliant order; he had made a special study of 'sand', which burns up all scent, and he was deeply versed in 'change-off', 'fence' and 'double', as well as 'hole-up', which is a trick requiring longer notice, and yet he never forgot that 'lay-low' is the beginning of all wisdom and 'brierbrush' the only trick that is always safe.

He was taught the signs by which to know all his foes and then the way to baffle them. For hawks, owls, foxes, hounds, curs, minks, weasels, cats, skunks, coons, and men, each have a different plan of pursuit, and for each and all of these evils he was taught a remedy.

And for knowledge of the enemy's approach he learnt to depend first on himself and his mother, and then on the bluejay. 'Never neglect the bluejay's warning,' said Molly; 'he is a mischief-maker, a marplot, and a thief all the time, but nothing escapes him. He wouldn't mind harming us, but he cannot, thanks to the briers, and his enemies are ours, so it is well to heed him. If the woodpecker cries a warning you can trust him, he is honest; but he is a fool beside the bluejay, and though the bluejay often tells lies for mischief you are safe to believe him when he brings ill news.'

The barbed-wire trick takes a deal of nerve and the best of legs. It was long before Rag ventured to play it, but as he came to his full powers it became one of his favourites.

'It's fine play for those who can do it,' said Molly. 'First you lead off your dog on a straightaway and warm him up a bit by nearly letting him catch you. Then keeping just one hop ahead, you lead him at a long slant full tilt into a breast-high barb-wire. I've seen many a dog and fox crippled, and one big hound killed outright this way. But I've also seen more than one rabbit lose his life in trying it.'

Rag early learnt what some rabbits never learn at all, that 'hole-up' is not such a fine ruse as it seems; it may be the certain safety of a wise rabbit, but soon or late is a sure death-trap to a fool. A young rabbit always thinks of it first, an old rabbit never tries it till all others fail. It means escape from a man or dog, a fox or a bird of prey, but it means sudden death if the foe is a ferret, mink, skunk, or weasel.

There were but two ground-holes in the Swamp. One on the Sunning Bank, which was a dry sheltered knoll in the South-end. It was open and sloping to the sun, and here on fine days the Cottontails took their sunbaths. They stretched out among the fragrant pine needles and winter-green in odd, cat-like positions, and turned slowly over as though roasting and wishing all sides well done. And they blinked and panted, and squirmed as if in dreadful pain; yet this was one of the keenest enjoyments they knew.

Just over the brow of the knoll was a large pine stump. Its grotesque roots wriggled out above the yellow sand-bank like dragons, and under their protecting claws a sulky old woodchuck had dug a den long ago. He became more sour and ill-tempered as weeks went by, and one day waited to quarrel with Olifant's dog instead of going in, so that Molly Cottontail was able to take possession of the den an hour later.

This, the pine-root hole, was afterward very coolly taken by a self-sufficient young skunk, who with less valour might have enjoyed greater longevity, for he imagined that even man with a gun would fly from him. Instead of keeping Molly from the den for good, therefore, his reign, like that of a certain Hebrew king, was over in four days.

The other, the fern-hole, was in a fern thicket next the clover field. It was small and damp, and useless except as a last retreat. It also was the work of a woodchuck, a well-meaning, friendly neighbour, but a hare-brained youngster whose skin in the form of a whip-lash was now developing higher horse-power in the Olifant working team.

'Simple justice,' said the old man, 'for that hide was raised on stolen feed that the team would 'a' turned into horse-power anyway.'

The Cottontails were now sole owners of the holes, and did not go near them when they could help it, lest anything like a path should be made that might betray these last retreats to an enemy.

There was also the hollow hickory, which, though nearly fallen, was still green, and had the great advantage of being open at both ends. This had long been the residence of one Lotor, a solitary old coon whose ostensible calling was frog-hunting, and who, like the monks of old, was supposed to abstain from all flesh food. But it was shrewdly suspected that he needed but a chance to indulge in a diet of rabbit.

When at last one dark night he was killed while raiding Olifant's hen-house, Molly, so far from feeling a pang of regret, took possession of his cosy nest with a sense of unbounded relief.

IV

Bright August sunlight was flooding the Swamp in the morning. Everything seemed soaking in the warm radiance. A little brown swamp-sparrow was teetering on a long rush in the pond. Beneath him there were open spaces of dirty water that brought down a few scraps of the blue sky, and worked it and the yellow duckweed into an exquisite mosaic, with a little wrong-side picture of the bird in the middle. On the bank behind was a great vigourous growth of golden green skunk-cabbage, that cast a dense shadow over the brown swamp tussocks.

The eyes of the swamp-sparrow were not trained to take in the colour glories, but he saw what we might have missed; that two of the numberless leafy brown bumps under the broad cabbage-leaves were furry, living things, with noses that never ceased to move up and down whatever else was still.

It was Molly and Rag. They were stretched under the skunk-cabbage, not because they liked its rank smell, but because the winged ticks could not stand it at all and so left them in peace.

Rabbits have no set time for lessons, they are always learning; but what the lesson is depends on the present stress, and that must arrive before it is known. They went to this place for a quiet rest, but had not been long there when suddenly a warning note from the ever-watchful bluejay caused Molly's nose and ears to go up and her tail to tighten to her back. Away across the Swamp was Olifant's big black and white dog, coming straight toward them.

'Now,' said Molly, 'squat while I go and keep that fool out of mis-chief.' Away she went to meet him and she fearlessly dashed across the dog's path.

'Bow-ow-ow,' he fairly yelled as he bounded after Molly, but she kept just beyond his reach and led him where the million daggers struck fast and deep, till his tender ears were scratched raw, and guided him at last plump into a hidden barbed-wire fence, where he got such a gashing that he went homeward howling with pain. After making a short double, a loop and a baulk in case the dog should come back, Molly returned to find that Rag in his eagerness was standing bolt upright and craning his neck to see the sport.

This disobedience made her so angry that she struck him with her hind foot and knocked him over in the mud.

One day as they fed on the near clover field a red-tailed hawk came swooping after them. Molly kicked up her hind legs to make fun of him and skipped into the briers along one of their old pathways, where of course the hawk could not follow. It was the main path from the Creekside Thicket to the Stove-pipe brush-pile. Several creepers had grown across it, and Molly, keeping one eye on the hawk, set to work and cut the creepers off. Rag watched her, then ran on ahead, and cut some more that were across the path. 'That's right,' said Molly, 'always keep the runways clear, you will need them often enough. Not wide, but clear. Cut everything like a creeper across them and some day you will find you have cut a snare. 'A what?' asked Rag, as he scratched his right ear with his left hind foot.

'A snare is something that looks like a creeper, but it doesn't grow and it's worse than all the hawks in the world,' said Molly, glancing at the now far-away red-tail, 'for there it hides night and day in the runway till the chance to catch you comes.'

'I don't believe it could catch me,' said Rag, with the pride of youth as he rose on his heels to rub his chin and whiskers high up on a smooth sapling. Rag did not know he was doing this, but his mother saw and knew it was a sign, like the changing of a boy's voice, that her little one was no longer a baby but would soon be a grown-up Cottontail.

V

There is magic in running water. Who does not know it and feel it? The railroad builder fearlessly throws his bank across the wide bog or lake, or the sea itself, but the tiniest rill of running water he treats with great respect, studies its wish and its way and gives it all it seems to ask. The thirst-parched traveller in the poisonous alkali deserts holds back in deadly fear from the sedgy ponds till he finds one down whose centre is a thin, clear line, and a faint flow, the sign of running, living water, and joyfully he drinks.

There is magic in running water, no evil spell can cross it. Tam O'Shanter proved its potency in time of sorest need. The wild-wood creature with its deadly foe following tireless on the trail scent, realizes its nearing doom and feels an awful spell. Its strength is spent, its every trick is tried in vain till the good Angel leads it to the water, the running, living water, and dashing in it follows the cooling stream, and then with force renewed takes to the woods again.

There is magic in running water. The hounds come to the very spot and halt and cast about; and halt and cast in vain. Their spell is broken by the merry stream, and the wild thing lives its life.
And this was one of the great secrets that Raggylug learned from his mother – 'after the Brierrose, the Water is your friend'.

One hot, muggy night in August, Molly led Rag through the woods. The cotton-white cushion she wore under her tail twinkled ahead and was his guiding lantern, though it went out as soon as she stopped and sat on it. After a few runs and stops to listen, they came to the edge of the pond. The hylas in the trees above them were singing '*sleep, sleep,*' and away out on a sunken log in the deep water, up to his chin in the cooling bath, a bloated bullfrog was singing the praises of a '*jug o' rum.*'

'Follow me still,' said Molly, in rabbit, and 'flop' she went into the pond and struck out for the sunken log in the middle. Rag flinched but plunged with a little 'ouch', gasping and wobbling his nose very fast but still copying his mother. The same movements as on land sent him through the water, and thus he found he could swim. On he went till he reached the sunken log and scrambled up by his dripping mother on the high dry end, with a rushy screen around them and the Water that tells no tales. After this in warm, black nights, when that old fox from Springfield came prowling through the Swamp, Rag would note the place of the bullfrog's voice, for in case of direst need it might be a guide to safety. And thenceforth the words of the song that the bull-frog sang were, '*Come, come, in danger come*'.

This was the latest study that Rag took up with his mother-it was really a post-graduate course, for many little rabbits never learn it at all.

VI

No wild animal dies of old age. Its life has soon or late a tragic end. It is only a question of how long it can hold out against its foes. But Rag's life was proof that once a rabbit passes out of his youth he is likely to outlive his prime and be killed only in the last third of life, the downhill third we call old age.

The Cottontails had enemies on every side. Their daily life was a series of escapes. For dogs, foxes, cats, skunks, coons, weasels, minks, snakes, hawks, owls, and men, and even insects were all plotting to kill them. They had hundreds of adventures, and at least once a day they had to fly for their lives and save themselves by their legs and wits.

More than once that hateful fox from Springfield drove them to taking refuge under the wreck of a barbed-wire hog-pen by the spring. But once there they could look calmly at him while he spiked his legs in vain attempts to reach them.

Once or twice Rag when hunted had played off the hound against a skunk that had seemed likely to be quite as dangerous as the dog.

Once he was caught alive by a hunter who had a hound and a ferret to help him. But Rag had the luck to escape next day, with a yet deeper distrust of ground holes. He was several times run into the water by the cat, and many times was chased by hawks and owls, but for each kind of danger there was a safeguard. His mother taught him the principal dodges, and he improved on them and made many new ones as he grew older. And the older and wiser he grew the less he trusted to his legs, and the more to his wits for safety.

Ranger was the name of a young hound in the neighbourhood. To train him his master used to put him on the trail of one of the Cottontails. It was nearly always Rag that they ran, for the young buck enjoyed the runs as much as they did, the spice of danger in them being just enough for zest. He would say:

'Oh, mother! here comes the dog again, I must have a run today.'

'You are too bold, Raggy, my son!' she might reply. 'I fear you will run once too often.'

'But, mother, it is such glorious fun to tease that fool dog, and it's all good training. I'll thump if I am too hard pressed, then you can come and change off while I get my second wind.'

On he would come, and Ranger would take the trail and follow till Rag got tired of it. Then he either sent a thumping telegram for help, which brought Molly to take charge of the dog, or he got rid of the dog by some clever trick. A description of one of these shows how well Rag had learned the arts of the woods.

He knew that his scent lay best near the ground, and was strongest when he was warm. So if he could get off the ground, and be left in peace for half an hour to cool off, and for the trail to stale, he knew he would be safe. When, therefore, he tired of the chase, he made for the Creekside brier-patch, where he 'wound' – that is, zigzagged – till he left a course so crooked that the dog was sure to be greatly delayed in working it out. He then went straight to D in the woods, passing one hop to windward of the high log E. Stopping at D, he followed his back trail to F, here he leaped aside and ran toward G. Then, returning on his trail to J, he waited till the hound passed on his trail at I. Rag then got back on his old trail at H, and followed it to E, where, with a scent-baulk or great leap aside, he reached the high log, and running to its higher end, he sat like a bump.

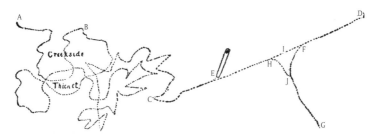

Ranger lost much time in the bramble maize, and the scent was very poor when he got it straightened out and came to D. Here he began to circle to pick it up, and after losing much time, struck the trail which ended suddenly at G. Again he was at fault, and had to circle to find the trail. Wider and wider the circles, until at last, he passed right under the log Rag was on. But a cold scent, on a cold day, does not go downward much. Rag never budged nor winked, and the hound passed.

Again the dog came round. This time he crossed the low part of the log, and stopped to smell it. 'Yes, clearly it was rabbity', but it was a stale scent now; still he mounted the log.

It was a trying moment for Rag, as the great hound came sniff-sniffing along the log. But his nerve did not forsake him; the wind was right; he had his mind made up to bolt as soon as Ranger came half way up. But he didn't come. A yellow cur would have seen the rabbit sitting there, but the hound did not, and the scent seemed stale, so he leaped off the log, and Rag had won.

VII

Rag had never seen any other rabbit than his mother. Indeed he had scarcely thought about there being any other. He was more and more away from her now, and yet he never felt lonely, for rabbits do not hanker for company. But one day in December, while he was among the red dogwood brush, cutting a new path to the great Creekside thicket, he saw all at once against the sky over the Sunning Bank the head and ears of a strange rabbit. The new-comer had the air of a well-pleased discoverer and soon came hopping Rag's way along one of *his* paths into *his* Swamp. A new feeling rushed over him, that boiling mixture of anger and hatred called jealousy.

The stranger stopped at one of Rag's rubbing-trees – that is, a tree against which he used to stand on his heels and rub his chin as far up as he could reach. He thought he did this simply because he liked it; but all buck-rabbits do so, and several ends are served. It makes the tree rabbity, so that other rabbits know that this swamp already belongs to a rabbit family and is not open for settlement. It also lets the next one know by the scent if the last caller was an acquaintance, and the height from the ground of the rubbing-places shows how tall the rabbit is.

Now to his disgust Rag noticed that the new-comer was a head taller than himself, and a big, stout buck at that. This was a wholly new experience and filled Rag with a wholly new feeling. The spirit of murder entered his heart; he chewed very hard with nothing in his mouth, and hopping forward onto a smooth piece of hard ground he struck slowly:

'*Thump–thump–thump*', which is a rabbit telegram for 'Get out of my swamp, or fight'.

The new-comer made a big V with his ears, sat upright for a few seconds, then, dropping on his fore-feet, sent along the ground a louder, stronger, '*Thump–thump–thump*'.

And so war was declared.

They came together by short runs sidewise, each one trying to get the wind of the other and watching for a chance advantage. The stranger was a big, heavy buck with plenty of muscle, but one or two trifles such as treading on a turnover and failing to close when Rag was on low ground showed that he had not much cunning and counted on winning his battles by his weight. On he came at last and Rag met him like a little fury. As they came together they leaped up and struck out with their hind feet.

Thud, *thud* they came, and down went poor little Rag. In a moment the stranger was on him with his teeth and Rag was bitten, and lost several tufts of hair before he could get up. But he was swift of foot and got out of reach. Again he charged and again he was knocked down and bitten severely. He was no match for his foe, and it soon became a question of saving his own life.

Hurt as he was he sprang away, with the stranger in full chase, and bound to kill him as well as to oust him from the Swamp where he was born. Rag's legs were good and so was his wind. The stranger was big and so heavy that he soon gave up the chase, and it was well for poor Rag that he did, for he was getting stiff from his wounds as well as tired. From that day began a reign of terror for Rag. His training had been against owls, dogs, weasels, men, and so on, but what to do when chased by another rabbit, he did not know. All he knew was to lay low till he was found, then run.

Poor little Molly was completely terrorized; she could not help Rag and sought only to hide. But the big buck soon found her out. She tried to run from him, but she was not now so swift as Rag. The stranger made no attempt to kill her, but he made love to her, and because she hated him and tried to get away, he treated her shamefully.

Day after day he worried her by following her about, and often, furious at her lasting hatred, he would knock her down and tear out mouthfuls of her soft fur till his rage cooled somewhat, when he would let her go for awhile. But his fixed purpose was to kill Rag, whose escape seemed hopeless. There was no other swamp he could go to, and whenever he took a nap now he had to be ready at any moment to dash for his life. A dozen times a day the big stranger came creeping up to where he slept, but each time the watchful Rag awoke in time to escape. To escape yet not to escape. He saved his life indeed, but oh! what a miserable life it had become. How maddening to be thus helpless, to see his little mother daily beaten and torn, as well as to see all his favourite feeding-grounds, the cosey nooks, and the pathways he had made with so much labour, forced from him by this hateful brute. Unhappy Rag realized that to the victor belong the spoils, and he hated him more than ever he did fox or ferret.

How was it to end? He was wearing out with running and watching and bad food, and little Molly's strength and spirit were breaking down under the long persecution. The stranger was ready to go to all lengths to destroy poor Rag, and at last stooped to the worst crime known among rabbits. However much they may hate each other, all good rabbits forget their feuds when their common enemy appears. Yet one day when a great goshawk came swooping over the Swamp, the stranger, keeping well under cover himself, tried again and again to drive Rag into the open.

Once or twice the hawk nearly had him, but still the briers saved him, and it was only when the big buck himself came near being caught that he gave it up. And again Rag escaped, but was no better off. He

made up his mind to leave, with his mother, if possible, next night and go into the world in quest of some new home when he heard old Thunder, the hound, sniffing and searching about the outskirts of the swamp, and he resolved on playing a desperate game. He deliberately crossed the hound's view, and the chase that then began was fast and furious. Thrice around the Swamp they went till Rag had made sure that his mother was hidden safely and that his hated foe was in his usual nest. Then right into that nest and plump over him he jumped, giving him a rap with one hind foot as he passed over his head.

'You miserable fool, I kill you yet,' cried the stranger, and up he jumped only to find himself between Rag and the dog and heir to all the peril of the chase.

On came the hound baying hotly on the straight-away scent. The buck's weight and size were great advantages in a rabbit fight, but now they were fatal. He did not know many tricks. Just the simple ones like 'double,' 'wind,' and 'hole-up,' that every baby Bunny knows. But the chase was too close for doubling and winding, and he didn't know where the holes were.

It was a straight race. The brier-rose, kind to all rabbits alike, did its best, but it was no use. The baying of the hound was fast and steady. The crashing of the brush and the yelping of the hound each time the briers tore his tender ears were borne to the two rabbits where they crouched in hiding. But suddenly these sounds stopped, there was a scuffle, then loud and terrible screaming.

Rag knew what it meant and it sent a shiver through him, but he soon forgot that when all was over and rejoiced to be once more the master of the dear old Swamp.

VIII

Old Olifant had doubtless a right to burn all those brush-piles in the east and south of the Swamp and to clear up the wreck of the old barbed-wire hog-pen just below the spring. But it was none the less hard on Rag and his mother. The first were their various residences and outposts, and the second their grand fastness and safe retreat.

They had so long held the Swamp and felt it to be their very own in every part and suburb – including Olifant's grounds and buildings – that they would have resented the appearance of another rabbit even about the adjoining barnyard.

Their claim, that of long, successful occupancy, was exactly the same as that by which most nations hold their land, and it would be hard to find a better right.

During the time of the January thaw the Olifants had cut the rest of the large wood about the pond and curtailed the Cottontails' domain on all sides. But they still clung to the dwindling Swamp, for it was their home and they were loath to move to foreign parts. Their life of daily perils went on, but they were still fleet of foot, long of wind, and bright of wit. Of late they had been somewhat troubled by a mink that had wandered up-stream to their quiet nook. A little judicious guidance had transferred the uncomfortable visitor to Olifant's hen-house. But they were not yet quite sure that he had been properly looked after. So for the present they gave up using the ground-holes, which were, of course, dangerous blind-alleys, and stuck closer than ever to the briers and the brush-piles that were left.

That first snow had quite gone and the weather was bright and warm until now. Molly, feeling a touch of rheumatism, was somewhere in the lower thicket seeking a tea-berry tonic. Rag was sitting in the weak sunlight on a bank in the east side. The smoke from the familiar gable chimney of Olifant's house came fitfully drifting a pale blue haze through the under-woods and showing as a dull brown against the brightness of the sky. The sun-gilt gable was cut off midway by the banks of brier-brush, that purple in shadow shone like rods of blazing crimson and gold in the light. Beyond the house the barn with its gable and roof, new gilt as the house, stood up like a Noah's ark.

The sounds that came from it, and yet more the delicious smell that mingled with the smoke, told Rag that the animals were being fed cabbage in the yard. Rag's mouth watered at the idea of the feast. He blinked and blinked as he snuffed its odourous promises, for he loved cabbage dearly. But then he had been to the barnyard the night before after a few paltry clover-tops, and no wise rabbit would go two nights running to the same place.

Therefore he did the wise thing. He moved across where he could not smell the cabbage and made his supper of a bundle of hay that had been blown from the stack. Later, when about to settle for the night, he was joined by Molly, who had taken her tea-berry and then eaten her frugal meal of sweet birch near the Sunning Bank.

Meanwhile the sun had gone about his business elsewhere, taking all his gold and glory with him. Off in the east a big black shutter came pushing up and rising higher and higher; it spread over the whole sky, shut out all light, and left the world a very gloomy place indeed. Then another mischief-maker, the wind, taking advantage of the sun's absence, came on the scene and set about brewing trouble. The weather turned colder and colder; it seemed worse than when the ground had been covered with snow.

'Isn't this terribly cold? How I wish we had our stove-pipe brush-pile,' said Rag.

'A good night for the pine-root hole,' replied Molly, 'but we have not yet seen the pelt of that mink on the end of the barn, and it is not safe till we do.'

The hollow hickory was gone – in fact at this very moment its trunk, lying in the wood-yard, was harboring the mink they feared. So the Cottontails hopped to the south side of the pond and, choosing a brush-pile, they crept under and snuggled down for the night, facing the wind but with their noses in different directions so as to go out different ways in case of alarm. The wind blew harder and colder as the hours went by, and about midnight a fine, icy snow came ticking down on the dead leaves and hissing through the brush heap. It might seem a poor night for hunting, but that old fox from Springfield was out. He came pointing up the wind in the shelter of the Swamp and chanced in the lee of the brush-pile, where he scented the sleeping Cottontails. He halted for a moment, then came stealthily sneaking up toward the brush under which his nose told him the rabbits were crouching. The noise of the wind and the sleet enabled him to come quite close before Molly heard the faint crunch of a dry leaf under his paw. She touched Rag's whiskers, and both were fully awake just as the fox sprang on them; but they always slept with their legs ready for a jump. Molly darted out into the blinding storm. The fox missed his spring but followed like a racer, while Rag dashed off to one side.

There was only one road for Molly; that was straight up the wind, and bounding for her life she gained a little over the unfrozen mud that would not carry the fox, till she reached the margin of the pond. No chance to turn now, on she must go.

Splash! splash! through the weeds she went, then plunge into the deep water.

And plunge went the fox close behind. But it was too much for Reynard on such a night. He turned back, and Molly, seeing only one course, struggled through the reeds into the deep water and struck out for the other shore. But there was a strong headwind. The little waves, icy cold, broke over her head as she swam, and the water was full of snow that blocked her way like soft ice, or floating mud. The dark line of the other shore seemed far, far away, with perhaps the fox waiting for her there.

But she laid her ears flat to be out of the gale, and bravely put forth all her strength with wind and tide against her. After a long, weary swim in the cold water, she had nearly reached the farther reeds when a great mass of floating snow barred her road; then the wind on the bank made strange, fox-like sounds that robbed her of all force, and she was drifted far backward before she could get free from the floating bar.

Again the struck Out, but slowly—oh so slowly now. And when at last she reached the lee of the tall reeds, her limbs were numbed, her strength spent, her brave little heart was sinking, and she cared no more whether the fox were there or not. Through the reeds she did indeed pass, but once in the weeds her course wavered and slowed, her feeble strokes no longer sent her landward, the ice forming around her stopped her altogether. In a little while the cold, weak limbs ceased to move, the furry nose-tip of the little mother Cottontail wobbled no more, and the soft brown eyes were closed in death.

But there was no fox waiting to tear her with ravenous jaws. Rag had escaped the first onset of the foe, and as soon as he regained his wits he came running back to change-off and so help his mother. He met the old fox going round the pond to meet Molly and led him far and away, then dismissed him with a barbed-wire gash on his head, and came to the bank and sought about and trailed and thumped, but all his searching was in vain; he could not find his little mother. He never saw her again, and he never knew whither she went, for she slept her never-waking sleep in the ice-arms of her friend the Water that tells no tales.

Poor little Molly Cottontail! She was a true heroine, yet only one of unnumbered millions that without a thought of heroism have lived and done their best in their little world, and died. She fought a good fight in the battle of life. She was good stuff; the stuff that never dies. For flesh of her flesh and brain of her brain was Rag. She lives in him, and through him transmits a finer fibre to her race.

And Rag still lives in the Swamp. Old Olifant died that winter, and the unthrifty sons ceased to clear the Swamp or mend the wire fences. Within a single year it was a wilder place than ever; fresh trees and brambles grew, and falling wires made many Cottontail castles and last retreats that dogs and foxes dared not storm. And there to this day lives Rag. He is a big strong buck now and fears no rivals. He has a large family of his own, and a pretty brown wife that he got I know not where. There, no doubt, he and his children's children will flourish for many years to come, and there you may see them any sunny evening if you have learnt their signal S code, and, choosing a good spot on the ground, know just how and when to thump it.

THE SPRINGFIELD FOX

I

The hens had been mysteriously disappearing for over a month; and when I came home to Springfield for the summer holidays it was my duty to find the cause. This was soon done. The fowls were carried away bodily one at a time, before going to roost or else after leaving, which put tramps and neighbours out of court; they were not taken from the high perches, which cleared all coons and owls; or left partly eaten, so that weasels, skunks, or minks were not the guilty ones, and the blame, therefore, was surely left at Reynard's door.

The great pine wood of Erindale was on the other bank of the river, and on looking carefully about the lower ford I saw a few fox-tracks and a barred feather from one of our Plymouth Rock chickens. On climbing the farther bank in search of more dews, I heard a great outcry of crows behind me, and turning, saw a number of these birds darting down at something in the ford. A better view showed that it was the old story, thief catch thief, for there in the middle of the ford was a fox with something in his jaws – he was returning from our barnyard with another hen. The crows, though shameless robbers themselves, are ever first to cry 'Stop thief,' and yet more than ready to take 'hush-money' in the form of a share in the plunder.

And this was their game now. The fox to get back home must cross the river, where he was exposed to the full brunt of the crow mob. He made a dash for it, and would doubtless have gotten across with his booty had I not joined in the attack, whereupon he dropped the hen, scarce dead, and disappeared in the woods.

This large and regular levy of provisions wholly carried off could mean but one thing, a family of little foxes at home; and to find them I now was bound.

That evening I went with Ranger, my hound,

across the river into the Erindale woods. As soon as the hound began to circle, we heard the short, sharp bark of a fox from a thickly wooded ravine close by. Ranger dashed in at once, struck a hot scent and went off on a lively straight-away till his voice was lost in the distance away over the upland.

After nearly an hour he came back, panting and warm, for it was baking August weather, and lay down at my feet.

But almost immediately the same foxy 'Yap yurrr' was heard close at hand and off dashed the dog on another chase.

Away he went in the darkness, baying like a foghorn, straight away to the north. And the loud 'Boo, boo,' became a low 'oo,oo,' and that a feeble 'o-o' and then was lost. They must have gone some miles away, for even with ear to the ground I heard nothing of them though a mile was easy distance for Ranger's brazen voice.

As I waited in the black woods I heard a sweet sound of dripping water: 'Tink tank tenk tink, Ta tink tank tenk tonk'.

I did not know of any spring so near, and in the hot night it was a glad find. But the sound led me to the bough of a oak-tree, where I found its source. Such a soft sweet song; full of delightful suggestion on such a night:

> Tonk tank tenk tink
> Ta tink a tonk a tank a tink a
> Ta ta tink tank ta ta tonk tink
> Drink a tank a drink a drunk.

It was the 'water-dripping' song of the saw-whet owl.

But suddenly a deep raucous breathing and a rustle of leaves showed that Ranger was back. He was completely fagged out. His tongue hung almost to the ground and was dripping with foam, his flanks were heaving and spume-flecks dribbled from his breast and sides. He stopped panting a moment to give my hand a dutiful lick, then flung himself flop on the leaves to drown all other sounds with his noisy panting.

But again that tantilizing 'Yap yurr' was heard a few feet away, and the meaning of it all dawned on me.

We were close to the den where the little foxes were, and the old ones were taking turns in trying to lead us away.

It was late night now, so we went home feeling sure that the problem was nearly solved.

II

It was well known that there was an old fox with his family living in the neighbourhood, but no one supposed them so near.

This fox had been called 'Scarface', because of a scar reaching from his eye through and back of his ear; this was supposed to have been given him by a barbed-wire fence during a rabbit hunt, and as the hair came in white after it healed it was always a strong mark.

The winter before I had met with him zand had had a sample of his craftiness. I was out shooting, after a fall of snow, and had crossed the open fields to the edge of the brushy hollow back of the old mill. As my head rose to a view of the hollow I caught sight of a fox trotting at long range down the other side, in line to cross my course. Instantly I held motionless, and did not even lower or turn my head lest I should catch his eye by moving, until he went on out of sight in the thick cover at the bottom. As soon as he was hidden I bobbed down and ran to head him off where he should leave the cover on the other side, and was there in good time awaiting, but no fox came forth. A careful look showed the fresh track of a fox that had bounded from the cover, and following it with my eye I saw old Scarface himself far out of range behind me, sitting on his haunches and grinning as though much amused.

A study of the trail made all clear. He had seen me at the moment I saw him, but he, also like a true hunter, had concealed the fact, putting on an air of unconcern till out of sight, when he had run for his life around behind me and amused himself by watching my still born trick.

In the springtime I had yet another instance of Scarface's cunning. I was walking with a friend along the road over the high pasture. We passed within thirty feet of a ridge on which were several grey and brown boulders. When at the nearest point my friend said:

'Stone number three looks to me very much like a fox curled up.'

But I could not see it, and we passed. We had not gone many yards farther when the wind blew on this boulder as on fur.

My friend said, 'I am sure that is a fox, lying asleep.'

'We'll soon settle that,' I replied, and turned back, but as soon as I had taken one step from the road, up jumped Scarface, for it was he, and ran. A fire had swept the middle of the pasture, leaving a broad belt of black; over this he scurried till he came to the unburnt yellow grass again, where he squatted down and was lost to view. He had been watching us all the time, and would not have moved had we kept to the road. The wonderful part of this is, not that be resembled the round stones and dry grass, but that he *knew he did*, and was ready to profit by it.

We soon found that it was Scarface and his wife Vixen that had made our woods their home and our barnyard their base of supplies.

Next morning a search in the pines showed a great bank of earth that had been scratched up within a few months. It must have come from a hole, and yet there was none to be seen. It is well known that a really cute fox, on digging a new den, brings all the earth out at the first hole made, but carries on a tunnel into some distant thicket. Then closing up for good the first made and too well-marked door, uses only the entrance hidden in the thicket.

So after a little search at the other side of a knoll, I found the real entry and good proof that there was a nest of little foxes inside.

Rising above the brush on the hillside was a great hollow basswood. It leaned a good deal and had a large hole at the bottom, and a smaller one at top.

We boys had often used this tree in playing Swiss Family Robinson, and by cutting steps in its soft punky walls had made it easy to go up and down in the hollow. Now it came in handy, for next day when the sun was warm I went there to watch, and from this perch on the roof, I soon saw the interesting family that lived in the cellar near by. There were four little foxes; they looked curiously like little lambs, with their woolly coats, their long thick legs and innocent expressions, and yet a second glance at their broad, sharp-nosed, sharp-eyed visages showed that each of these innocents was the makings of a crafty old fox.

They played about, basking in the sun, or wrestling with each other till a slight sound made them scurry under ground. But their alarm was needless, for the cause of it was their mother; she stepped from the bushes bringing another hen – number seventeen as I remember. A low call from her and the little fellows came tumbling out. Then began a scene that I thought charming, but which my uncle would not have enjoyed at all.

They rushed on the hen, and tussled and fought with it, and each other, while the mother, keeping a sharp eye for enemies, looked on with fond delight. The expression on her face was remarkable. It was first a grinning of delight, but her usual look of wildness and cunning was there, nor were cruelty and nervousness lacking, but over all was the unmistakable look of the mother's pride and love.

The base of my tree was hidden in bushes and much lower than the knoll where the den was. So I could come and go at will without scaring the foxes.

For many days I went there and saw much of the training of the young ones. They early learned to turn to turn to statuettes sound, and then on hearing it again or finding other cause for fear, to run for shelter.

Some animals have so much mother-love that it over flows and benefits outsiders. Not so old Vixen it would seem. Her pleasure in the cubs led to most refined cruelty. For she often brought home to them mice and birds alive, and with diabolic gentleness would avoid doing them serious hurt so that the cubs might have larger scope to torment them.

There was a woodchuck that lived over in the hill orchard. He was neither handsome nor interesting, but he knew how to take care of himself. He had dug a den between the roots of an old pine stump, so that the foxes could not follow him by digging. But hard work was not their way of life; wits they believed worth more then elbowgrease. This woodchuck usually sunned himself on the stump each morning. If he saw a fox near he went down in the door of his den, or if the enemy was very near he went inside and stayed long enough for the danger to pass.

One morning Vixen and her mate seemed to decide that it was time the children knew something about the broad subject of Woodchucks, and further that this orchard woodchuck would serve nicely for an object-lesson. So they went together to the orchard-fence unseen by old Chuckie on his stump. Scarface then showed himself in the orchard and quietly walked in a line so as to pass by the stump at a distance, but never once turned his head or allowed the ever-watchful wood-chuck to think himself seen. When the fox entered the field the wood-chuck quietly dropped down to the mouth of his den: here he waited as the fox passed – but concluding that after all wisdom is the better part, went into his hole.

This was what the foxes wanted. Vixen had kept out of sight, but now ran swiftly to the stump and hid behind it. Scarface had kept straight on, going very slowly. The woodchuck had not been fright-ened, so before long his head popped up between the roots and he looked around. There was that fox still going on, farther and farther away. The woodchuck grew bold as the fox went, and came out farther, and then seeing the coast clear, he scrambled onto the stump, and with one spring Vixen had him and shook him till he lay senseless. Scarface had watched out of the corner of his eye and now came running back. But Vixen took the chuck in her jaws and made for the den, so he saw he wasn't needed.

Back to the den came Vix, and carried the chuck so carefully that he was able to struggle a little when she got there. A low 'woof' at the den brought the little fellows out like schoolboys to play. She threw the wounded animal to them and they set on him like four little furies, uttering little growls and biting little bites with all the strength of their baby jaws, but the woodchuck fought for his life and beating them off slowly hobbled to the shelter of a thicket. The little ones pursued like a pack of hounds and dragged at his tail and flanks, but could not hold him back. So Vixen overtook him with a couple of bounds and dragged him again into the open for the children to worry. Again and again this rough sport went on till one of the little ones was badly bitten, and his squeal of pain roused Vix to end the woodchuck's misery and serve him up at once.

Not far from the den was a hollow overgrown with coarse grass, the playground of a colony of field-mice. The earliest lesson in woodcraft that the little ones took, away from the den, was in this hollow. Here they had their first course of mice, the easiest of all game. In teaching, the main thing was example, aided by a deep-set instinct. The old fox, also, had one or two signs meaning 'lie still and watch,' 'come, do as I do,' and so on, that were much used.

So the merry lot went to this hollow one calm evening and Mother Fox made them lie still in the grass. Presently a faint squeak showed that the game was astir. Vix rose up and went on tiptoe into the grass – not crouching but as high as she could stand, sometimes on her hind legs so as to get a better view. The runs that the mice follow are hidden under the grass tangle, and the only way to know the whereabouts of a mouse is by seeing the slight shaking of the grass, which is the reason why mice are hunted only on calm days.

And the trick is to locate the mouse and seize him first and see him afterward. Vix soon made a spring, and in the middle of the bunch of dead grass that she grabbed was a field-mouse squeaking his last squeak.

He was soon gobbled, and the four awkward little foxes tried to do the same as their mother, and when at length the eldest for the first time in his life caught game, he quivered with excitement and ground his pearly little milk-teeth into the mouse with a rush of inborn savageness that must have surprised even himself.

Another home lesson was on the red-squirrel. One of these noisy, vulgar creatures, lived close by and used to waste part of each day scolding the foxes, from some safe perch. The cubs made many vain attempts to catch him as he ran across their glade from one tree to an other, or spluttered and scolded at them a foot or so out of reach. But old Vixen was up in natural history – she knew squirrel nature and took the case in hand when the proper time came. She hid the children and lay down flat in the middle of the open glade. The saucy low-minded squirrel came and scolded as usual. But she moved no hair. He came nearer and at last right over head to chatter:

'You brute you, you brute you.'

But Vix lay as dead. This was very perplexing, so the squirrel came down the trunk and peeping about made a nervous dash across the grass, to another tree, again to scold from a safe perch.

'You brute you, you useless brute, scarrr-scarrrr.'

But flat and lifeless on the grass lay Vix. Ths was most tantilizing to the squirrel. He was naturally curious and disposed to be venturesome, so again he came to the ground and scurried across the glade nearer than before. Still as death lay Vix, 'surely she was dead'. And the little foxes began to wonder if their mother wasn't asleep.

But the squirrel was working himself into a little craze of foolhardy curiosity. He had dropped a piece of bark on Vix's head, he had used up his list of bad words and he had done it all over again, without getting a sign of life. So after a couple more dashes across the glade he ventured within a few feet of the really watchful Vix, who sprang to her feet and pinned him in a twinkling.

'And the little ones picked the bones e-oh.'

Thus the rudiments of their education were laid, and afterward as they grew stronger they were taken farther afield to begin the higher branches of trailing and scenting.

For each kind of prey they were taught a way to hunt, for every animal has some great strength or it could not live, and some great weakness or the others could not live. The squirrel's weakness was foolish curiosity; the fox's that he can't climb a tree. And the training of the little foxes was all shaped to take advantage of the weakness of the other creatures and to make up for their own by defter play where they are strong.

From their parents they learned the chief axioms of the fox world. How, is not easy to say. But that they learned this in company with their parents was clear.

Here are some that foxes taught me, without saying a word: –

Never sleep on your straight track.

Your nose is before your eyes, then trust it first.

A fool runs down the wind.

Running rills cure many ills.

Never take the open if you can keep the cover.

Never leave a straight trail if a crooked one will do.

If it's strange, it's hostile.

Dust and water burn the scent.

Never hunt mice in a rabbit-woods, or rabbits in a henyard.

Keep off the grass.

Inklings of the meanings of these were already entering the little ones' minds– thus, 'Never follow what you can't smell', was wise, they could see, because if you can't smell it, then the wind is so that it must smell you.

One by one they learned the birds and beasts of their home woods, and then as they were able to go abroad with their parents they learned new animals. They were beginning to think they knew the scent of everything that moved. But one night the mother took them to a field where there was a strange black flat thing on the ground. She brought them on purpose to smell it, but at the first whiff their every hair stood on end, they trembled, they knew not why – it seemed to tingle through their blood and fill them with instinctive hate and fear. And when she saw its full effect she told them –

'*That is man-scent.*'

III

Meanwhile the hens continued to disappear. I had not betrayed the den of cubs. Indeed, I thought a good deal more of the little rascals than I did of the hens; but uncle was dreadfully wrought up and made most disparaging remarks about my woodcraft. To please him I one day took the hound across to the woods and seating myself on a stump on the open hillside, I bade the dog go on. Within three minutes he sang out in the tongue all hunters know so well, 'Fox! fox! fox! straight away down the valley.'

After awhile I heard them coming back. There I saw the fox – Scarface – loping lightly across the river-bottom to the stream. In he went and trotted along in the shallow water near the margin for two hundred yards, then came out straight toward me. Though in full view, he saw me not but came up the hill watching over his shoulder for the hound. Within ten feet of me he turned and sat with his back to me while he craned his neck and showed an eager interest in the doings of the hound. Ranger came bawling along the trail till he came to the running water, the killer of scent, and here he was puzzled; but there was only one thing to do; that was by going up and down both banks find where the fox had left the river.

The fox before me shifted his position a little to get a better view and watched with a most human interest all the circling of the hound. He was so close that I saw the hair of his shoulder bristle a little when the dog came in sight. I could see the jumping of his heart on his ribs, and the gleam of his yellow eye. When the dog was wholly baulked by the water trick, it was comical to see: – he could not sit still, but rocked up and down in glee, and reared on his hind feet to get a better view of the slow-plodding hound. With mouth opened nearly to his ears, though not at all winded, he panted noisily for a moment, or rather he laughed gleefully, just as a dog laughs by grinning and panting.

Old Scarface wriggled in huge enjoyment as the hound puzzled over the trail so long that when he did find it, it was so stale he could barely follow it, and did not feel justified in tonguing on it at all.

As soon as the hound was working up the hill, the fox quietly went into the woods. I had been sitting in plain view only ten feet away, but I had the wind and kept still and the fox never knew that his life had for twenty minutes been in the power of the foe he most feared. Ranger also would have passed me as near as the fox, but I spoke to him, and with a little nervous start he quit the trail and looking sheepish lay down by my feet.

This little comedy was played with variations for several days, but it was all in plain view from the house across the river. My uncle, impatient at the daily loss of hens, went out himself, sat on the open knoll, and when old Scarface trotted to his lookout to watch the dull hound on the river fiat below, my uncle remorselessly shot him in the back, at the very moment when he was grinning over a new triumph.

IV

But still the hens were disappearing. My uncle was wrathy. He determined to conduct the war himself, and sowed the woods with poison baits, trusting to luck that our own dogs would not get them. He indulged in contemptuous remarks on my by-gone woodcraft, and went out evenings with a gun and the two dogs, to see what he could destroy.

Vix knew right well what a poisoned bait was; she passed them by or else treated them with active contempt, but one she dropped down the hole of an old enemy, a skunk, who was never afterward seen. Formerly old Scarface was always ready to take charge of the dogs, and keep them out of mischief. But now that Vix had the whole burden of the brood she could no longer spend time in breaking every track to the den, and was not always at hand to meet and mislead the foes that might be coming too near.

The end is easily foreseen. Ranger followed a hot trail to the den, and Spot, the fox-terrier, announced that the family was at home, and then did his best to go in after them.

The whole secret was now out, and the whole family doomed. The hired man came around with pick and shovel to dig them out, while we and the dogs stood by. Old Vix soon showed herself in the near woods, and led the dogs away off down the river, where she shook them off when she thought proper, by the simple device of springing on a sheep's back. The frightened animal ran for several hundred yards, then Vix got off, knowing that there was now a hopeless gap in the scent, and returned to the den. But the dogs, baffled by the break in the trail, soon did the same, to find Vix hanging about in despair, vainly trying to decoy us away from her treasures.

Meanwhile Paddy plied both pick and shovel with vigour and effect. The yellow, gravelly sand was heaping on both sides, and the shoulders of the sturdy digger were sinking below the level. After an hour's digging, enlivened by frantic rushes of the dogs after the old fox, who hovered near in the woods, Pat called:

'Here they are, sor!'

It was the den at the end of the burrow, and cowering as far back as they could, were the four little woolly cubs.

Before I could interfere, a murderous blow from the shovel, and a sudden rush for the fierce little terrier, ended the lives of three. The fourth and smallest was barely saved by holding him by his tail high out of reach of the excited dogs.

He gave one short squeal, and his poor mother came at the cry, and circled so near that she would have been shot but for the accidental protection of the dogs, who somehow always seemed to get between, and whom she once more led away on a fruitless chase.

The little one saved alive was dropped into a bag, where he lay quite still. His unfortunate brothers were thrown back into their nursery bed, and buried under a few shovelfuls of earth.

We guilty ones then went back into the house, and the little fox was soon chained in the yard. No one knew just why he was kept alive, but in all a change of feeling had set in, and the idea of killing him was without a supporter.

He was a pretty little fellow, like a cross between a fox and a lamb. His woolly visage and form were strangely lamb-like and innocent, but one could find in his yellow eyes a gleam of cunning and savageness as unlamb-like as it possibly could be.

As long as anyone was near he crouched sullen and cowed in his shelter-box, and it was a full hour after being left alone before he ventured to look out.

My window now took the place of the hollow bass wood. A number of hens of the breed he knew so well were about the cub in the yard. Late that afternoon as they strayed near the captive there was a sudden rattle of the chain, and the young-ster dashed at the nearest one and would have caught him but for the chain which brought him up with a jerk. He got on his feet and slunk back to his box, and though he afterward made several rushes he so gauged his leap as to win or fail within the length of the chain and never again was brought up by its cruel jerk.

As night came down the little fellow became very uneasy, sneaking out of his box, but going back at each slight alarm, tugging at his chain, or at times biting it in fury while he held it down with his fore paws. Suddenly he paused as though listening, then raising his little black nose he poured out a short quavering cry.

Once or twice this was repeated, the time between being occupied in worrying the chain and running about. Then an answer came. The far-away *Yap-yurrr* of the old fox. A few minutes later a shadowy form appeared on the wood-pile. The little one slunk into his box, but at once returned and ran to meet his mother with all the gladness that a fox could show. Quick as a flash she seized him and turned to bear him away by the road she came. But the moment the end of the chain was reached the cub was rudely jerked from the old one's mouth, and she, scared by the opening of a window, fled over the wood-pile.

An hour afterward the cub had ceased to run about or cry. I peeped out, and by the light of the moon saw the form of the mother at full length on the ground by the little one, gnawing at something – the clank of iron told what, it was that cruel chain. And Tip, the little one, meanwhile was helping himself to a warm drink.

On my going out she fled Into the dark woods, but there by the shelter-box were two little mice, bloody and still warm, food for the cub brought by the devoted mother. And in the morning I found the chain was very bright for a foot or two next the little one's collar.

On walking across the woods to the ruined den, I again found signs of Vixen. The poor heart-broken mother had come and dug out the bedraggled bodies of her little ones.

There lay the three little baby foxes all licked smooth now, and by them were two of our hens fresh killed. The newly heaved earth was printed all over with telltale signs--signs that told me that here by the side of her dead she had watched like Rizpah. Here she had brought their usual meal, the spoil of her nightly hunt. Here she had stretched herself beside them and vainly offered them their natural drink and yearned to feed and warm them as of old, but only stiff little bodies under their soft wool she found, and little cold noses still and unresponsive.

A deep impress of elbows, breasts, and hocks showed where she had laid in silent grief and watched them for long and mourned as a wild mother can mourn for its young. But from that time she came no more to the ruined den, for now she surely knew that her little ones were dead.

V

Tip the captive, the weakling of the brood, was now the heir to all her love. The dogs were loosed to guard the hens. The hired man had orders to shoot the old fox on sight – so had I but was resolved never to see her. Chicken-heads, that a fox loves and a dog will not touch, had been poisoned and scattered through the woods; and the only way to the yard where Tip was tied, was by climbing the wood-pile after braving all other dangers. And yet each night old Vix was there to nurse her baby and bring it fresh-killed hens and game. Again and again I saw her, although she came now without awaiting the querulous cry of the captive.

The second night of the captivity I heard the rattle of the chain, and then made out that the old fox was there, hard at work digging a hole by the little one's kennel. When it was deep enough to half bury her, she gathered into it all the slack of the chain, and filled it again with earth. Then in triumph thinking she had gotten rid of the chain, she seized little Tip by the neck and turned to dash off up the wood-pile, but alas! only to have him jerked roughly from her grasp.

Poor little fellow, he whimpered sadly as he crawled into his box. After half an hour there was a great out cry among the dogs, and by their straight-away tonguing through the far wood I knew they were chasing Vix. Away up north they went in the direction of the railway and their noise faded from hearing. Next morning the hound had not come back. We soon knew why. Foxes long ago learned what a railroad is; they soon devised several ways of turning it to account. One way is when hunted to walk the rails for a long distance just before a train comes. The scent, always poor on iron, is destroyed by the train and there is always a chance of hounds being killed by the engine. But another way more sure, but harder to play, is to lead the hounds straight to a high trestle just ahead of the train, so that the engine overtakes them on it and they are surely dashed to destruction.

This trick was skilfully played, and down below we found the mangled remains of old Ranger and learned that Vix was already wreaking her revenge.

That same night she returned to the yard before Spot's weary limbs could bring him back and killed another hen and brought it to Tip, and stretched her panting length beside him that he might quench his thirst. For she seemed to think he had no food but what she brought.

It was that hen that betrayed to my uncle the nightly visits.

My own sympathies were all turning to Vix, and I would have no hand in planning further murders. Next night my uncle himself watched, gun in hand, for an hour. Then when it became cold and the moon clouded over he remembered other important business elsewhere, and left Paddy in his place.

But Paddy was 'onaisy' as the stillness and anxiety of watching worked on his nerves. And the loud bang! bang! an hour later left us sure only that powder had been burned.

In the morning we found Vix had not failed her young one. Again next night found my uncle on guards for another hen had been taken. Soon after dark a single shot was heard, but Vix dropped the game she was bringing and escaped. Another attempt made that night called forth another gunshot. Yet next day it was seen by the brightness of the chain that she had come again and vainly tried for hours to cut that hateful bond.

Such courage and staunch fidelity were bound to win respect, if not toleration. At any rate, there was no gunner in wait next night, when all was still. Could it be of any use? Driven off thrice with gunshots, would she make another try to feed or free her captive young one? Would she? Hers was a mother's love. There was but one to watch them this time, the fourth night, when the quavering whine of the little one was followed by that shadowy form above the wood pile.

But carrying no fowl or food that could be seen. Had the keen huntress failed at last? Had she no head of game for this her only charge, or had she learned to trust his captors for his food?

No, far from all this. The wild-wood mother's heart and hate were true. Her only thought had been to set him free. All means she knew she tried, and every danger braved to tend him well and help him to be free. But all had failed.

Like a shadow she came and in a moment was gone, and Tip seized on something dropped, and crunched and chewed with relish what she brought. But even as he ate, a knife-like pang shot through and a scream of pain escaped him. Then there was a momentary struggle and the little fox was dead.

The mother's love was strong in Vix, but a higher thought was stronger. She knew right well the poison's power; she knew the poison bait, and would have taught him had he lived to know and shun it too. But now at last when she must choose for him a wretched prisoner's life or sudden death, she quenched the mother in her breast and freed him by the one remaining door.

It is when the snow is on the ground that we take the census of the woods, and when the winter came it told me that Vix no longer roamed the woods of Erindale. Where she went it never told, but only this, that she was gone.

Gone, perhaps, to some other far-off haunt to leave behind the sad remembrance of her murdered little ones and mate. Or gone, may be, deliberately, from the scene of a sorrowful life, as many a wild-wood mother has gone, by the means that she herself had used to free her young one, the last of all her brood.

THE BIOGRAPHY OF A GRIZZLY

PART I

THE CUBHOOD OF WAHB

I

He was born over a score of years ago, away up in the wildest part of the wild West, on the head of the Little Piney, above where the Palette Ranch is now.

His Mother was just an ordinary Silvertip, living the quiet life that all Bears prefer, minding her own business and doing her duty by her family, asking no favours of any one excepting to let her alone. It was July before she took her remarkable family down the Little Piney to the Greybull, and showed them what strawberries were, and where to find them.

Notwithstanding their Mother's deep conviction, the cubs were not remarkably big or bright; yet they were a remarkable family, for there were four of them, and it is not often a Grizzly Mother can boast of more than two.

The woolly-coated little creatures were having a fine time, and reveled in the lovely mountain summer and the abundance of good things. Their Mother turned over each log and flat stone they came to, and

the moment it was lifted they all rushed under it like a lot of little pigs to lick up the ants and grubs there hidden.

It never once occurred to them that Mammy's strength might fail sometime, and let the great rock drop just as they got under it; nor would any one have thought so that might have chanced to see that huge arm and that shoulder sliding about under the great yellow robe she wore. No, no; that arm could never fail. The little ones were quite right. So they hustled and tumbled one another at each fresh log in their haste to be first, and squealed little squeals, and growled little growls, as if each was a pig, a pup, and a kitten all rolled into one.

They were well acquainted with the common little brown ants that harbor under logs in the uplands, but now they came for the first time on one of the hills of the great, fat, luscious Wood-ant, and they all crowded around to lick up those that ran out. But they soon found that they were licking up more cactus-prickles and sand than ants, till their Mother said in Grizzly, 'Let me show you how.'

She knocked off the top of the hill, then laid her great paw flat on it for a few moments, and as the angry ants swarmed on to it she licked them up with one lick, and got a good rich mouthful to crunch, without a grain of sand or a cactus-stinger in it. The cubs soon learned. Each put up both his little brown paws, so that there was a ring of paws all around the ant-hill, and there they sat, like children playing 'hands,' and each licked first the right and then the left paw, or one cuffed his brother's ears for licking a paw that was not his own, till the ant-hill was cleared out and they were ready for a change.

Ants are sour food and made the Bears thirsty, so the old one led down to the river. After they had drunk as much as they wanted, and dabbled their feet, they walked down the bank to a pool, where the old one's keen eye caught sight of a number of Buffalo-fish basking on the bottom. The water was very low, mere pebbly rapids between these deep holes, so Mammy said to the little ones:

'Now you all sit there on the bank and learn something new.'

First she went to the lower end of the pool and stirred up a cloud of mud which hung in the still water, and sent a long tail floating like a curtain over the rapids just below. Then she went quietly round by land, and sprang into the upper end of the pool with all the noise she could. The fish had crowded to that end, but this sudden attack sent them off in a panic, and they dashed blindly into the mud-cloud. Out of fifty fish there is always a good chance of some being fools, and half a dozen of these dashed through the darkened water into the current, and before they knew it they were struggling over the shingly shallow. The old Grizzly jerked them out to the bank, and the little ones rushed noisily on these funny, short snakes that could not get away, and gobbled and gorged till their little bellies looked like balloons.

They had eaten so much now, and the sun was so hot, that all were quite sleepy. So the Mother-bear led them to a quiet little nook, and as soon as she lay down, though they were puffing with heat, they all snuggled around her and went to sleep, with their little brown paws curled in, and their little black noses tucked into their wool as though it were a very cold day.

After an hour or two they began to yawn and stretch themselves, except little Fuzz, the smallest; she poked out her sharp nose for a moment, then snuggled back between her Mother's great arms, for she was a gentle, petted little thing. The largest, the one afterward known as Wahb, sprawled over on his back and began to worry a root that stuck up, grumbling to himself as he chewed it, or slapped it with his paw for not staying where he wanted it. Presently Mooney, the mischief, began tugging at Frizzle's ears, and got his own well boxed. They clenched for a tussle; then, locked in a tight, little grizzly yellow ball, they sprawled over and over on the grass, and, before they knew it, down a bank, and away out of sight toward the river.

Almost immediately there was an outcry of yells for help from the little wrestlers. There could be no mistaking the real terror in their voices. Some dreadful danger was threatening.

Up jumped the gentle Mother, changed into a perfect demon, and over the bank in time to see a huge Range-bull make a deadly charge at what he doubtless took for a yellow dog. In a moment all would have been over with Frizzle, for he had missed his footing on the bank; but there was a thumping of heavy feet, a roar that startled even the great Bull, and, like a huge bounding ball of yellow fur, Mother Grizzly was upon him.

Him! the monarch of the herd, the master of all these plains, what had he to fear? He bellowed his deep war-cry, and charged to pin the old one to the bank; but as he bent to tear her with his shining horns, she dealt him a stunning blow, and before he could recover she was on his shoulders, raking the flesh from his ribs with sweep after sweep of her terrific claws.

The Bull roared with rage, and plunged and reared, dragging Mother Grizzly with him; then, as he hurled heavily off the slope, she let go to save herself, and the Bull rolled down into the river.

This was a lucky thing for him, for the Grizzly did not want to follow him there; so he waded out on the other side, and bellowing with fury and pain, slunk off to join the herd to which he belonged.

II

Old Colonel Pickett, the cattle king, was out riding the range. The night before, he had seen the new moon descending over the white cone of Pickett's Peak.

'I saw the last moon over Frank's Peak,' said he, 'and the luck was against me for a month; now I reckon it's my turn.'

Next morning his luck began. A letter came from Washington granting his request that a post-office be established at his ranch, and contained the polite inquiry, 'What name do you suggest for the new post-office?'

The Colonel took down his new rifle, a 45-90 repeater. 'May as well,' he said; 'this is my month;' and he rode up the Greybull to see how the cattle were doing.

As he passed under the Rimrock Mountain he heard a far-away roaring as of Bulls fighting, but thought nothing of it till he rounded the point and saw on the flat below a lot of his cattle pawing the dust and bellowing as they always do when they smell the blood of one of their number. He soon saw that the great Bull, 'the boss of the bunch,' was covered with blood. His back and sides were torn as by a Mountain-lion, and his head was battered as by another Bull.

'Grizzly,' growled the Colonel, for he knew the mountains. He quickly noted the general direction of the Bull's back trail, then rode toward a high bank that offered a view. This was across the gravelly ford of the Greybull, near the mouth of the Piney. His horse splashed through the cold water and began jerkily to climb the other bank.

As soon as the rider's head rose above the bank his hand grabbed the rifle, for there in full sight were five Grizzly Bears, an old one and four cubs. 'Run for the woods,' growled the Mother Grizzly, for she knew that men carried guns. Not that she feared for herself; but the idea of such things among her darlings was too horrible to think of. She set off to guide them to the timber-tangle on the Lower Piney. But an awful, murderous fusillade began.

Bang! and Mother Grizzly felt a deadly pang.

Bang! and poor little Fuzz rolled over with a scream of pain and lay still.

With a roar of hate and fury Mother Grizzly turned to attack the enemy.

Bang! and she fell paralyzed and dying with a high shoulder shot. And the three little cubs, not knowing what to do, ran back to their Mother.

Bang! bang! and Mooney and Frizzle sank in dying agonies beside her, and Wahb, terrified and stupefied, ran in a circle about them. Then, hardly knowing why, he turned and dashed into the timber-tangle, and disappeared as a last bang left him with a stinging pain and a useless, broken hind paw.

THAT is why the post-office was called Four-Bears. The Colonel seemed pleased with what he had done; indeed, he told of it himself.

But away up in the woods of Anderson's Peak that night a little lame Grizzly might have been seen wandering, limping along, leaving a bloody spot each time he tried to set down his hind paw; whining and whimpering, 'Mother! Mother! Oh, Mother, where are you?' for he was cold and hungry, and had such a pain in his foot. But there was no

Mother to come to him, and he dared not go back where he had left her, so he wandered aimlessly about among the pines.

Then he smelled some strange animal smell and heard heavy footsteps; and not knowing what else to do, he climbed a tree. Presently a band of great, long-necked, slim-legged animals, taller than his Mother, came by under the tree. He had seen such once before and had not been afraid of them then, because he had been with his Mother. But now he kept very quiet in the tree, and the big creatures stopped picking the grass when they were near him, and blowing their noses, ran out of sight.

He stayed in the tree till near morning, and then he was so stiff with cold that he could scarcely get down. But the warm sun came up, and he felt better as he sought about for berries and ants, for he was very hungry. Then he went back to the Piney and put his wounded foot in the ice-cold water.

He wanted to get back to the mountains again, but still he felt he must go to where he had left his Mother and brothers. When the afternoon grew warm, he went limping down the stream through the timber, and down on the banks of the Greybull till he came to the place where yesterday they had had the fish-feast; and he eagerly crunched the heads and remains that he found. But there was an odd and horrid smell on the wind. It frightened him, and as he went down to where he last had seen his Mother the smell grew worse. He peeped out cautiously at the place, and saw there a lot of Coyotes, tearing at something. What it was he did not know; but he saw no Mother, and the smell that sickened and terrified him was worse than ever, so he quietly turned back toward the timber-tangle of the Lower Piney, and nevermore came back to look for his lost family. He wanted his Mother as much as ever, but something told him it was no use.

As cold night came down, he missed her more and more again, and he whimpered as he limped along, a miserable, lonely, little, motherless Bear – not lost in the mountains, for he had no home to seek, but so sick and lonely, and with such a pain in his foot, and in his stomach a craving for the drink that would nevermore be his. That night he found a hollow log, and crawling in, he tried to dream that his Mother's great, furry arms were around him, and he snuffled himself to sleep.

III

Wahb had always been a gloomy little Bear; and the string of misfortunes that came on him just as his mind was forming made him more than ever sullen and morose. It seemed as though every one were against him. He tried to keep out of sight in the upper woods of the Piney, seeking his food by day and resting a night in the hollow log. But one evening he found it occupied by a Porcupine as big as himself and as bad as a cactus-bush. Wahb could do nothingwith him. He had to give up the log and seek another nest.

One day he went down on the Greybull flat to dig some roots that his Mother had taught him were good. But before he had well begun, a greyish-looking animal came out of a hole in the ground and rushed at him, hissing and growling. Wahb did not know it was a Badger, but he saw it was a fierce animal as big as himself. He was sick, and lame too, so he limped away and never stopped till he was on a ridge in the next canyon. Here a Coyote saw him, and came bounding after him, calling at the same time to another to come and join the fun. Wahb was near a tree, so he scrambled up to the branches. The Coyotes came bounding and yelping below, but their noses told them that this was a young Grizzly they had chased, and they soon decided that a young Grizzly in a tree means a Mother Grizzly not far away, and they had better let him alone.

After they had sneaked off Wahb came down and returned to the Piney. There was better feeding on the Greybull, but every one seemed against him there now that his loving guardian was gone, while on the Piney he had peace at least sometimes, and there were plenty of trees that he could climb when an enemy came.

His broken foot was a long time in healing; indeed, it never got quite well. The wound healed and the soreness wore off, but it left a stiffness that gave him a slight limp, and the sole-balls grew together quite unlike those of the other foot. It particularly annoyed him when he had to climb a tree or run fast from his enemies; and of them he found no end, though never once did a friend cross his path. When he lost his Mother he lost his best and only friend. She would have taught him much that he had to learn by bitter experience, and would have saved him from most of the ills that befell him in his cubhood − ills so many and so dire that but for his native sturdiness he never could have passed through alive.

The piñons bore plentifully that year, and the winds began to shower down the ripe, rich nuts. Life was becoming a little easier for Wahb. He was gaining in health and strength, and the creatures he daily met now let him alone. But as he feasted on the piñons one morning after a gale, a great Black-bear came marching down the hill. 'No one meets a friend in the woods,' was a byword that Wahb had learned already. He swung up the nearest tree. At first the Black-bear was scared, for he smelled the smell of Grizzly; but when he saw it was only a cub, he took courage and came growling at Wahb. He could climb as well as the little Grizzly, or better, and high as Wahb went, the Blackbear followed, and when Wahb got out on the smallest and highest twig that would carry him, the Blackbear cruelly shook him off, so that he was thrown to the ground, bruised and shaken and half-stunned. He limped away moaning, and the only thing that kept the Blackbear from following him up and perhaps killing him was the fear that the old Grizzly might be about. So Wahb was driven away down the creek from all the good piñon woods.

There was not much food on the Greybull now. The berries were nearly all gone; there were no fish or ants to get, and Wahb, hurt, lonely, and miserable, wandered on and on, till he was away down to-ward the Meteetsee. A Coyote came bounding and barking through the sage-brush after him. Wahb tried to run, but it was no use; the Coyote was soon up with him. Then with a sudden rush of desperate courage Wahb turned and charged his foe. The astonished Coyote gave a scared yowl or two, and fled with his tail between his legs. Thus Wahb learned that war is the price of peace.

But the forage was poor here; there were too many cattle; and Wahb was making for a far-away piñon woods in the Meteetsee Canyon when he saw a man, just like the one he had seen on that day of sorrow. At the same moment he heard a bang, and some sage-brush rattled and fell just over his back. All the dreadful smells and dangers of that day came back to his memory, and Wahb ran as he never had run before.

He soon got into a gully and followed it into the canyon. An opening between two cliffs seemed to offer shelter, but as he ran toward it a Range-cow came trotting between, shaking her head at him and snorting threats against his life.

He leaped aside upon a long log that led up a bank, but at once a savage Bobcat appeared on the other end and warned him to go back. It was no time to quarrel. Bitterly Wahb felt that the world was full of enemies. But he turned and scrambled up a rocky bank into the piñon woods that border the benches of the Meteetsee.

The Pine Squirrels seemed to resent his coming, and barked furiously. They were thinking about their piñon-nuts. They knew that this Bear was coming to steal their provisions, and they followed him overhead to scold and abuse him, with such an outcry that an enemy might have followed him by their noise, which was exactly what they intended.

There was no one following, but it made Wahb uneasy and nervous. So he kept on till he reached the timberline, where both food and foes we scarce, and here on the edge of the Mountain-sheep land at last he got a chance to rest.

IV

Wahb never was sweet-tempered like his baby sister, and the persecutions by his numerous foes were making him more and more sour. Why could not they let him alone in his misery? Why was every one against him? If only he had his Mother back! If he could only have killed that Black-bear that had driven him from his woods! It did not occur to him that some day he himself would be big. And that spiteful Bobcat, that took advantage of him; and the man that had tried to kill him. He did not forget any of them, and he hated them all.

Wahb found his new range fairly good, because it was a good nut year. He learned just what the Squirrels feared he would, for his nose directed him to the little granaries where they had stored up great quantities of nuts for winter's use. It was hard on the Squirrels, but it was good luck for Wahb, for the nuts were delicious food. And when the days shortened and the nights began to be frosty, he had grown fat and well-favoured.

He travelled over all parts of the canyon now, living mostly in the higher woods, but coming down at times to forage almost as far as the river. One night as he wandered by the deep-water a peculiar smell reached his nose. It was quite pleasant, so he followed it up to the water's edge. It seemed to come from a sunken log. As he reached over toward this, there was a sudden clank, and one of his paws was caught in a strong, steel Beaver-trap.

Wahb yelled and jerked back with all his strength, and tore up the stake that held the trap. He tried to shake it off, then ran away through the bushes trailing it. He tore at it with his teeth; but there it hung, quiet, cold, strong, and immovable. Every little while he tore at it with his teeth and claws, or beat it against the ground. He buried it in the earth, then climbed a low tree, hoping to leave it behind; but still it clung, biting into his flesh. He made for his own woods, and sat down to try to puzzle it out. He did not know what it was, but his little green-brown eyes glared with a mixture of pain, fright, and fury as he tried to understand his new enemy.

He lay down under the bushes, and, intent on deliberately crushing the thing, he held it down with one paw while he tightened his teeth on the other end, and bearing down as it slid away, the trap jaws opened and the foot was free. It was mere chance, of course, that led him to squeeze both springs at once. He did not understand it, but he did not forget it, and he got these not very clear ideas: 'There is a dreadful little enemy that hides by the water and waits for one. It has an odd smell. It bites one's paws and is too hard for one to bite. But it can be got off by hard squeezing.'

For a week or more the little Grizzly had another sore paw, but it was not very bad if he did not do any climbing.

It was now the season when the Elk were bugling on the mountains. Wahb heard them all night, and once or twice had to climb to get away from one of the big-antlered Bulls. It was also the season when the trappers were coming into the mountains, and the Wild Geese were honking overhead. There were several quite new smells in the woods, too. Wahb followed one of these up, and it led to a place where were some small logs piled together; then, mixed with the smell that had drawn him, was one that he hated – he remembered it from the time when he had lost his Mother. He sniffed about carefully, for it was not very strong, and learned that this hateful smell was on a log in front, and the sweet smell that made his mouth water was under some brush behind. So he went around, pulled away the brush till he got the prize, a piece of meat, and as he grabbed it, the log in front went down with a heavy *chock*.

It made Wahb jump; but he got away all right with the meat and some new ideas, and with one old idea made stronger, and that was, 'When that hateful smell is around it always means trouble'.

As the weather grew colder, Wahb became very sleepy; he slept all day when it was frosty. He had not any fixed place to sleep in; he knew a number of dry ledges for sunny weather, and one or two sheltered nooks for stormy days. He had a very comfortable nest under a root, and one day, as it began to blow and snow, he crawled into this and curled up to sleep. The storm howled without. The snow fell deeper and deeper. It draped the pine-trees till they bowed, then shook themselves clear to be draped anew. It drifted over the mountains and poured down the funnel-like ravines, blowing off the peaks and ridges, and filling up the hollows level with their rims. It piled up over Wahb's den, shutting out the cold of the winter, shutting out itself: and Wahb slept and slept.

V

He slept all winter without waking, for such is the way of Bears, and yet when spring came and aroused him, he knew that he had been asleep a long time. He was not much changed – he had grown in height, and yet was but little thinner. He was now very hungry, and forcing his way through the deep drift that still lay over his den, he set out to look for food. There were no piñon-nuts to get, and no berries or ants; but Wahb's nose led him away up the canyon to the body of a winter-killed Elk, where he had a fine feast, and then buried the rest for future use.

Day after day he came back till he had finished it. Food was very scarce for a couple of months, and after the Elk was eaten, Wahb lost all the fat he had when he awoke. One day he climbed over the Divide into the Warhouse Valley. It was warm and sunny there, vegetation was well advanced, and he found good forage. He wandered down toward the thick timber, and soon smelled the smell of another Grizzly. This grew stronger and led him to a single tree by a Bear-trail. Wahb reared up on his hind feet to smell this tree. It was strong of Bear, and was plastered with mud and Grizzly hair far higher, than he could reach; and Wahb knew that it must have been a very large Bear that had rubbed himself there. He felt uneasy. He used to long to meet one of his own kind, yet now that there was a chance of it he was filled with dread.

No one had shown him anything but hatred in his lonely, unprotected life, and he could not tell what this older Bear might do. As he stood in doubt, he caught sight of the old Grizzly himself slouching along a hillside, stopping from time to time to dig up the quamash-roots and wild turnips.

He was a monster. Wahb instinctively distrusted him, and sneaked away through the woods and up a rocky bluff where he could watch. Then the big fellow came on Wahb's track and rumbled a deep growl of anger; he followed the trail to the tree, and rearing up, he tore the bark with his claws, far above where Wahb had reached. Then he strode rapidly along Wahb's trail. But the cub had seen enough. He fled back over the Divide into the Meteetsee Canyon, and realized in his dim,bearish way that he was at peace there because the Bear-forage was so poor.

As the summer came on, his coat was shed. His skin got very itchy, and he found pleasure in rolling in the mud and scraping his back against some convenient tree. He never climbed now: his claws were too long, and his arms, though growing big and strong, were losing that suppleness of wrist that makes cub Grizzlies and all Black-bears great climbers. He now dropped naturally into the Bear habit of seeing how high he could reach with his nose on the rubbing-post, whenever he was near one.

He may not have noticed it, yet each time he came to a post, after a week or two away, he could reach higher, for Wahb was growing fast and coming into his strength.

Sometimes he was at one end of the country that he felt was his, and sometimes at another, but he had frequent use for the rubbing-tree, and thus it was that his range was mapped out by posts with his own mark on them.

One day late in summer he sighted a stranger on his land,a glossy Black-bear, and he felt furious against the interloper. As the Black-bear came nearer Wahb noticed the tan-red face, the white spot on his breast, and then the bit out of his ear, and last of all the wind brought a whiff. There could be no further doubt; it was the very smell: this was the black coward that had chased him down the Piney long ago. But how he had shrunken! Before, he had looked like a giant; now Wahb felt he could crush him with one paw. Revenge is sweet, Wahb felt, though he did not exactly say it, and he went for that red-nosed Bear. But the Black one went up a small tree like a Squirrel. Wahb tried to follow as the other once followed him, but somehow he could not. He did not seem to know how to take hold now, and after a while he gave it up and went away, although the Blackbear brought him back more than once by coughing in derision. Later on that day, when the Grizzly passed again, the red-nosed one had gone.

As the summer waned, the upper forage-grounds began to give out, and Wahb ventured down to the Lower Meteetsee one night to explore. There was a pleasant odour on the breeze, and following it up, Wahb came to the carcass of a Steer. A good distance away from it were some tiny Coyotes, mere dwarfs compared with those he remembered. Right by the carcass was another that jumped about in the moonlight in a foolish way. For some strange reason it seemed unable to get away. Wahb's old hatred broke out. He rushed up. In a flash the Coyote bit him several times before, with one blow of that great paw, Wahb smashed him into a limp, furry rag; then broke in all his ribs with a crunch or two of his jaws. Oh, but it was good to feel the hot, bloody juices oozing between his teeth!

The Coyote was caught in a trap. Wahb hated the smell of the iron, so he went to the other side of the carcass, where it was not so strong, and had eaten but little before clank, and his foot was caught in a Wolf-trap that he had not seen.

But he remembered that he had once before been caught and had escaped by squeezing the trap. He set a hind foot on each spring and pressed till the trap opened and released his paw. About the carcass was the smell that he knew stood for man, so he left it and wandered down-stream; but more and more often he got whiffs of that horrible odour, so he turned and went back to his quiet piñon benches.

PART II

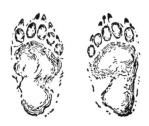

THE DAYS OF HIS STRENGTH

I

Wahb's third summer had brought him the stature of a large-sized Bear, though not nearly the bulk and power that in time were his. He was very light-coloured now, and this was why Spahwat, a Shoshone Indian who more than once hunted him, called him the Whitebear, or Wahb.

Spahwat was a good hunter, and as soon as he saw the rubbing-tree on the Upper Meteetsee he knew that he was on the range of a big Grizzly. He bushwhacked the whole valley, and spent many days before he found a chance to shoot; then Wahb got a stinging flesh-wound in the shoulder. He growled horribly, but it had seemed to take the fight out of him; he scrambled up the valley and over the lower hills till he reached a quiet haunt, where he lay down.

His knowledge of healing was wholly instinctive. He licked the wound and all around it, and sought to be quiet. The licking removed the dirt, and by massage reduced the inflammation, and it plastered the hair down as a sort of dressing over the wound to keep out the air, dirt, and microbes. There could be no better treatment.

But the Indian was on his trail. Before long the smell warned Wahb that a foe was coming, so he quietly climbed farther up the mountain to another resting-place. But again he sensed the Indian's approach, and made off. Several times this happened, and at length there was a second shot and another galling wound. Wahb was furious now. There was nothing that really frightened him but that horrible odour of man, iron, and guns, that he remembered from the day when he lost his

Mother; but now all fear of these left him. He heaved painfully up the mountain again, and along under a six-foot ledge, then up and back to the top of the bank, where he lay flat. On came the Indian, armed with knife and gun; deftly, swiftly keeping on the trail; floating joyfully over each bloody print that meant such anguish to the hunted Bear. Straight up the slide of broken rock he came, where Wahb, ferocious with pain, was waiting on the ledge. On sneaked the dogged hunter; his eye still scanned the bloody slots or swept the woods ahead, but never was raised to glance above the ledge. And Wahb, as he saw this shape of Death relentless on his track, and smelled the hated smell, poised his bulk at heavy cost upon his quivering, mangled arm, there held until the proper instant came, then to his sound arm's matchless native force he added all the weight of desperate hate as down he struck one fearful, crushing blow. The Indian sank without a cry, and then dropped out of sight. Wahb rose, and sought again a quiet nook where he might nurse his wounds. Thus he learned that one must fight for peace; for he never saw that Indian again, and he had time to rest and recover.

II

The years went on as before, except that each winter Wahb slept less soundly, and each spring he came out earlier and was a bigger Grizzly, with fewer enemies that dared to face him. When his sixth year came he was a very big, strong, sullen Bear, with neither friendship nor love in his life since that evil day on the Lower Piney.

No one ever heard of Wahb's mate. No one believes that he ever had one. The love-season of Bears came and went year after year, but left him alone in his prime as he had been in his youth. It is not good for a Bear to be alone; it is bad for him in every way. His habitual moroseness grew with his strength, and any one chancing to meet him now would have called him a dangerous Grizzly.

He had lived in the Meteetsee Valley since first he betook himself there, and his character had been shaped by many little adventures with traps and his wild rivals of the mountains. But there was none of the latter that he now feared, and he knew enough to avoid the first, for that penetrating odour of man and iron was a never-failing warning, especially after an experience which befell him in his sixth year.

His ever-reliable nose told him that there was a dead Elk down among the timber.

He went up the wind, and there, sure enough, was the great delicious carcass, already torn open at the very best place. True, there was that terrible man-and-iron taint, but it was so slight and the feast so tempting that after circling around and inspecting the carcass from his eight feet of stature, as he stood erect, he went cautiously forward, and at once was caught by his left paw in an enormous Bear-trap. He roared with pain and slashed about in a fury. But this was no Beaver-trap; it was a big forty-pound Bear-catcher, and he was surely caught.

Wahb fairly foamed with rage, and madly grit his teeth upon the trap. Then he remembered his former experiences. He placed the trap between his hind legs, with a hind paw on each spring, and pressed down with all his weight. But it was not enough. He dragged off the trap and its clog, and went clanking up the mountain. Again and again he tried to free his foot, but in vain, till he came where a great trunk crossed the trail a few feet from the ground. By chance, or happy thought, he reared again under this and made a new attempt. With a hind foot on each spring and his mighty shoulders underneath the tree, he bore down with his titanic strength: the great steel springs gave way, the jaws relaxed, and he tore out his foot. So Wahb was free again, though he left behind a great toe which had been nearly severed by the first snap of the steel.

Again Wahb had a painful wound to nurse, and as he was a left-handed Bear, – that is, when he wished to turn a rock over he stood on the right paw and turned with the left, – one result of this disablement was to rob him for a time of all those dainty foods that are found under rocks or logs.

The wound healed at last, but he never forgot that experience, and thenceforth the pungent smell of man and iron, even without the gun smell, never failed to enrage him.

Many experiences had taught him that it is better to run if he only smelled the hunter or heard him far away, but to fight desperately if the man was close at hand. And the cowboys soon came to know that the Upper Meteetsee was the range of a Bear that was better let alone.

III

One day after a long absence Wahb came into the lower part of his range, and saw to his surprise one of the wooden dens that men make for themselves. As he came around to get the wind, he sensed the taint that never failed to infuriate him now, and a moment later he heard a loud bang and felt a stinging shock in his left hind leg, the old stiff leg. He wheeled about, in time to see a man running toward the new-made shanty. Had the shot been in his shoulder Wahb would have been helpless, but it was not.

Mighty arms that could toss pine logs like broomsticks, paws that with one tap could crush the biggest Bull upon the range, claws that could tear huge slabs of rock from the mountain-side – what was even the deadly rifle to them!

When the man's partner came home that night he found him on the reddened shanty floor. The bloody trail from outside and a shaky, scribbled note on the back of a paper novel told the tale.

It was Wahb done it. I seen him by the spring and wounded him. I tried to git on the shanty, but he ketched me. My God, how I suffer! JACK.

It was all fair. The man had invaded the Bear's country, had tried to take the Bear's life, and had lost his own. But Jack's partner swore he would kill that Bear.

He took up the trail and followed it up the canyon, and there bushwhacked and hunted day after day. He put out baits and traps, and at length one day he heard a crash, clatter, thump, and a huge rock bounded down a bank into a wood, scaring out a couple of deer that floated away like thistle-down. Miller thought at first that it was a landslide; but he soon knew that it was Wahb that had rolled the boulder over merely for the sake of two or three ants beneath it.

The wind had not betrayed him, so on peering through the bush Miller saw the great Bear as he fed, favouring his left hind leg and growling sullenly to himself at a fresh twinge of pain. Miller steadied himself, and thought, 'Here goes a finisher or a dead miss'. He gave a sharp whistle, the Bear stopped every move, and, as he stood with ears acock, the man fired at his head.

But at that moment the great shaggy head moved, only an infuriating scratch was given, the smoke betrayed the man's place, and the Grizzly made savage, three-legged haste to catch his foe.

Miller dropped his gun and swung lightly into a tree, the only large one near. Wahb raged in vain against the trunk. He tore off the bark with his teeth and claws; but Miller was safe beyond his reach. For fully four hours the Grizzly watched, then gave it up, and slowly went off into the bushes till lost to view. Miller watched him from the tree, and afterward waited nearly an hour to be sure that the Bear was gone. He then slipped to the ground, got his gun, and set out for camp. But Wahb was cunning; he had only seemed to go away, and then had sneaked back quietly to watch. As soon as the man was away from the tree, too far to return, Wahb dashed after him. In spite of his wounds the Bear could move the faster. Within a quarter of a mile – well, Wahb did just what the man had sworn to do to him.

Long afterward his friends found the gun and enough to tell the tale.

The claim-shanty on the Meteetsee fell to pieces. It never again was used, for no man cared to enter a country that had but few allurements to offset its evident curse of ill luck, and where such a terrible Grizzly was always on the war-path.

IV

Then they found good gold on the Upper Meteetsee. Miners came in pairs and wandered through the peaks, rooting up the ground and spoiling the little streams – grizzly old men mostly, that had lived their lives in the mountain and were themselves slowly turning into Grizzly Bears; digging and grubbing everywhere, not for good, wholesome roots, but for that shiny yellow sand that they could not eat; living the lives of Grizzlies, asking nothing but to be let alone to dig.

They seemed to understand Grizzly Wahb. The first time they met, Wahb reared up on his hind legs, and the wicked green lightnings began to twinkle in his small eyes. The elder man said to his mate:

'Let him alone, and he won't bother you.'

'Ain't he an awful size, though?' replied the other, nervously.

Wahb was about to charge, but something held him back – a something that had no reference to his senses, that was felt only when they were still; a something that in Bear and Man is wiser than his wisdom, and that points the way at every doubtful fork in the dim and winding trail.

Of course Wahb did not understand what the men said, but he did feel that there was something different here. The smell of man and iron was there, but not of that maddening kind, and he missed the pungent odour that even yet brought back the dark days of his cubhood.

The men did not move, so Wahb rumbled a subterranean growl, dropped down on his four feet, and went on.

Late the same year Wahb ran across the red-nosed Blackbear. How that Bear did keep on shrinking! Wahb could have hurled him across the Greybull with one tap now.

But the Black-bear did not mean to let him try. He hustled his fat, podgy body up a tree at a rate that made him puff. Wahb reached up nine feet from the ground, and with one rake of his huge claws tore off the bark clear to the shining white wood and down nearly to the ground; and the Blackbear shivered and whimpered with terror as the scraping of those awful claws ran up the trunk and up his spine in a way that was horribly suggestive.

What was it that the sight of that Blackbear stirred in Wahb? Was it memories of the Upper Piney, long forgotten; thoughts of a woodland rich in food?

Wahb left him trembling up there as high as he could get, and without any very clear purpose swung along the upper benches of the Meteetsee down to the Greybull, around the foot of the Rimrock Mountain; on, till hours later he found himself in the timber-tangle of the Lower Piney, and among the berries and ants of the old times.

He had forgotten what a fine land the Piney was: plenty of food, no miners to spoil the streams, no hunters to keep an eye on, and no mosquitos or flies, but plenty of open, sunny glades and sheltering woods, backed up by high, straight cliffs to turn the colder winds. There were, moreover, no resident Grizzlies, no signs even of passing travelers, and the Black-bears that were in possession did not count.

Wahb was well pleased. He rolled his vast bulk in an old Buffalo-wallow, and rearing up against a tree where the Piney Canyon quits the Greybull Canyon, he left on it his mark fully eight feet from the ground.

In the days that followed he wandered farther and farther up among the rugged spurs of the Shoshones, and took possession as he went. He found the signboards of several Black-bears, and if they were small dead trees he sent them crashing to earth with a drive of his giant paw. If they were green, he put his own mark over the other mark, and made it clearer by slashing the bark with the great pickaxes that grew on his toes.

The Upper Piney had so long been a Black-bear range that the Squirrels had ceased storing their harvest in hollow trees, and were now using the spaces under flat rocks, where the Black-bears could not get at them; so Wahb found this a land of plenty: every fourth or fifth rock in the pine woods was the roof of a Squirrel or Chipmunk granary, and when he turned it over, if the little owner were there, Wahb did not scruple to flatten him with his paw and devour him as an agreeable relish to his own provisions. And wherever Wahb went he put up his sign-board:

TRESPASSERS BEWARE!

It was written on the trees as high up as he could reach, and every one that came by understood that the scent of it and the hair in it were those of the great Grizzly Wahb.

If his Mother had lived to train him, Wahb would have known that a good range in spring may be a bad one in summer. Wahb found out by years of experience that a total change with the seasons is best. In the early spring the Cattle and Elk ranges, with their winter-killed carcasses, offer a bountiful feast. In early summer the best forage is on the warm hill-sides where the quamash and the Indian turnip grow. In late summer the berry-bushes along the river-flat are laden with fruit, and in autumn the pine woods gave good chances to fatten for the winter. So he added to his range each year. He not only cleared out the

Black-bears from the Piney and the Meteetsee, but he went over the Divide and killed that old fellow that had once chased him out of the Warhouse Valley. And, more than that, he held what he had won, for he broke up a camp of tenderfeet that were looking for a ranch location on the Middle Meteetsee; he stampeded their horses, and made general smash of the camp. And so all the animals, including man, came to know that the whole range from Frank's Peak to the Shoshone spurs was the proper domain of a king well able to defend it, and the name of that king was Meteetsee Wahb.

Any creature whose strength puts him beyond danger of open attack is apt to lose in cunning. Yet Wahb never forgot his early experience with the traps. He made it a rule never to go near that smell of man and iron, and that was the reason that he never again was caught.

So he led his lonely life and slouched around on the mountains, throwing boulders about like pebbles, and huge trunks like matchwood, as he sought for his daily food. And every beast of hill and plain soon came to know and fly in fear of Wahb, the one time hunted, persecuted cub. And more than one Black-bear paid with his life for the ill-deed of that other, long ago. And many a cranky Bobcat flying before him took to a tree, and if that tree were dead and dry, Wahb heaved it down, and tree and Cat alike were dashed to bits. Even the proud-necked Stallion, leader of the mustang band, thought well for once to yield the road. The great, grey Timberwolves, and the Mountain Lions too, left their new kill and sneaked in sullen fear aside when Wahb appeared. And if, as he hulked across the sage-covered river-flat sending the scared Antelope skimming like birds before him, he was faced perchance, by some burly Range-bull, too young to be wise and too big to be afraid, Wahb smashed his skull with one blow of that giant paw, and served him as the Range-cow would have served himself long years ago.

The All-mother never fails to offer to her own, twin cups, one gall, and one of balm. Little or much they may drink, but equally of each. The mountain that is easy to descend must soon be climbed again. The grinding hardship of Wahb's early days, had built his mighty frame. All usual pleasures of a grizzly's life had been denied him but power bestowed in more than double share. So he lived on year after year, unsoftened by mate or companion, sullen, fearing nothing, ready to fight, but asking only to be let alone – quite alone. He had but one keen pleasure in his sombre life – the lasting glory in his matchless strength – the small but never failing thrill of joy as the foe fell crushed and limp, or the riven boulders grit and heaved when he turned on them the measure of his wondrous force.

V

Everything has a smell of its own for those that have noses to smell. Wahb had been learning smells all his life, and knew the meaning of most of those in the mountains. It was as though each and every thing had a voice of its own for him; and yet it was far better than a voice, for every one knows that a good nose is better than eyes and ears together. And each of these myriads of voices kept on crying, 'Here and such am I.'

The juniper-berries, the rosehips, the strawberries, each had a soft, sweet little voice, calling, 'Here we are – Berries, Berries.'

The great pine woods had a loud, far-reaching voice, 'Here are we, the Pine-trees,' but when he got right up to them Wahb could hear the low, sweet call of the piñon-nuts, 'Here are we, the Piñon-nuts.'

And the quamash beds in May sang a perfect chorus when the wind was right: 'Quamash beds, Quamash beds.'

And when he got among them he made out each single voice.

Each root had its own little piece to say to his nose: 'Here am I, a big Quamash, rich and ripe,' or a tiny, sharp voice, 'Here am I, a good-for-nothing, stringy little root.'

And the broad, rich russulas in the autumn called aloud, 'I am a fat, wholesome Mushroom,' and the deadly amanita cried, 'I am an Amanita. Let me alone, or you'll be a sick Bear.' And the fairy harebell of the canyon-banks sang a song too, as fine as its threadlike stem, and as soft as its dainty blue; but the warden of the smells had learned to report it not, for this, and a million other such, were of no interest to Wahb.

So every living thing that moved, and every flower that grew, and every rock and stone and shape on earth told out its tale and sang its little story to his nose. Day or night, fog or bright, that great, moist nose told him most of the things he needed to know, or passed unnoticed those of no concern, and he depended on it more and more. If his eyes and ears together reported so and so, he would not even then believe it until his nose said, 'Yes; that is right.'

But this is something that man cannot understand, for he has sold the birthright of his nose for the privilege of living in towns.

While hundreds of smells were agreeable to Wahb, thousands were indifferent to him, a good many were unpleasant, and some actually put him in a rage.

He had often noticed that if a west wind were blowing when he was at the head of the Piney Canyon there was an odd, new scent. Some days he did not mind, it, and some days it disgusted him; but he never followed it up. On other days a north wind from the high Divide brought a most awful smell, something unlike any other, a smell that he wanted only to get away from.

Wahb was getting well past his youth now, and he began to have pains in the hind leg that had been wounded so often. After a cold night or a long time of wet weather he could scarcely use that leg, and one day, while thus crippled, the west wind came down the canyon with an odd message to his nose. Wahb could not clearly read the message, but it seemed to say, 'Come,' and something within him said, 'Go.' The smell of food will draw a hungry creature and disgust a gorged one. We do not know why, and all that any one can learn is that the desire springs from a need of the body. So Wahb felt drawn by what had long disgusted him, and he slouched up the mountain path, grumbling to himself and slapping savagely back at branches that chanced to switch his face.

The odd odour grew very strong; it led him where he had never been before – up a bank of whitish sand to a bench of the same colour, where there was unhealthy-looking water running down, and a kind of fog coming out of a hole. Wahb threw up his nose suspiciously – such a peculiar smell! He climbed the bench.

A snake wriggled across the sand in front. Wahb crushed it with a blow that made the near trees shiver and sent a balanced boulder toppling down, and he growled a growl that rumbled up the valley like distant thunder. Then he came to the foggy hole. It was full of water that moved gently and steamed. Wahb put in his foot, and found it was quite warm and that it felt pleasantly on his skin. He put in both feet, and little by little went in farther, causing the pool to overflow on all sides, till he was lying at full length in the warm, almost hot, sulphur-spring, and sweltering in the greenish water, while the wind drifted the steam about overhead.

There are plenty of these sulphur-springs in the Rockies, but this chanced to be the only one on Wahb's range. He lay in it for over an hour; then, feeling that he had had enough, he heaved his huge bulk up on the bank, and realized that he was feeling remarkably well and supple. The stiffness of his hind leg was gone.

He shook the water from his shaggy coat. A broad ledge in full sun-heat invited him to stretch himself out and dry. But first he reared against the nearest tree and left a mark that none could mistake. True, there were plenty of signs of other animals using the sulphur-bath for their ills; but what of it? Thenceforth that tree bore this inscription, in a language of mud, hair, and smell, that every mountain creature could read:

My bath. Keep away!
(Signed) WAHB.

Wahb lay on his belly till his back was dry, then turned on his broad back and squirmed about in a ponderous way till the broiling sun had wholly dried him. He realized that he was really feeling very well now. He did not say to himself, 'I am troubled with that unpleasant disease called rheumatism, and sulphur-bath treatment is the thing to cure it.' But what he did know was, 'I have dreadful pains; I feel better when I am in this stinking pool.' So thenceforth he came back whenever the pains began again, and each time he was cured.

PART III

The Waning

I

Years went by. Wahb grew no bigger – there was no need for that – but he got whiter, crosser, and more dangerous. He really had an enormous range now. Each spring, after the winter storms had removed his notice-boards, he went around and renewed them. It was natural to do so, for, first of all, the scarcity of food compelled him to travel all over the range. There were lots of clay wallows at that season, and the itching of his skin, as the winter coat began to shed, made the dressing of cool, wet clay very pleasant, and the exquisite pain of a good scratching was one of the finest pleasures he knew. So, whatever his motive, the result was the same: the signs were renewed each spring.

At length the Palette Ranch outfit appeared on the Lower Piney, and the men got acquainted with the 'ugly old fellow'. The cowpunchers, when they saw him, decided they 'hadn't lost any Bears and they had better keep out of his way and let him mind his business.'

They did not often see him, although his tracks and sign-boards were everywhere. But the owner of this outfit, a born hunter, took a keen interest in Wahb. He learned something of the old Bear's history from Colonel Pickett, and found out for himself more than the colonel ever knew.

He learned that Wahb ranged as far south as the Upper Wiggins Fork and north to the Stinking Water, and from the Meteetsee to the Shoshones.

He found that Wahb knew more about bear-traps than most trappers do; that he either passed them by or tore open the other end of the bait-pen and dragged out the bait without going near the trap, and by accident or design Wahb sometimes sprang the trap with one of the logs that formed the pen. This ranch-owner found also that Wahb disappeared from his range each year during the heat of the summer, as completely as he did each winter during his sleep.

II

Many years ago a wise government set aside the head waters of the Yellowstone to be a sanctuary of wild life forever. In the limits of this great Wonderland the ideal of the Royal Singer was to be realized, and none were to harm or make afraid. No violence was to be offered to any bird or beast, no ax was to be carried into its primitive forests, and the streams were to flow on forever unpolluted by mill or mine. All things were to bear witness that such as this was the West before the white man came.

The wild animals quickly found out all this. They soon learned the boundaries of this unfenced Park, and, as every one knows, they show a different nature within its sacred limits. They no longer shun the face of man, they neither fear nor attack him, and they are even more tolerant of one another in this land of refuge.

Peace and plenty are the sum of earthly good; so, finding them here, the wild creatures crowd into the Park from the surrounding country in numbers not elsewhere to be seen.

The Bears are especially numerous about the Fountain Hotel. In the woods, a quarter of a mile away, is a smooth open place where the steward of the hotel has all the broken and waste food put out daily for the Bears, and the man whose work it is has become the Steward of the Bears' Banquet. Each day it is spread, and each year there are more Bears to partake of it. It is a common thing now to see a dozen Bears feasting there at one time. They are of all kinds – Black, Brown, Cinnamon, Grizzly, Silvertip, Roachbacks, big and small, families and rangers, from all parts of the vast surrounding country. All seem to realize that in the Park no violence is allowed, and the most ferocious of them have here put on a new behaviour. Although scores of Bears roam about this choice resort, and sometimes quarrel among themselves, not one of them has ever yet harmed a man.

Year after year they have come and gone. The passing travellers see them. The men of the hotel know many of them well. They know that they show up each summer during the short season when the hotel is in use, and that they disappear again, no man knowing whence they come or whither they go.

One day the owner of the Palette Ranch came through the Park. During his stay at the Fountain Hotel, he went to the Bear banquet-hall at high meal-tide. There were several Blackbears feasting, but they made way for a huge Silvertip Grizzly that came about sundown.

'That,' said the man who was acting as guide, 'is the biggest Grizzly in the Park; but he is a peaceable sort, or Lud knows what'd happen.'

'That!' said the ranchman, in astonishment, as the Grizzly came hulking nearer, and loomed up like a load of hay among the piney pillars

of the Banquet Hall. 'That! It that is not Meteetsee Wahb, I never saw a Bear in my life! Why, that is the worst Grizzly that ever rolled a log in the Big Horn Basin.' 'It ain't possible,' said the other, 'for he's here every summer, July and August, an' I reckon he don't live so far away.'

'Well, that settles it,' said the ranchman; 'July and August is just the time we miss him on the range; and you can see for yourself that he is a little lame behind and has lost a claw of his left front foot. Now I know where he puts in his summers; but I did not suppose that the old reprobate would know enough to behave himself away from home.'

The big Grizzly became very well known during the successive hotel seasons. Once only did he really behave ill, and that was the first season he appeared, before he fully knew the ways of the Park.

He wandered over to the hotel, one day, and in at the front door. In the hall he reared up his eight feet of stature as the guests fled in terror; then he went into the clerk's office. The man said: 'All right; if you need this office more than I do, you can have it,' and leaping over the counter, locked himself in the telegraph-office, to wire the superintendent of the Park: 'Old Grizzly in the office now, seems to want to run hotel; may we shoot?'

The reply came: 'No shooting allowed in Park; use the hose.' Which they did, and, wholly taken by surprise, the Bear leaped over the counter too, and ambled out the back way, with a heavy thud-thudding of his feet, and a rattling of his claws on the floor. He passed through the kitchen as he went, and, picking up a quarter of beef, took it along.

This was the only time he was known to do ill, though on one occasion he was led into a breach of the peace by another Bear. This was a large she-Blackbear and a noted mischief-maker. She had a wretched, sickly cub that she was very proud of – so proud that she went out of her way to seek trouble on his behalf. And he, like all spoiled children, was the cause of much bad feeling. She was so big and fierce that she could bully all the other Blackbears, but when she tried to drive off old Wahb she received a pat from his paw that sent her tumbling like a football. He followed her up, and would have killed her, for she had broken the peace of the Park, but she escaped by climbing a tree, from the top of which her miserable little cub was apprehensively squealing at the pitch of his voice. So the affair was ended; in future the Blackbear kept out of Wahb's way, and he won the reputation of being a peaceable, well-behaved Bear. Most persons believed that he came from some remote mountains where were neither guns nor traps to make him sullen and revengeful.

III

Every one knows that a Bitter-root Grizzly is a bad Bear. The Bitter-root Range is the roughest part of the mountains. The ground is everywhere cut up with deep ravines and overgrown with dense and tangled underbrush.

It is an impossible country for horses, and difficult for gunners, and there is any amount of good Bear-pasture. So there are plenty of Bears and plenty of trappers.

The Roachbacks, as the Bitter-root Grizzlies are called, are a cunning and desperate race. An old Roachback knows more about traps than half a dozen ordinary trappers; he knows more about plants and roots than a whole college of botanists. He can tell to a certainty just when and where to find each kind of grub and worm, and he knows by a whiff whether the hunter on his trail a mile away is working with guns, poison, dogs, traps, or all of them together. And he has one general rule, which is an endless puzzle to the hunter: 'Whatever you decide to do, do it quickly and follow it right up'. So when a trapper and a Roachback meet, the Bear at once makes up his mind to run away as hard as he can, or to rush at the man and fight to a finish.

The Grizzlies of the Bad Lands did not do this: they used to stand on their dignity and growl like a thunder-storm, and so gave the hunters a chance to play their deadly lightning; and lightning is worse than thunder any day. Men can get used to growls that rumble along the ground and up one's legs to the little house where one's courage lives; but Bears cannot get used to 45-90 soft-nosed bullets, and that is why the Grizzlies of the Bad Lands were all killed off.

So the hunters have learned that they never know what a Roachback will do; but they do know that he is going to be quick about it.

Altogether these Bitter-root Grizzlies have solved very well the problem of life, in spite of white men, and are therefore increasing in their own wild mountains.

Of course a range will hold only so many Bears, and the increase is crowded out; so that when that slim young Bald-faced Roachback found he could not hold the range he wanted, he went out perforce to seek his fortune in the world.

He was not a big Bear, or he would not have been crowded out; but he had been trained in a good school, so that he was cunning enough to get on very well elsewhere. How he wandered down to the Salmon River Mountains and did not like them; how he travelled till he got among the barb-wire fences of the Snake Plains and of course could not stay there; how a mere chance turned him from going eastward to the Park, where he might have rested; how he made for the Snake River Mountains and found more hunters than berries; how he crossed into the Tetons and looked down with disgust on the teeming man colony of Jackson's Hole, does not belong to this history of Wahb. But when Baldy Roachback crossed the Gros Ventre Range and over the Wind River Divide to the head of the Greybull, he does come into the story, just as he did into the country and the life of the Meteetsee Grizzly.

The Roachback had not found a man-sign since he left Jackson's

Hole, and here he was in a land of plenty of food. He feasted on all the delicacies of the season, and enjoyed the easy, brushless country till he came on one of Wahb's sign-posts.

'Trespassers beware!' it said in the plainest manner. The Roachback reared up against it.

'Thunder! what a Bear!' The nose-mark was a head and neck above Baldy's highest reach. Now, a simple Bear would have gone quietly away after this discovery; but Baldy felt that the mountains owed him a living, and here was a good one if he could keep out of the way of the big fellow. He nosed about the place, kept a sharp lookout for the present owner, and went on feeding wherever he ran across a good thing.

A step or two from this ominous tree was an old pine stump. In the Bitter-roots there are often mice-nests under such stumps, and Baldy jerked it over to see. There was nothing. The stump rolled over against the sign-post. Baldy had not yet made up his mind about it; but a new notion came into his cunning brain. He turned his head on this side, then on that. He looked at the stump, then at the sign, with his little pig--like eyes. Then he deliberately stood up on the pine root, with his back to the tree, and put his mark away up, a head at least above that of Wahb. He rubbed his back long and hard, and he sought some mud to smear his head and shoulders, then came back and made the mark so big, so strong, and so high, and emphasized it with such claw-gashes in the bark, that it could be read only in one way – a challenge to the present claimant from some monstrous invader, who was ready, nay anxious, to fight to a finish for this desirable range.

Maybe it was accident and maybe design, but when the Roach-back jumped from the root it rolled to one side. Baldy went on down the canyon, keeping the keenest lookout for his enemy.

It was not long before Wahb found the trail of the interloper, and all the ferocity of his outside-the-Park nature was aroused.

He followed the trail for miles on more than one occasion. But the small Bear was quick-footed as well as quick-witted, and never showed himself. He made a point, however, of calling at each sign-post, and if there was any means of cheating, so that his mark might be put higher, he did it with a vim, and left a big, showy record. But if there was no chance for any but a fair register, he would not go near the tree, but looked for a fresh tree near by with some log or side-ledge to reach from.

Thus Wahb soon found the interloper's marks towering far above his own – a monstrous Bear evidently, that even he could not be sure of mastering. But Wahb was no coward. He was ready to fight to a finish any one that might come; and he hunted the range for that invader. Day after day Wahb sought for him and held himself ready to fight. He found his trail daily, and more and more often he found that towering record far above his own. He often smelled him on the wind; but he never saw him, for the old Grizzly's eyes had grown very dim of late years; things but a little way off were blurs to him. The continual menace could not but fill Wahb with uneasiness, for he was not young now, and his teeth and claws were worn and blunted. He was more than ever troubled with pains in his old wounds, and though he could have risen on the spur of the moment to fight any number of Grizzlies of any size, still the continual apprehension, the knowledge that he must hold himself ready at any moment to fight this young monster, weighed on his spirits and began to tell on his general health.

IV

The Roachback's life was one of continual vigilance, always ready to run, doubling and shifting to avoid the encounter that must mean in-stant death to him. Many a time from some hiding-place he watched the great Bear, and trembled lest the wind should betray him. Several times his very impudence saved him, and more than once he was nearly cornered in a box-canyon. Once he escaped only by climbing up a long crack in a cliff, which Wahb's huge frame could not have entered. But still, in a mad persistence, he kept on marking the trees farther into the range.

At last he scented and followed up the sulphur-bath. He did not understand it at all. It had no appeal to him, but hereabouts were the tracks of the owner. In a spirit of mischief the Roachback scratched dirt into the spring, and then seeing the rubbing-tree, he stood sidewise on the rocky ledge, and was thus able to put his mark fully five feet above that of Wahb. Then he nervously jumped down, and was running about, defiling the bath and keeping a sharp lookout, when he heard a noise in the woods below. Instantly he was all alert. The sound drew near, then the wind brought the sure proof, and the Roachback, in terror, turned and fled into the woods.

It was Wahb. He had been failing in health of late; his old pains were on him again, and, as well as his hind leg, had seized his right shoulder, where were still lodged two rifle-balls. He was feeling very ill, and crippled with pain. He came up the familiar bank at a jerky limp, and there caught the odour of the foe; then he saw the track in the mud – his eyes said the track of a small Bear, but his eyes were dim now, and his nose, his unerring nose, said, 'This is the track of the huge invader.' Then he noticed the tree with his sign on it, and there beyond doubt was the stranger's mark far above his own. His eyes and nose were agreed on this; and more, they told him that the foe was close at hand, might at any moment come.

Wahb was feeling ill and weak with pain. He was in no mood for a desperate fight. A battle against such odds would be madness now. So, without taking the treatment, he turned and swung along the bench away from the direction taken by the stranger – the first time since his cubhood that he had declined to fight.

That was a turning-point in Wahb's life. If he had followed up the stranger he would have found the miserable little craven trembling, cowering, in an agony of terror, behind a log in a natural trap, a walled-in glade only fifty yards away, and would surely have crushed him. Had he even taken the bath, his strength and courage would have been renewed, and if not, then at least in time he would have met his foe, and his after life would have been different. But he had turned. This was the fork in the trail, but he had no means of knowing it.

He limped along, skirting the lower spurs of the Shoshones, and soon came on that horrid smell that he had known for years, but never followed up or understood. It was right in his road, and he traced it to a small, barren ravine that was strewn over with skeletons and dark objects, and Wahb, as he passed, smelled a smell of many different animals, and knew by its quality that they were lying dead in this treeless, grassless hollow. For there was a cleft in the rocks at the upper end, whence poured a deadly gas; invisible but heavy, it filled the little gulch like a brimming poison bowl, and at the lower end there was a steady overflow. But Wahb knew only that the air that poured from it as he passed made him dizzy and sleepy, and repelled him, so that he got quickly away from it and was glad once more to breathe the piny wind. Once Wahb decided to retreat, it was all too easy to do so next time; and the result worked double disaster.

For, since the big stranger was allowed possession of the sulphur-spring, Wahb felt that he would rather not go there. Sometimes when he came across the traces of his foe, a spurt of his old courage would come back. He would rumble that thunder-growl as of old, and go painfully lumbering along the trail to settle the thing right then and there. But he never overtook the mysterious giant, and his rheumatism, growing worse now that he was barred from the cure, soon made him daily less capable of either running or fighting.

Sometimes Wahb would sense his foe's approach when he was in a bad place for fighting, and, without really running, he would yield to a wish to be on a better footing, where he would have a fair chance. This better footing never led him nearer the enemy, for it is well known that the one awaiting has the advantage.

Some days Wahb felt so ill that it would have been madness to have staked everything on a fight, and when he felt well or a little better, the stranger seemed to keep away.

Wahb soon found that the stranger's track was most often on the Warhouse and the west slope of the Piney, the very best feeding-grounds. To avoid these when he did not feel equal to fighting was only natural, and as he was always in more or less pain now, it amounted to abandoning to the stranger the best part of the range.

Weeks went by. Wahb had meant to go back to his bath, but he never did. His pains grew worse; he was now crippled in his right shoulder as well as in his hind leg.

The long strain of waiting for the fight begot anxiety, that grew to be apprehension, which, with the sapping of his strength, was breaking down his courage, as it always must when courage is founded on muscular force. His daily care now was not to meet and fight the invader, but to avoid him till he felt better.

Thus that first little retreat grew into one long retreat. Wahb had to go farther and farther down the Piney to avoid an encounter. He was daily worse fed, and as the weeks went by was daily less able to crush a foe.

He was living and hiding at last on the Lower Piney – the very place where once his Mother had brought him with his little brothers. The life he led now was much like the one he led after that dark day. Perhaps for the same reason. If he had had a family of his own all might have been different. As he limped along one morning, seeking among the barren aspen groves for a few roots, or the wormy partridge-berries that were too poor to interest the Squirrel and the Grouse, he heard a stone rattle down the western slope into the woods, and, a little later, on the wind was borne the dreaded taint. He waded through the ice-cold Piney, – once he would have leaped it, – and the chill water sent through and up each great hairy limb keen pains that seemed to reach his very life. He was retreating again – which way? There seemed but one way now – toward the new ranch-house.

But there were signs of stir about it long before he was near enough to be seen. His nose, his trustiest friend, said, 'Turn, turn and seek the hills,' and turn he did even at the risk of meeting there the dreadful foe. He limped painfully along the north bank of the Piney, keeping in the hollows and among the trees. He tried to climb a cliff that of old he had often bounded up at full speed. When half-way up his footing gave way, and down he rolled to the bottom. A long way round was now the only road, for onward he must go – on – on. But where? There seemed no choice now but to abandon the whole range to the terrible stranger.

And feeling, as far as a Bear can feel, that he is fallen, defeated, dethroned at last, that he is driven from his ancient range by a Bear too strong for him to face, he turned up the west fork, and the lot was drawn. The strength and speed were gone from his once mighty limbs; he took three times as long as he once would to mount each well-known ridge, and as he went he glanced backward from time to time to know if he were pursued. Away up the head of the little branch were the Shoshones, bleak, forbidding; no enemies were there, and the Park was beyond it all – on, on he must go. But as he climbed with shaky limbs, and short uncertain steps, the west wind brought the odour of Death Gulch, that fearful little valley where everything was dead, where the very air was deadly. It used to disgust him and drive him away, but now Wahb felt that it had a message for him; he was drawn by it. It was in his line of flight, and he hobbled slowly toward the place. He went nearer, nearer, until he stood upon the entering ledge. A Vulture that had descended to feed on one of the victims was slowly going to sleep on the untouched carcass. Wahb swung his great grizzled muzzle and his long white beard in the wind. The odour that he once had hated was attractive now. There was a strange biting quality in the air. His body craved it. For it seemed to numb his pain and it promised sleep, as it did that day when first he saw the place.

Far below him, to the right and to the left and on and on as far as the eye could reach, was the great kingdom that once had been his; where he had lived for years in the glory of his strength; where none had dared to meet him face to face. The whole earth could show no view more beautiful. But Wahb had no thought of its beauty; he only knew that it was a good land to live in; that it had been his, but that now it was gone, for his strength was gone, and he was flying to seek a place where he could rest and be at peace.

Away over the Shoshones, indeed, was the road to the Park, but it was far, far away, with a doubtful end to the long, doubtful journey. But why so far? Here in this little gulch was all he sought; here were peace and painless sleep. He knew it; for his nose, his never-erring nose, said, 'Here! here now!'

He paused a moment at the gate, and as he stood the wind-borne fumes began their subtle work. Five were the faithful wardens of his life, and the best and trustiest of them all flung open wide the door he long had kept. A moment still Wahb stood in doubt. His lifelong guide was silent now, had given up his post. But another sense he felt within. The Angel of the Wild Things was standing there, beckoning, in the little vale. Wahb did not understand. He had no eyes to see the tear in the Angel's eyes, nor the pitying smile that was surely on his lips. He could not even see the Angel. But he felt him beckoning, beckoning. A rush of his ancient courage surged in the Grizzly's rugged breast. He turned aside into the little gulch. The deadly vapours entered in, filled his huge chest and tingled in his vast, heroic limbs as he calmly lay down on the rocky, herbless floor and as gently went to sleep, as he did that day in his Mother's arms by the Greybull, long ago.

A STREET TROUBADOUR

BEING THE ADVENTURES OF A COCK SPARROW

I

Such a chirruping, such a twittering, and such a squirming, fluttering mass! Half a dozen English Sparrows rolling over and chattering around one another in the Fifth Avenue gutter, and in the middle of the mob, when it scattered somewhat, could be seen the cause of it all – a little Hen Sparrow, vigourously, indignantly defending herself against her crowd of noisy suitors. They seemed to be making love to her, but their methods were so rough they might have been a lynching party. They plucked, worried, and harried the indignant little lady in a manner utterly disgraceful, except that it was noticeable they did her no serious harm. She, however, laid about her with a will. Under no compulsion to spare her tormentors, apparently she would have slaughtered them all if she could.

It seemed clear that they were making love to her, but it seemed equally clear that she wanted none of them, and having partly convinced them of this at the point of her beak, she took advantage of a brief scattering of the assailants to fly up to the nearest eaves, displaying in one wing, as she went, some white feathers that afforded a mark to know her by, and may have been one of her chief charms.

II

A COCK SPARROW, in the pride of his black cravat and white collar-points, was hard at work building in a bird-house that some children had set on a pole in the garden for such as he. He was a singular Bird in several respects. The building-material that he selected was all twigs, that must have been brought from Madison or Union Square, and in the early morning he sometimes stopped work for a minute to utter a loud sweet song, much like that of a Canary.

It is not usual for a Cock Sparrow to build alone. But then this was an unusual Bird. After a week he had apparently finished the nest, for the bird-house was crammed to the very door with twig purloined from the municipal shade-trees. He had now more leisure for music, and astonished the people about by frequent rendering of his long, un-sparrow-like ditty; and he might have gone down to history as an unaccountable mystery, but that a barber bird-fancier on Sixth Avenue supplied the missing chapters of his early life.

This man, it seems, had put a Sparrow's egg into the wicker basket-nest of his Canaries. The youngster had duly hatched, and had been trained by the foster-parents. Their specialty was song. He had the lungs and robustness of his own race. The Canaries had trained him well, and the result was a songster who made up in energy what he lacked in native talent. Strong and pugnacious, as well as musical, this vociferous roustabout had soon made himself master of the cage. He had no hesitation in hammering into silence a Canary that he could not put down by musical superiority, and after one of these little victories his strains were so unusually good that the barber had a stuffed Canary provided for the boisterous musician to vanquish whenever he wished to favour some visitor with Randy's exultant paeans of victory. He worried into silent subjection all of the Canaries he was caged with, and when finally kept by himself nothing angered him more than to be near some voluble songster that he could neither silence nor get at. On these occasions he forgot his music, and his own Sparrow nature showed in the harsh *chirrup, chirrup* that has apparently been developed to make itself appreciated in the din of street traffic.

By the time his black bib had appeared he had made himself one of the chief characters and quite the chief attraction of the barber-shop. But one day the shelf on which the bird-cages stood gave way, all the cages were dashed to the floor, and in the general smash many of the Birds escaped. Among them was Randy, or, more properly, Bertrand, as this pugnacious songster was named after the famous Troubadour. The Canaries had voluntarily returned to their cages, or permitted themselves to be caught.

But Randy hopped out of a back window,

chirruped a few times, sang a defiant answer to the elevated-railway whistle, and keeping just out of reach of all attempts to capture him, he began to explore the brick wilderness about. He had not been a prisoner for generations. He readily accepted the new condition of freedom, and within a week was almost as wild as any of his kin, and had degenerated into a little street rowdy like the others, squabbling among them in the gutter, giving them blow for blow, or surprising all hearers with occasional bursts of Canary music delivered with Sparrow energy.

III

THIS, then, was Randy, who had selected the bird-house for a nesting-place, and the reason for his intemperance in the matter of twigs is now clear. The only nest he had ever known was of basketwork; therefore a proper nest is made of twigs.

Within a few days Randy appeared with a mate. I might have forgotten the riot scene in the gutter, as such things are common, but that I now recognized in Randy's bride the little white-winged Biddy Sparrow that had caused it. She had apparently accepted Randy, but she was still putting on airs, pecking at him when he came near. He was squirming around with drooping wings and tilted tail, chirping like any other ardent Cock Sparrow, but occasionally stopping to show off his Canary accomplishment.

Any objections she may have had were apparently overcome, possibly by this astonishing display of genius, and he escorted her to the ready-made nest, running in ahead to show the way, and hopping proudly, noisily, officiously about her. She followed him, but came out again quickly, with Randy after her chirping and beseeching. He chattered a long time before he could persuade her to re-enter, but again she came out immediately, this time sputtering and scolding. Again he seemed to exert his power of persuasion, and finally she went in chattering, reappeared with a twig in her bill, dropped it, and flew away out of sight. Randy came out. All his joy and pride in his house were gone. This was a staggering blow, when he had looked for unmitigated commendation. He sat disconsolately on the door-step for a minute, and chirruped in a way that probably meant, 'Come back, come back!' But his bride did not come. He turned into the house. There was a scratching sound, and he came out at once with a large stick and flung it from the door to the ground. He returned for another, sent that flying after the first, and so went on, dragging out and hurling down all the sticks he had so carefully and labouriously carried in. That wonderful forked one that had given so much trouble to get here from Union Square, and those two smooth ones, just like the ones in his foster-mother's nest – all must go. For over an hour he toiled away in silence and alone. Then, apparently, he had ended his task, for on the ground below was a pile of sticks, as big as a bonfire, the labour of a week undone. Randy glared fiercely at them and at the empty house, gave a short, harsh chirp, probably a Sparrow bad word, then flew away.

Next day he reappeared with Biddy, fussing about her in passerine exuberance once more, and chirping as he led her to the door again. She hopped in, then out, looked aslant at the twigs below, went back in, reappeared with a very small twig that had been overlooked, dropped it, and with evident satisfaction watched it fall on the pile below. After running in and out a dozen times they set off together, and presently returned, Biddy with her bill full of hay, Randy with one straw. These were carried in and presumably arranged satisfactorily. Then they went for more hay, and having got Randy set right, she remained in the box to arrange the hay as he brought it, only occasionally going for a load when he was long in coming. It was marvellous to see how the chivalry in this aggressive musician was reducing him to subjection. It seemed a good opportunity to try their tastes. I put out thirty short strings and ribbons in a row on a balcony near. Fifteen were common strips, eight were gaudy strips, and seven were bright silk ribbons. Every other one in the row was a dull string. Biddy was the first to see this array of material. She flew down, looked over it, around it, left eye, right eye; then decided to let it alone. But Randy came closer; he was not unfamiliar with threads. He hopped this way, then that, pulled at a thread, started back, but came nearer, nibbled at one or two, then made a. dart at a string and bore it away. Next time Biddy came, and each bore off a string. They took only the dull ones, but after these were gone Biddy selected some of the brighter material, though even she did not venture on the gaudiest ribbons, and Randy would have no hand in bringing home any but the soberest and most stick-like materials. The nest was now half done. Randy once more ventured to carry in a stick, but a moment later it was whirling down to the pile below, with Biddy triumphantly gazing after it. Poor Randy! no toleration for *his* hobby – all those splendid sticks wasted. His mother had had a stick nest, – a beautiful nest it was, – but he was overruled. Nothing but straw now; then, not sticks, but softer material. He submitted – liberty had brought daily lessons of submission. He used to think that the barber-shop was the whole world and himself the most important living being. But of late both these ideas had been badly shaken. Biddy found that his education had been sadly neglected in all useful matters, and in each new kind of material she had to instruct him anew.

When the nest was two-thirds finished, Biddy, whose ideas were quite luxurious, began to carry in large soft feathers. But now Randy thought this was going too far. He must draw the line somewhere. He drew it at feather beds. His earliest cradle had had no such lining. He proceeded to bundle out the objectionable feather bedding, and Biddy, returning with a new load, was just in time to see the first lot float downward from the door to join the stick pile below. She fluttered after them, seized them in the air, and returned to meet her lord coming out of the door with more of the obnoxious plumes, and there they stood, glaring at each other, chattering their loudest, their mouths full of feathers, and their hearts full of indignation.

How is it that when it is a question of home furnishing we sympathize with the female? I felt that Biddy had first right, and in the end she got her way. First there was a stormy time in which quantities of feathers were carried in and out of the house, or wind-borne about the garden. Then there was a lull, and next day all the feathers were carried back to the nest. Just how they arranged the matter will never be known, but it is sure that Randy himself did the greater part of the work, and never stopped till the box was crammed with the largest and softest of feathers. During all this they were usually together, but one day Biddy went off and stayed for some time. Raridy looked about, chirruped, got no answer, looked up, then down, and far below he saw the pile of sticks that he had toiled to bring. Those dear sticks, just like the home of his early days! Randy fluttered down. There was the curious forked one still. The temptation was irresistible. Randy picked it up and hurried to the nest, then in. It had always been a difficult twig to manage – that side prong would catch at the door; but he had carried it so often now that he knew how. After half a minute's delay inside, while he was placing it, I suppose, he came out again, looked perkily about, preened and shook himself, then sang his Canary song from beginning to end several times, tried some new bars, and seemed extremely happy.

When Biddy came with more feathers, he assiduously helped her to place them inside, and then the nest was finished. Two days later I got up to the nest, and in it found one egg. The Sparrows saw me go up, but did not fly chattering about my head, as do most Birds. They flew away to a distance, and watched anxiously from the shelter of some chimneys.

The third day there was a great commotion in the box, a muffled scuffling and chattering, and once or twice a tail appeared at the door as though the owner were trying to back out. Then it seemed that something was being dragged about.

At length the owner of the tail came out far enough to show that it was Biddy; but, apparently, she was pulled in again.

Evidently a disgraceful family brawl was on. It was quite unaccountable, until finally Biddy struggled out of the door, dragging Randy's pet twig to throw it contemptuously on the ground below. She had discovered it in the bedding where he had hidden it; hence the row. But I do not see how she could drag it out when he was resisting. I suspect that he really weakened for the sake of peace. In the scuffle and general upset the egg – their first arrival – was unfortunately tumbled out with the stick, and fell down to lie below, in porcelain fragments, on a wet yellow background. The Sparrows did not seem to trouble about the remains. Having dropped from the nest, it had dropped out of their world.

IV

AFTER this the pair got along peaceably for several days. Egg after egg was added to the nest. In a week there were five, and the two seemed now to be quite happy together. Randy sang to the astonishment of all the neighbourhood, and Biddy carried in more feathers as though preparing to set and anticipating a blizzard. But about this time it occurred to me to try a little experiment with the pair. Watching my chance, late one evening, I dropped a marble into the luxurious nest. What happened at once I do not know, but early the next morning I was out on Fifth Avenue near the corner of Twenty-first Street. It was Sunday. The street was very quiet, but a ring of perhaps a dozen people were standing gazing at something in the gutter. As I came near I heard occasional chirruping, and getting a view into the ring, I saw two Sparrows locked in fierce combat, chirruping a little, but hammering and pecking away in deadly earnest. They scuffled around, regardless of the bystanders, for some time; but when at length they paused for breath, and sat back on their tails and heels to gasp, I was quite shocked to recognize Biddy and Randy. After another round they were shooed away by one of the onlookers, who evidently disapproved of Sunday brawling. They then flew to the nearest roof to go on as before. That afternoon I found below the nest not only the intrusive marble, but also the remains of the five eggs, all alike thrown out, and I suspect that the presence of that curious hard round egg in the nest, arid the obvious implication, were the cause of the brawl.

Whether Biddy had been able to explain it or not I do not know, but it seemed that the couple decided to forget the past and begin again. There was evidently neither luck nor peace in that bird-box, so they abandoned it, feathers and all; and Biddy, whose ideas were distinctly original, selected the site this time, nothing less than the top of an electric lamp in the middle of Madison Square. All week they laboured, and in spite of a high wind most of the time, they finished the nest. It is hard to see how the Birds could sleep at night with that great glaring buzzing light under their noses. Still, Biddy seemed pleased, Randy was learning to suppress his own opinion, and all would have gone well but that before the first egg was laid the carbon-points of the light burned out, and the man who put in the new ones thought proper to consign remorselessly the whole of the Biddy-Randy mansion to the garbage-can. A Robin or a Swallow might have felt this a crushing blow, but there is no limit to a Sparrow's energy and hopefulness. Evidently it was the wrong kind of a nest. Probably the material was at fault. At any rate, a radical change would be much better. After embezzling some long straws from the nest of an absent neighbour, Biddy laid them in the high fork of an elm-tree in Madison Square Park, by way of letting Randy know that this was the place now selected; and Randy, having learned by this time that it was less trouble to accept her decision than to offer an opinion of his own, sang a Canary trill on two chirps, and set about rummaging in the garbage-heaps for choice building-material, winking hard and looking the other way when a nice twig presented itself.

V

ON the other side of the Square was the nest of a pair of very unpopular Sparrows. The male bird in particular had made himself thoroughly disliked. He was a big, handsome fellow with an enormous black cravat, but an out-and-out bully. Might is right in Sparrow world. Their causes for quarrel are food, mates, quarters, and nesting-material – pretty much as with ourselves. This arrogant little Bird, by reason of his strength, had the mate of his choice and the best nesting-site, and was adding to it all the most-admired material in the Square. My Sparrows had avoided the gaudy ribbons I offered. They were not educated up to that pitch, but they certainly had their esthetic preferences. A few Guinea-fowl feathers that originally came from Central Park Menagerie had been stolen from one nest to another, till now they rested in the sumptuous home with which Cravat and his wife had embellished one of the marble capitals of the new bank. The Bully did much as he pleased in the Park, and one day, on hearing Randy's song, flew at him. Randy had been a terror among Canaries, but against Cravat he had but little chance. He did his best, but was defeated, and took refuge in flight. Puffed up by this victory, the Bully flew to Randy's new nest, and after a more or less scornful scrutiny proceeded to drag out some strings that he thought he might use at home. Randy had been worsted, but the sight of this pillage roused the doughty Troubadour again, and he flew at the Bully as before. From the branches they tumbled to the ground. Other Sparrows joined in, and, shame to tell! they joined with the big fellow against the comparative stranger. Randy was getting very roughly handled, feathers began to float away, when into the ring flashed a little Hen Sparrow with white wing-feathers, chirrup, chirrup, wallop, wallop, she went into it. Oh, how she did lay about her! The Sparrows that had joined in for fun now went off: there was no longer any fun in it, nothing but hard pecks, and the tables were completely turned on Cravat. He quickly lost heart, then, and fled toward his own quarter of the Square, with Biddy holding on to his tail like a little bulldog; and there she continued to hang till the feather came out by the roots, and she afterward had the satisfaction of working it into the coarser make-up of her nest along with the rescued material. It is hardly possible that Sparrows have refined ideas of justice and retribution, but it is sure that things which look like it do crop up among them. Within two days the Guinea-fowl feathers that had so long been the chief glory of the Cravat's nest now formed part of the furnishing of Biddy's new abode, and none had the temerity to dispute her claim.

It was now late in the season, feathers were scarce, and Biddy could not find enough for the lining that she was so particular about. But she found a substitute that appealed to her love of the novel. In the Square was the cab-stand, and scattering near were usually more or less horsehairs. These seemed to be good and original linings. A most happy thought, and with appropriate enthusiasm the ever-hopeful couple set about gathering horsehairs, two or three at a time. Possibly the nest of a Chipping Sparrow in one of the parks gave them the idea. The Chippy always lines with horse-hair, and gets an admirable spring-mattress effect by curling the hair round and round the inside of the nest. The result is good, but one must know how to get it. It would have been well had the Sparrows learned how to handle the hair. When a Chippy picks up a horsehair to bring home it takes only one at a time, and is careful to lift it by the end, for the harmless-looking hair is not without its dangers. The Sparrows had no notion of handling it except as they did the straw. Biddy seized a hair near the middle, found it somewhat long, so took a second hold, several inches away. In most cases this made a great loop in the hair over her head or beyond her beak. But it was a convenient way to manage, and at first no mischief came, though Chippy, had she seen, might well have shuddered at the idea of that threatening noose.

It was the last day of the lining. Biddy had in some way given Randy to understand that no more hair was needed, and, proud and bustling, she was adding a few finishing touches and a final hair while he was trying some new variations of his finest bars on top of Farragut's head, when a loud alarm chirrup from Biddy caught his ear. He looked toward the new home to see her struggling up and down without apparent reason, and yet unable to get more than her length away from the nest. She had at last put her head through one of those dangerous hair nooses, made by herself, and by mischance had tightened and twisted it so that she was caught. The more she struggled and twisted the tighter became the noose. Randy now discovered that he was deeply attached to this wilful little termagant. He became greatly excited, and flew about chattering. He tried to release her by pulling at her foot, but that only made matters worse. All their efforts were in vain. Several new kinks were added to the hair. Other hairs from the nest seemed to join in the plot, and, tangled and intermeshed, they tightened even more, till the group of wondering, upturned child faces in the Park below were centred on a tousled feathery form hanging still and silent in the place of the bustling, noisy, energetic Biddy Sparrow.

Poor Randy seemed deeply distressed. The neighbour Sparrows had come at the danger-call note, and joined their cries with his, but had not been able to help the victim. Now they went off to their own squabbles and troubles, and Randy hopped about chirping or sat still with drooping wings. It was long before he realized that she was dead, and all that day he exerted himself to interest her and make her join in their usual life. At night he rested alone in one of the trees, and at grey dawn was bustling about, singing occasionally and chirruping around the nest, from whose rim, in the fateful horse-hair, hung Biddy, stiff and silent now.

VI

Randy had never been an alert Sparrow. His Canary training had really handicapped him. He was venturesome and heedless with carnages as well as with children. This peculiarity was greatly increased by his present preoccupation, and while foraging somewhat listlessly on Madison Avenue, that afternoon, a messenger-boy on a wheel came silently up, and before Randy realized his danger, the wheel was on his tail. As he struggled to get away, even at the price of his tail, his right wing flashed under the hind wheel, and then he was crippled. The boy rode on, and Randy managed to flutter and hop away toward the sheltering trees. A little girl, assisted by her small dog, captured the cripple, after an exciting chase among the benches. She took him home, and moved by what her brothers considered sadly misplaced tenderness, she caged and nursed him. When he began to recover, he one day surprised them by singing his Canary song.

This created quite a stir in the household. In time a newspaper reporter heard of it. The inevitable write-up followed, and this met the eye of the Sixth Avenue barber. He came with many witnesses to claim his bird, and at length his claim was allowed.

So Randy is once more in a cage, carefully watched and fed, the central figure in a small world, and not at all unhappy. After all, he was never a truly wild Bird. It was an accident that set him free originally. An accident had mated him with Biddy. Their brief life together had been a succession of storms and accidents. An accident had taken her away, and another accident had renewed his cage life. This life, comparatively calm and uneventful, has given him an opportunity to cultivate his musical gifts, for he is in a very conservatory of music, and close at hand are his old tutors and foster-parents.

Sometimes when left alone he amuses himself by beginning a rude nest of sticks, but he looks guilty, and leaves that corner of the cage when any one comes near. If a few feathers are given him they are worked into the nest at first, but next morning are invariably found on the floor below. These persistent attempts at nesting suggested that he wanted a mate, and several were furnished on approval, but the result was not happy. Prompt interference was needed each time to prevent bloodshed and to rescue the intended bride. So the attempt was given up. Evidently this Troubadour wants no new lady-love. His songs seem to be rather of war, for the barber has discovered that when he wishes to provoke Randy into his most rapturous musical expression it is only necessary to let him demolish, not the effigy of a Canary, but a stuffed Cock Sparrow. And on these occasions Randy develops an enthusiasm almost amounting to inspiration if the dummy have a very well marked black patch on the throat.

This, however, is mere by-play. All his best energies are devoted to song. And if you stumble on the right barber-shop you may see this energetic recluse, forgetting the cares, joys, and sorrows of active life in his devotion to music, like some monk who has tried the world, found it too hard for him, and has gladly returned to his cell, there to devote the rest of his days to purely spiritual pleasures.

WULLY

The Story of a Yaller Dog

Wully was a little yaller dog. A yaller dog, be it understood, is not necessarily the same as a yellow dog. He is not simply a canine whose capillary covering is highly charged with yellow pigment. He is the mongrelest mixture of all mongrels, the least common multiple of all dogs, the breedless union of all breeds, and though of no breed at all, he is yet of older, better breed than any of his aristocratic relations, for he is nature's attempt to restore the ancestral jackal, the parent stock of all dogs.

Indeed, the scientific name of the jackal (*Canis aureus*) means simply 'yellow dog', and not a few of that animal's characteristics are seen in his domesticated representative. For the plebeian cur is shrewd, active, and hardy, and far better equipped for the real struggle of life than any of his 'thoroughbred' kinsmen.

If we were to abandon a yaller dog, a greyhound, and a bulldog on a desert island, which of them after six months would be alive and well? Unquestionably it would be the despised yellow cur. He has not the speed of the greyhound, but neither does he bear the seeds of lung and skin diseases. He has not the strength or reckless courage of the bulldog, but he has something a thousand times better, he has *common sense*. Health and wit are no mean equipment for the life struggle, and when the dog-world is not 'managed' by man, they have never yet failed to bring out the yellow mongrel as the sole and triumphant survivor.

Once in a while the reversion to the jackal type is more complete, and the yaller dog has pricked and pointed ears. Beware of him then. He is cunning and plucky and can bite like a wolf. There is a strange, wild streak in his nature too, that under cruelty or long adversity may develop into deadliest treachery in spite of the better traits that are the foundation of man's love for the dog.

I

Away up in the Cheviots little Wully was born. He and one other of the litter were kept; his brother because he resembled the best dog in the vicinity, and himself because he was a little yellow beauty.

His early life was that of a sheep-dog, in company with an experienced collie who trained him, and an old shepherd who was scarcely inferior to them in intelligence. By the time he was two years old Wully was full grown and had taken a thorough course in sheep. He knew them from ram-horn to lamb-hoof, and old Robin, his master, at length had such confidence in his sagacity that he would frequently stay at the tavern all night while Wully guarded the woolly idiots in the hills. His education had been wisely bestowed and in most ways he was a very bright little dog with a future before him, Yet he never learned to despise that addlepated Robin. The old shepherd, with all his faults, his continual striving after his ideal state – intoxication – and his mind-shrivelling life in general was rarely brutal to Wully, and Wully repaid him with an exaggerated worship that the greatest and wisest in the land would have aspired to in vain.

Wully could not have imagined any greater being than Robin, and yet for the sum of five shillings a week all Robin's vital energy and mental force were pledged to the service of a not very great cattle and sheep dealer, the real proprietor of Wully's charge, and when this man, really less great than the neighbouring laird, or dered Robin to drive his flock by stages to the Yorkshire moors and markets, of all the 376 mentalities concerned, if Wully's was the most interested and interesting.

The journey through Northumberland was uneventful. At the River Tyne the sheep were driven on to the ferry and landed safely in smoky

South Shields. The great factory chimneys were just starting up for the day and belching out fogbanks and thunder-rollers of opaque leaden smoke that darkened the air and hung low like a storm-cloud over the streets. The sheep thought that they recognized the fuming dun of an unusually heavy Cheviot storm. They became alarmed, and in spite of their keepers stampeded through the town in 374 different directions.

Robin was vexed to the inmost recesses of his tiny soul. He stared stupidly after the sheep for half a minute, then gave the order, 'Wully, fetch them in.' After this mental effort he sat down, lit his pipe, and taking out his knitting began work on a half-finished sock.

To Wully the voice of Robin was the voice of God. Away he ran in 374 different directions, and headed off and rounded up the 374 different wanderers, and brought them back to the ferry-house before Robin, who was stolidly watching the process, had toed off his sock. Finally Wully – not Robin – gave the sign that all were in. The old shepherd proceeded to count them – 370, 371, 372, 373.

'Wully,' he said reproachfully, 'thar no' a' here. Thur's anither.' And Wully, stung withshame, bounded off to scour the whole city for the missing one. He was not long gone when a small boy pointed out to Robin that the sheep were all there, the whole 374. Now Robin was in a quandary. His order was to hasten on to Yorkshire, and yet he knew that Wully's pride would prevent his coming back without another sheep, even if he had to steal it. Such things had happened before, and resulted in embarrassing complications. What should he do?

There was five shillings a week at stake. Wully was a good dog, it was a pity to lose him, but then, his orders from the master; and again, if Wully stole an extra sheep to make up the number, then what – in a foreign land too? He decided to abandon Wully, and push on alone with the sheep. And how he fared no one knows or cares.

Meanwhile, Wully careered through miles of streets hunting in vain for his lost sheep. All day he searched, and at night, famished and worn out, he sneaked shamefacedly back to the ferry, only to find that master and sheep had gone. His sorrow was pitiful to see. He ran about

whimpering, then took the ferryboat across to the other side, and searched everywhere for Robin. He returned to South Shields and searched there, and spent the rest of the night seeking for his wretched idol. The next day he continued his search, he crossed and re-crossed the river many times. He watched and smelt everyone that came over, and with significant shrewdness he sought unceasingly in the neighbouring taverns for his master. The next day he set to work systematically to smell everyone that might cross the ferry.

The ferry makes fifty trips a day, with an average of one hundred persons a trip, yet never once did Wully fail to be on the gang-plank and smell every pair of legs that crossed – 5,000 pairs, 10,000 legs that day did Wully examine after his own fashion. And the next day, and the next, and all the week he kept his post, and seemed indifferent to feeding himself. Soon starvation and worry began to tell on him. He grew thin and ill-tempered. No one could touch him, and any attempt to interfere with his daily occupation of leg-smelling roused him to desperation.

Day after day, week after week Wully watched and waited for his master, who never came. The ferry men learned to respect Wully's fidelity. At first he scorned their proffered food and shelter, and lived no one knew how, but starved to it at last, he accepted the gifts and learned to tolerate the givers. Although embittered against the world, his heart was true to his worthless master.

Fourteen months afterward I made his acquaintance. He was still on rigid duty at his post. He had regained his good looks. His bright, keen face set off by his white ruff and pricked ears made a dog to catch the eye anywhere. But he gave me no second glance, once he found my legs were not those he sought, and in spite of my friendly overtures during the ten months following that he continued his watch. I got no farther into his confidence than any other stranger.

For two whole years did this devoted creature attend that ferry. There was only one thing to prevent him going home to the hills, not the distance nor the chance of getting lost, but the conviction that Robin, the godlike Robin, wished him to stay by the ferry; and he stayed.

But he crossed the water as often as he felt it would serve his purpose. The fare for a dog was one penny, and it was calculated that Wully owed the company hundreds of pounds before he gave up his quest. He never failed to sense every pair of nethers that crossed the gangplank – 6,000,000 legs by computation had been pronounced upon by this expert. But all to no purpose.

His unswerving fidelity never faltered, though his temper was obviously souring under the long strain.

We had never heard what became of Robin, but one day a sturdy drover strode down the ferry-slip and Wully mechanically assaying the new personality, suddenly started, his mane bristled, he trembled, a low growl escaped him, and he fixed his every sense on the drover.

One of the ferry hands not understanding, called to the stranger, 'Hoot mon, ye maunna hort oor dawg.'

'Whaes hortin 'im, ye fule; he is mair like to hort me.' But further explanation was not necessary. Wully's manner had wholly changed. He fawned on the drover, and his tail was wagging violently for the first time in years. A few words made it all clear. Dorley, the drover, had known Robin very well, and the mittens and comforter he wore were of Robin's own make and had once been part of his wardrobe. Wully recognized the traces of his master, and despairing of any nearer approach to his lost idol, he abandoned his post at the ferry and plainly announced his intention of sticking to the owner of the mittens, and Dorley was well pleased to take Wully along to his home among the hills of Derbyshire, where he became once more a sheep-dog in charge of a flock.

II

Monsaldale is one of the best-known valleys in Derbyshire. The Pig and Whistle is its single but celebrated inn, and Jo Greatorex, the landlord, is a shrewd and sturdy Yorkshireman. Nature meant him for a frontiersman, but circumstances made him an innkeeper and his inborn tastes made him a – well, never mind; there was a great deal of poaching done in that country.

Wully's new home was on the upland east of the valley above Jo's inn, and that fact was not without weight in bringing me to Monsaldale. His master, Doricy, farmed in a small way on the lowland, and on the moors had a large number of sheep. These Wully guarded with his old-time sagacity, watching them while they fed and bringing them to the fold at night. He was reserved and preoccupied for a dog, and rather too ready to show his teeth to strangers, but he was so unremitting in his attention to his flock that Dorley did not lose a lamb that year, although the neighbouring farmers paid the usual tribute to eagles and to foxes.

The dales are poor fox-hunting country at best. The rocky ridges, high stone walls, and precipices are too numerous to please the riders, and the final retreats in the rocks are so plentiful that it was a marvel the foxes did not overrun Monsaldale. But they didn't. There had been but little reason for complaint until the year 1881, when a sly old fox quartered himself on the fat parish, like a mouse inside a cheese, and laughed equally at the hounds of the huntsmen and the lurchers of the farmers.

He was several times run by the Peak hounds, and escaped by making for the Devil's Hole. Once in this gorge, where the cracks in the rocks extend unknown distances, he was safe. The country folk began to see something more than chance in the fact that he always escaped at the Devil's Hole, and when one of the hounds who nearly caught this Devil's Fox soon after went mad, it removed all doubt as to the spiritual paternity of said fox.

He continued his career of rapine, making audacious raids and hair-breadth escapes, and finally began, as do many old foxes, to kill from a mania for slaughter. Thus it was that Digby lost ten lambs in one night. Carroll lost seven the next night. Later, the vicarage duck-pond was wholly devastated, and scarcely a night passed but someone in the region had to report a carnage of poultry, lambs or sheep, and, finally even calves.

Of course all the slaughter was attributed to this one fox of the Devil's Hole. It was known only that he was a very large fox, at least one that made a very large track. He never was clearly seen, even by the huntsmen. And it was noticed that Thunder and Bell, the stanuchest hounds in the pack, had refused to tongue or even to follow the trail when he was hunted.

His reputation for madness sufficed to make the master of the Peak hounds avoid the neighbourhood. The farmers in Monsaldale, led by Jo, agreed among themselves that if it would only come on a snow, they would assemble and beat the whole country, and in defiance of all rules of the hunt, get rid of the 'daft' fox in any way they could. But the snow did not come, and the red-haired gentleman lived his life. Notwithstanding his madness, he did not lack method. He never came two successive nights to the same farm. He never ate where he killed, and he never left a track that betrayed his retreat. He usually finished up his night's trail on the turf, or on a public highway.

Once I saw him. I was walking to Monsaldale from Bakewell late one night during a heavy storm, and as I turned the corner of Stead's sheep-fold there was a vivid flash of lightning. By its light, there was fixed on my retina a picture that made me start. Sitting on his haunches by the roadside, twenty yards away, was a very large fox gazing at me with malignant eyes, and licking his muzzle in a suggestive manner. All this I saw, but no more, and might have forgotten it, or thought myself mistaken, but the next morning, in that very fold, were found the bodies of twenty-three lambs and sheep, and the unmistakable signs that brought home the crime to the well-known marauder.

There was only one man who escaped,and that was Dorley. This was the more remarkable because he lived in the centre of the region raided, and within one mile of the Devil's Hole. Faithful Wully proved himself worth all the dogs in the neighbourhood. Night after night he brought in the sheep, and never one was missing. The Mad Fox might prowl about the Dorley homestead if he wished, but Wully, shrewd, brave, active Wully was more than a match for him, and not only saved his master's flock, but himself escaped with a whole skin. Everyone entertained a profound respect for him, and he might have been a popular pet but for his temper which, never genial, became more and more crabbed. He seemed to like Dorley, and Huldah, Dorley's eldest daughter, a shrewd, handsome, young woman, who, in the capacity of general manager of the house, was Wully's special guardian. The other members of Doricy's family Wully learned to tolerate, but the rest of the world, men and dogs, he seemed to hate.

His uncanny disposition was well shown in the last meeting I had with him. I was walking on a pathway across the moor behind Dorley's house. Wully was lying on the doorstep. As I drew near he arose, and without appearing to see me trotted toward my pathway and placed himself across it about ten yards ahead of me. There he stood silently and intently regarding the distant moor, his slightly bristling mane the only sign that he had not been suddenly turned to stone. He did not stir as I came up, and not wishing to quarrel, I stepped around past his nose and walked on. Wully at once left his position and in the same eerie silence trotted on some twenty feet and again stood across the pathway. Once more I came up and, stepping into the grass, brushed past his nose. Instantly, but without a sound, he seized my left heel. I kicked out with the other foot, but he escaped. Not having a stick, I flung a large stone at him. He leaped forward and the stone struck him in the ham, bowling him over into a ditch. He gasped out a savage growl as he fell, but scrambled out of the ditch and limped away in silence.

Yet sullen and ferocious as Wully was to the world, he was always gentle with Dorley's sheep. Many were the tales of rescues told of him. Many a poor lamb that had fallen into a pond or hole would have perished but for his timely and sagacious aid, many a far-weltered ewe did he turn right side up; while his keen eye discerned and his fierce courage baffled every eagle that had appeared on the moor in his time.

III

The Monsaldale farmers were still paying their nightly tribute to the Mad Fox, when the snow came, late in December. Poor Widow Cot lost her entire flock of twenty sheep, and the fiery cross went forth early in the morning. With guns unconcealed the burly farmers set out to follow to the finish the tell-tale tracks in the snow, those of a very large fox, undoubtedly the multo-murderous villain. For a while the trail was clear enough, then it came to the river and the habitual cunning of the animal was shown. He reached the water at a long angle pointing down stream and jumped into the shallow, unfrozen current. But at the other side there was no track leading out, and it was only after long searching that, a quarter of a mile higher up the stream, they found where he had come out. The track then ran to the top of Henley's high stone wall, where there was no snow left to tell tales. But the patient hunters persevered. When it crossed the smooth snow from the wall to the high road there was a difference of opinion. Some claimed that the track went up, others down the road. But Jo settled it, and after another long search they found where apparently the same trail, though some said a larger one, had left the road to enter a sheep-fold, and leaving this without harming the occupants, the track-maker had stepped in the footmarks of a countryman, thereby getting to the moor road, along which he had trotted straight to Dorley's farm.

That day the sheep were kept in on account of the snow and Wully, without his usual occupation, was lying on some planks in the sun. As the hunters drew near the house, he growled savagely and sneaked around to where the sheep were. Jo Greatorex walked up to where Wully had crossed the fresh snow, gave a glance, looked dumbfounded, then pointing to the retreating sheep-dog, he said, with emphasis:

'Lads, we're off the track of the Fox. But there's the killer of the Widder's yowes.'

Some agreed with Jo, others recalled the doubt in the trail and were for going back to make a fresh follow. At this juncture, Dorley himself came out of the house.

'Tom,' said Jo, 'that dog o' thine 'as killed twenty of Widder Gelt's sheep, last night. An' ah fur one don't believe as it 'is first killin'.'

'Why, mon, thou art crazy,' said Tom. 'Ah never 'ad a better sheepdog – 'e fair loves the sheep.'

'Aye! We's seen summat o' that in las' night's work,' replied Jo.

In vain the company related the history of the morning. Tom swore that it was nothing but a jealous conspiracy to rob him of Wully.

'Wully sleeps i' the kitchen every night. Never is oot till he's let to bide wi' the yowes. Why, mon, he's wi' oor sheep the year round, and never a hoof have ah lost.'

Tom became much excited over this abominable attempt against Wully's reputation and life. Jo and his partisans got equally angry, and it was a wise suggestion of Huldah's that quieted them.

'Feyther,' said she, 'ah'll sleep i' the kitchen the night. If Wully 'as ae way of gettin' oot ah'll see it, an' if he's no oot an' sheep's killed on the country-side, we'll ha' proof it's na Wully.'

That night Huldah stretched herself on the settee and Wully slept as usual underneath the table. As night wore on the dog became restless. He turned on his bed and once or twice got up, stretched, looked at Huldah and lay down again. About two o'clock he seemed no longer able to resist some strange impulse. He arose quietly, looked toward the low window, then at the motionless girl. Huldah lay still and breathed as though sleeping. Wully slowly came near and sniffed and breathed his doggy breath in her face. She made no move. He nudged her gently with his nose. Then, with his sharp ears forward and his head on one side he studied her calm face. Still no sign. He walked quietly to the window, mounted the table without noise, placed his nose under the sash-bar and raised the light frame until he could put one paw underneath. Then changing, he put his nose under the sash and raised it high enough to slip out, easing down the frame finally on his rump and tail with an adroitness that told of long practice. Then he disappeared into the darkness.

From her couch Huldah watched in amazement. After waiting for some time to make sure that he was gone, she arose, intending to call her father at once, but on second thought she decided to await more conclusive proof. She peered into the darkness, but no sign of Wully was to be seen. She put more wood on the fire, and lay down again. For over an hour she lay wide awake listening to the kitchen clock, and starting at each trifling sound, and wondering what the dog was doing. Could it be possible that he had really killed the widow's sheep? Then the recollection of his gentleness to their own sheep came, and completed her perplexity.

Another hour slowly tick-tocked. She heard a slight sound at the window that made her heart jump. The scratching sound was soon followed by the lifting of the sash, and in a short time Wully was back in the kitchen with the window closed behind him.

By the flickering fire-light Huldah could see a strange, wild gleam in his eye, and his jaws and snowy breast were dashed with fresh blood. The dog ceased his slight panting as he scrutinized the girl. Then, as she did not move, he lay down, and began to lick his paws and muzzle, growling lowly once or twice as though at the remembrance of some recent occurrence.

Huldah had seen enough. There could no longer be any doubt that Jo was right and more – a new thought flashed into her quick brain, she realized that the weird fox of Monsal was before her. Raising herself, she looked straight at Wully, and exclaimed:

'Wully! Wully! so it's a' true – oh, Wully, ye terrible brute.'

Her voice was fiercely reproachful, it rang in the quiet kitchen, and Wully recoiled as though shot. He gave a desperate glance toward the closed window. His eye gleamed, and his mane bristled. But he cowered under her gaze, and grovelled on the floor as though begging for mercy. Slowly he crawled nearer and nearer, as if to lick her feet, until quite close, then, with the fury of a tiger, but without a sound, he sprang for her throat.

The girl was taken unawares, but she threw up her arm in time, and Wully's long, gleaming tusks sank into her flesh, and grated on the bone.

'Help! help! feyther! feyther!' she shrieked.

Wully was a light weight, and for a moment she flung him off. But there could be no mistaking his purpose. The game was up, it was his life or hers now.

'Feyther! feyther!' she screamed, as the yellow fury, striving to kill her, bit and tore the unprotected hands that had so often fed him.

In vain she fought to hold him off, he would soon have had her by the throat, when in rushed Dorley.

Straight at him, now in the same horrid silence sprang Wully, and savagely tore him again and again before a deadly blow from the fagot-hook disabled him, dashing him, gasping and writhing, on the stone floor, desperate, and done for, but game and defiant to the last. Another quick blow scattered his brains on the hearthstone, where so long he had been a faithful and honoured retainer – and Wully, bright, fierce, trusty, treacherous Wully, quivered a moment, then straightened out, and lay forever still.

TITO:

The Story of the Coyote that Learned How

I

A raindrop may deflect a thunderbolt, or a hair may ruin an empire, as surely as a spider-web once turned the history of Scotland; and if it had not been for one little pebble, this history of Tito might never have happened.

That pebble was lying on a trail in the Dakota Badlands, and one hot, dark night it lodged in the foot of a Horse that was ridden by a tipsy cowboy. The man got off, as a matter of habit, to know what was laming his Horse. But he left the reins on its neck instead of on the ground, and the Horse, taking advantage of this technicality, ran off in the darkness. Then the cowboy, realizing that he was afoot, lay down in a hollow under some buffalo-bushes and slept the loggish sleep of the befuddled.

The golden beams of the early summer sun were leaping from top to top of the wonderful Badland Buttes, when an old Coyote might have been seen trotting homeward along the Garner's Creek Trail with a Rabbit in her jaws to supply her family's breakfast.

Fierce war had for a long time been waged against the Coyote kind by the cattlemen of Billings County. Traps, guns, poison, and Hounds had reduced their number nearly to zero, and the few survivors had learned the bitter need of caution at every step. But the destructive ingenuity of man knew no bounds, and their numbers continued to dwindle.

The old Coyote quit the trail very soon, for nothing that man has made is friendly. She skirted along a low ridge, then across a little hollow where grew a few buffalo-bushes, and, after a careful sniff at a very stale human trail-scent, she crossed another near ridge on whose sunny side was the home of her brood. Again she cautiously circled, peered about, and sniffed, but, finding no sign of danger, went down to the doorway and uttered a low *woof-woof*. Out of the den, beside a sage-bush, there poured a procession of little Coyotes, merrily tumbling over one another. Then, barking little barks and growling little puppy growls, they fell upon the feast that their mother had brought, and gobbled and tussled while she looked on and enjoyed their joy.

Wolver Jake, the cowboy, had awakened from his chilly sleep about sunrise, in time to catch a glimpse of the Coyote passing over the ridge. As soon as she was out of sight he got on his feet and went to the edge, there to witness the interesting scene of the family breakfasting and frisking about within a few yards of him, utterly unconscious of any danger.

But the only appeal the scene had to him lay in the fact that the county had set a price on every one of these Coyotes' lives. So he got out his big .45 navy revolver, and notwithstanding his shaky condition, he managed somehow to get a sight on the mother as she was caressing one of the little ones that had finished its breakfast, and shot her dead on the spot.

The terrified cubs fled into the den, and Jake, failing to kill another with his revolver, came forward, blocked up the hole with stones, and leaving the seven little prisoners quaking at the far end, set off on foot for the nearest ranch, cursing his faithless Horse as he went. In the afternoon he returned with his pard and tools for digging. The little ones had cowered all day in the darkened hole, wondering why their mother did not come to feed them, wondering at the darkness and the change. But late that day they heard sounds at the door. Then light was again let in. Some of the less cautious young ones ran forward to meet their mother, but their mother was not there – only two great rough brutes that began tearing open their home.

After an hour or more the diggers came to the end of the den, and here were the woolly, bright-eyed, little ones, all huddled in a pile at the farthest corner. Their innocent puppy faces and ways were not noticed by the huge enemy. One by one they were seized. A sharp blow, and each quivering, limp form was thrown into a sack to be carried to the nearest magistrate who was empowered to pay the bounties.

Even at this age there was a certain individuality of character among the puppies. Some of them squealed and some of them growled when dragged out to die. One or two tried to bite. The one that had been slowest to comprehend the danger, had been the last to retreat, and so was on top of the pile, and therefore the first killed. The one that had first realized the peril had retreated first, and now crouched at the bottom of the pile. Coolly and remorselessly the others were killed one by one, and then this prudent little puppy was seen to be the last of the family. It lay perfectly still, even when touched, its eyes being half closed, as, guided by instinct, it tried to 'play possum'. One of the men picked it up. It neither squealed nor resisted. Then Jake, realizing ever the importance of 'standing in with the boss', said: 'Say, let's keep that 'un for the children.' So the last of the family was thrown alive into the same bag with its dead brothers, and, bruised and frightened, lay there very still, understanding nothing, knowing only that after a long time of great noise and cruel jolting it was again half strangled by a grip on its neck and dragged out, where were a lot of creatures like the diggers.

These were really the inhabitants of the Chimney-pot Ranch, whose brand is the Broad-arrow; and among them were the children for whom the cub had been brought. The boss had no difficulty

in getting Jake to accept the dollar that the cub Coyote would have brought in bounty-money, and his present was turned over to the children. In answer to their question, 'What is it?' a Mexican cow-hand present said it was a Coyotito – that is, a 'little Coyote', – and this, afterward shortened to 'Tito', became the captive's name.

II

Tito was a pretty little creature, with woolly body, a puppy-like expression, and a head that was singularly broad between the ears.

But, as a children's pet, she – for it proved to be a female was not a success. She was distant and distrustful. She ate her food and seemed healthy, but never responded to friendly advances; never even learned to come out of the box when called. This probably was due to the fact that the kindness of the small children was offset by the roughness of the men and boys, who did not hesitate to drag her out by the chain when they wished to see her. On these occasions she .would suffer in silence, playing possum, shamming dead, for she seemed to know that that was the best thing to do. But as soon as released she would once more retire into the darkest corner of her box, and watch her tormentors with eyes that, at the proper angle, showed a telling glint of green.

Among the children of the ranchmen was a thirteen-year-old boy. The fact that he grew up to be like his father, a kind, strong, and thoughtful man, did not prevent him being, at this age, a shameless little brute.

Like all boys in that country, he practised lasso-throwing, with a view to being a cowboy. Posts and stumps are uninteresting things to catch. His little brothers and sisters were under special protection of the Home Government. The Dogs ran far away whenever they saw him coming with the rope in his hands. So he must needs practise on the unfortunate Coyotito. She soon learned that her only hope for peace was to hide in the kennel, or, if thrown at when outside, to dodge the rope by lying as flat as possible on the ground. Thus Lincoln unwittingly taught the Coyote the dangers and limitations of a rope, and so he proved a blessing in disguise – a very perfect disguise. When the Coyote had thoroughly learned how to baffle the lasso, the boy terror devised a new amusement. He got a large trap of the kind known as 'Fox-size'. This he set in the dust as he had seen Jake set a Wolf-trap, close to the kennel, and over it he scattered scraps of meat, in the most approved style for Wolf-trapping. After a while Tito, drawn by the smell of the meat, came hungrily sneaking out toward it, and almost immediately was caught in the trap by one foot. The boy terror was watching from a near hiding-place. He gave a wild Indian whoop of delight, then rushed forward to drag the Coyote out of the box into which she had retreated. After some more delightful thrills of excitement and struggle he got his lasso on Tito's body, and, helped by a younger brother, a most promising pupil, he succeeded in setting the Coyote free from the trap before the grown-ups had discovered his amusement. One or two experiences like this taught her a mortal terror of traps. She soon learned the smell of the steel, and could detect and avoid it, no matter how cleverly Master Lincoln might bury it in the dust, while the younger brother screened the operation from the intended victim by holding his coat over the door of Tito's kennel.

One day the fastening of her chain gave way, and Tito went off in an uncertain fashion, trailing her chain behind her. But she was seen by one of the men, who fired a charge of bird-shot at her. The burning, stinging, and surprise of it all caused her to retreat to the one place she knew, her own kennel. The chain was fastened again, and Tito added to her ideas this, a horror of guns and the smell of gunpowder; and this also, that the one safety from them is to 'lay low'. There were yet other rude experiences in store for the captive. Poisoning Wolves was a topic of daily talk at the Ranch, so it was not surprising that Lincoln should privately experiment on Coyotito.

The deadly strychnine was too well guarded to be available. So Lincoln hid some Rough on Rats in a piece of meat, threw it to the captive, and sat by to watch, as blithe and conscience-clear as any professor of chemistry trying a new combination.

Tito smelled the meat – everything had to be passed on by her nose. Her nose was in doubt. There was a good smell of meat, a familiar but unpleasant smell of human hands, and a strange new odour, but not the odour of the trap; so she bolted the morsel. Within a few minutes she began to have fearful pains in her stomach, followed by cramps. Now in all the Wolf tribe there is the instinctive habit to throw up anything that disagrees with them, and after a minute or two of suffering the Coyote sought relief in this way; and to make it doubly sure she hastily gobbled some blades of grass, and in less than an hour was quite well again.

Lincoln had put in poison enough for a dozen Coyotes. Had he put in less she could not have felt the pang till too late, but she recovered and never forgot that peculiar smell that means such awful after-pains. More than that, she was ready thenceforth to fly at once to the herbal cure that Nature had everywhere provided. An instinct of this kind grows quickly, once followed. It had taken minutes of suffering in the first place to drive her to the easement.

Thenceforth, having learned, it was her first thought on feeling pain. The little miscreant did indeed succeed in having her swallow another bait with a small dose of poison, but she knew what to do now and had almost no suffering.

Later on, a relative sent Lincoln a Bull-terrier, and the new combination was a fresh source of spectacular interest for the boy, and of tribulation for the Coyote. It all emphasized for her that old idea to 'lay low' – that is, to be quiet, unobtrusive, and hide when danger is in sight. The grown-ups of the household at length forbade these persecutions, and the Terrier was kept away from the little yard where the Coyote was chained up.

It must not be supposed that, in all this, Tito was a sweet, innocent victim. She had learned to bite. She had caught and killed several chickens by shamming sleep while they ventured to forage within the radius of her chain. And she had an inborn hankering to sing a morning and evening hymn, which procured for her many beatings. But she learned to shut up, the moment her opening notes were followed by a rattle of doors or windows, for these sounds of human nearness had frequently been followed by a '*bang*' and a charge of bird-shot, which somehow did no serious harm, though it severely stung her hide. And these experiences all helped to deepen her terror of guns and of those who used them. The object of these musical outpourings was not clear. They happened usually at dawn or dusk, but sometimes a loud noise at high noon would set her going. The song consisted of a volley of short barks, mixed with doleful squalls that never failed to set the Dogs astir in a responsive uproar, and once or twice had begotten a far away answer from some wild Coyote in the hills.

There was one little trick that she had developed which was purely instinctive – that is, an inherited habit. In the back end of her kennel she had a little *cache* of bones, and knew exactly where one or two lumps of unsavory meat were buried within the radius of her chain, for a time of famine which never came. If any one approached these hidden treasures she watched with anxious eyes, but made no other demonstration. If she saw that the meddler knew the exact place, she took an early opportunity to secrete them elsewhere.

After a year of this life Tito had grown to full size, and had learned many things that her wild kinsmen could not have learned without losing their lives in doing it. She knew and feared traps. She had learned to avoid poison baits, and knew what to do at once if, by some mistake, she should take one. She knew what guns were. She had learned to cut her morning and evening song very short. She had some acquaintance with Dogs, enough to make her hate and distrust them all. But, above all, she had this idea: whenever danger is near, the very best move possible is to lay low, be very quiet, do nothing to attract notice. Perhaps the little brain that looked out of those changing yellow eyes was the storehouse of much other knowledge about men, but what it was did not appear.

The Coyote was fully grown when the boss of the outfit bought a couple of thoroughbred Greyhounds, wonderful runners, to see whether he could not entirely extirpate the remnant of the Coyotes that still destroyed occasional Sheep and Calves on the range, and at the same time find amusement in the sport. He was tired of seeing that Coyote in the yard; so, deciding to use her for training the Dogs, he had her roughly thrown into a bag, then carried a quarter of a mile away and dumped out. At the same time the Greyhounds were slipped and chivvied on. Away they went bounding at their matchless pace, that nothing else on four legs could equal, and away went the Coyote, frightened by the noise of the men, frightened even to find herself free. Her quarter-mile start quickly shrank to one hundred yards, the one hundred to fifty, and on sped the flying Dogs. Clearly there was no chance for her. On and nearer they came. In another minute she would have been stretched out – not a doubt of it. But on a sudden she stopped, turned, and walked toward the Dogs with her tail serenely waving in the air and a friendly cock to her ears. Greyhounds are peculiar Dogs. Anything that runs away, they are going to catch and kill if they can. Anything that is calmly facing them becomes at once a non-combatant. They bounded over and past the Coyote before they could curb their own impetuosity, and returned completely nonplussed. Possibly they recognized the Coyote of the house-yard as she stood there wagging her tail. The ranchmen were nonplussed too. Every one was utterly taken aback, had a sense of failure, and the real victor in the situation was felt to be the audacious little Coyote.

The Greyhounds refused to attack an animal that wagged its tail and would not run; and the men, on seeing that the Coyote could *walk* far enough away to avoid being caught by hand, took their ropes (lassoes), and soon made her a prisoner once more.

The next day they decided to try again, but this time they added the white Bull-terrier to the chasers. The Coyote did as before. The Greyhounds declined to be party to any attack on such a mild and friendly acquaintance. But the Bull-terrier, who came puffing and panting on the scene three minutes later, had no such scruples. He was not so tall, but he was heavier than the Coyote, and, seizing her by her wool-protected neck, he shook her till, in a surprisingly short time, she lay limp and lifeless, at which all the men seemed pleased, and congratulated the Terrier, while the Greyhounds pottered around in restless perplexity.

A stranger in the party, a newly arrived Englishman, asked if he might have the brush, – the tail, he explained – and on being told to help himself, he picked up the victim by the tail, and with one awkward chop of his knife he cut it off at the middle, and the Coyote dropped, but gave a shrill yelp of pain. She was not dead, only playing possum, and now she leaped up and vanished into a near-by thicket of cactus and sage.

With Greyhounds a running animal is the signal for a run, so the two long-legged Dogs and the white, broad-chested Dog dashed after the Coyote. But right across their path, by happy chance, there flashed a brown streak ridden by a snowy powder-puff, the visible but evanescent sign for Cottontail Rabbit. The Coyote was not in sight now. The Rabbit was, so the Greyhounds dashed after the Cottontail, who took advantage of a Prairie-dog's hole to seek safety in the bosom of Mother Earth, and the Coyote made good her escape.

She had been a good deal jarred by the rude treatment of the Terrier, and her mutilated tail gave her some pain. But otherwise she was all right, and she loped lightly away, keeping out of sight in the hollows, and so escaped among the fantastic buttes of the Badlands, to be eventually the founder of a new life among the Coyotes of the Little Missouri.

Moses was preserved by the Egyptians till he had outlived the dangerous period, and learned from them wisdom enough to be the saviour of his people against those same Egyptians.  So the bobtailed Coyote was not only saved by man and carried over the dangerous period of puppyhood: she was also unwittingly taught by him how to baffle the traps, poisons, lassos, guns, and Dogs that had so long waged a war of extermination against her race.

III

Thus Tito escaped from man, and for the first time found herself face to face with the whole problem of life; for now she had her own living to get.

A wild animal has three sources of wisdom:

First, *the experience of its ancestors,* in the form of instinct, which is inborn learning, hammered into the race by ages of selection and tribulation. This is the most important to begin with, because it guards him from the moment he is born.

Second, *the experience of his parents and comrades,* learned chiefly by example. This becomes most important as soon as the young can run.

Third, *the personal experience* of the animal itself. This grows in importance as the animal ages.

The weakness of the first is its fixity; it cannot change to meet quickly changing conditions. The weakness of the second is the animal's inability freely to exchange ideas by language. The weakness of the third is the danger in acquiring it. But the three together are a strong arch.

Now, Tito was in a new case. Perhaps never before had a Coyote faced life with unusual advantages in the third kind of knowledge, none at all in the second, and with the first dormant. She travelled rapidly away from the ranchmen, keeping out of sight, and sitting down once in a while to lick her wounded tail-stump. She came at last to a Prairie-dog town. Many of the inhabitants were out, and they barked at the intruder, but all dodged down as soon as she came near. Her instinct taught her to try and catch one, but she ran about in vain for some time, and then gave it up. She would have gone hungry that night but that she found a couple of Mice in the long grass by the river. Her mother had not taught her to hunt, but her instinct did, and the accident that she had an unusual brain made her profit very quickly by her experience.

In the days that followed she quickly learned how to make a living; for Mice, Ground Squirrels, Prairie-dogs, Rabbits, and Lizards were abundant, and many of these could be captured in open chase. But open chase, and sneaking as near as possible before beginning the open chase, lead naturally to stalking for a final spring. And before the moon had changed the Coyote had learned how to make a comfortable living.

Once or twice she saw the men with the Grey-hounds coming her way. Most Coyotes would, perhaps, have barked in bravado, or would have gone up to some high place whence they could watch the enemy; but Tito did no such foolish thing. Had she run, her moving form would have caught the eyes of the Dogs, and then nothing could have saved her. She dropped where she was, and lay flat until the danger had passed. Thus her ranch training to lay low began to stand her in good stead, and so it came about that her weakness was her strength. The Coyote kind had so long been famous for their speed, had so long learned to trust in their legs, that they never dreamed of a creature that could run them down. They were accustomed to play with their pursuers, and so rarely bestirred themselves to run from Greyhounds, till it was too late. But Tito, brought up at the end of a chain, was a poor runner. She had no reason to trust her legs. She rather trusted her wits, and so lived.

During that summer she stayed about the Little Missouri, learning the tricks of small-game hunting that she should have learned before she shed her milk-teeth, and gaining in strength and speed. She kept far away from all the ranches, and always hid on seeing a man or a strange beast, and so passed the summer alone. During the daytime she was not lonely, but when the sun went down she would feel the impulse to sing that wild song of the West which means so much to the Coyotes.

It is not the invention of an individual nor of the present, but was slowly built out of the feelings of all Coyotes in all ages. It expresses their nature and the Plains that made their nature. When one begins it, it takes hold of the rest, as the fife and drum do with soldiers, or the ki-yi war-song with Indian braves. They respond to it as a bell-glass does to a certain note the moment that note is struck, ignoring other sounds. So the Coyote, no matter how brought up, must vibrate at the night song of the Plains, for it touches something in himself.

They sing it after sundown, when it becomes the rallying-cry of their race and the friendly call to a neighbour; and they sing it as one boy in the woods holloas to another to say, 'All's well! Here am I. Where are you?' A form of it they sing to the rising moon, for this is the time for good hunting to begin. They sing when they see the new camp-fire, for the same reason that a Dog barks at a stranger. Yet another weird chant they have for the dawning before they steal quietly away from the offing of the camp a wild, weird, squalling refrain:

Wow-wow-wow-wow-wow-w-o-o-o-o-o-o-w,

again and again; and doubtless with many another change that man cannot distinguish any more than the Coyote can distinguish the words in the cowboy's anathemas.

Tito instinctively uttered her music at the proper times. But sad experiences had taught her to cut it short and keep it low. Once or twice she had got a far-away reply from one of her own race, whereupon she had quickly ceased and timidly quit the neighbourhood.

One day, when on the Upper Garner's Creek, she found the trail where a piece of meat had been dragged along. It was a singularly inviting odour, and she followed it, partly out of curiosity. Presently she came on a piece of the meat itself. She was hungry; she was always hungry now. It was tempting, and although it had a peculiar odour, she swallowed it. Within a few minutes she felt a terrific pain. The memory of the poisoned meat the boy had given her, was fresh. With trembling, foaming jaws she seized some blades of grass, and her stomach threw off the meat; but she fell in convulsions on the ground.

The trail of meat dragged along and the poison baits had been laid the day before by Wolver Jake. This morning he was riding the drag, and on coming up from the draw he saw, far ahead, the Coyote struggling. He knew, of course, that it was poisoned, and rode quickly up; but the convulsions passed as he neared. By a mighty effort, at the sound of the Horses' hoofs the Coyote arose to her front feet. Jake drew his revolver and fired, but the only effect was fully to alarm her. She tried to run, but her hind legs were paralyzed. She put forth all her strength, dragging her hind legs. Now, when the poison was no longer in the stomach, will-power could do a great deal. Had she been allowed to lie down then she would have been dead in five minutes; but the revolver-shots and the man coming stirred her to strenuous action. Madly she struggled again and again to get her hind legs to work. All the force of desperate intent she brought to bear. It was like putting forth tenfold power to force the nervous fluids through their blocked-up channels as she dragged herself with marvellous speed downhill. What is nerve but will? The dead wires of her legs were hot with this fresh power, multiplied, injected, blasted into them. They had to give in. She felt them thrill with life again. Each wild shot from the gun lent vital help. Another fierce attempt, and one hind leg obeyed the call to duty. A few more bounds, and the other, too, fell in. Then lightly she loped away among the broken buttes, defying the agonizing gripe that still kept on inside.

Had Jake held off then she would yet have laid down and died; but he followed, and fired and fired, till in another mile she bounded free from pain, saved from her enemy by himself. He had compelled her to take the only cure, so she escaped.

And these were the ideas that she harvested that day: That curious smell on the meat stands for mortal agony. Let it alone! And she never forgot it; thenceforth she knew strychnine.

Fortunately, Dogs, traps, and strychnine do not wage war at once, for the Dogs are as apt to be caught or poisoned as the Coyotes. Had there been a single Dog in the hunt that day Tito's history would have ended.

IV

When the weather grew cooler toward the end of autumn Tito had gone far toward repairing the defects in her early training. She was more like an ordinary Coyote in her habits now, and she was more disposed to sing the sundown song.

One night, when she got a response, she yielded to the impulse again to call, and soon afterward a large, dark Coyote appeared. The fact that he was there at all was a guarantee of unusual gifts, for the war against his race was waged relentlessly by the cattlemen. He approached with caution. Tito's mane bristled with mixed feelings at the sight of one of her own kind. She crouched flat on the ground and waited. The newcomer came stiffly forward, nosing the wind; then up the wind nearly to her. Then he walked around so that she should wind him, and raising his tail, gently waved it. The first acts meant armed neutrality, but the last was a distinctly friendly signal. Then he approached, and she rose up suddenly and stood as high as she could to be smelled. Then she wagged the stump of her tail, and they considered themselves acquainted.

The newcomer was a very large Coyote, half as tall again as Tito, and the dark patch on his shoulders was so large and black that the cowboys, when they came to know him, called him Saddleback. From that time these two continued more or less together. They were not always close together, often were miles apart during the day, but toward night one or the other would get on some high, open place and sing the loud *Yap-yap-yap-yow-wow-wow -wow-wow,*
and they would foregather for some foray on hand.

The physical advantages were with Saddle-back, but the greater cunning was Tito's, so that she in time became the leader. Before a month a third Coyote had appeared on the scene and become also a member of this loose-bound fraternity, and later two more appeared. Nothing succeeds like success. The little bob-tailed Coyote had had rare advantages of training just where the others were lacking: she knew the devices of man. She could not tell about these in words, but she could by the aid of a few signs and a great deal of example. It soon became evident that her methods of hunting were successful, whereas, when they went without her, they often had hard luck. A man at Boxelder Ranch had twenty Sheep. The rules of the county did not allow any one to own more, as this was a Cattle-range. Tho Sheep were guarded by a large and fierce Collie. One day in winter two of the Coyotes tried to raid this flock by a bold dash, and all they got was a mauling from the Collie. A few days later the band returned at dusk. Just how Tito arranged it, man cannot tell. We can only guess how she taught them their parts, but we know that she surely did. The Coyotes hid in the willows. Then Saddleback, the bold and swift, walked openly toward the Sheep and barked a loud defiance. The Collie jumped up with bristling mane and furious growl, then, seeing the foe, dashed straight at him. Now was the time for the steady nerve and the unfailing limbs.

Saddleback let the Dog come near enough *almost* to catch him, and so beguiled him far and away into the woods, while the other Coyotes, led by Tito, stampeded the Sheep in twenty directions; then following the farthest, they killed several and left them in the snow.

In the gloom of descending night the Dog and his master laboured till they had gathered the bleating survivors; but next morning they found that four had been driven far away and killed, and the Coyotes had had, a banquet royal.

The shepherd poisoned the carcasses and left them. Next night the Coyotes returned. Tito sniffed the now frozen meat, detected the poison, gave a warning growl, and scattered filth over the meat, so that none of the band should touch it. One, however, who was fast and foolish, persisted in feeding in spite of Tito's warning, and when they came away he was lying poisoned and dead in the snow.

V

Jake now heard on all sides that the Coyotes were getting worse. So he set to work with many traps and much poison to destroy those on the Garner's Creek, and every little while he would go with the Hounds and scour the Little Missouri south and east of the Chimney-pot Ranch; for it was understood that he must never run the Dogs in country where traps and poison were laid. He worked in his erratic way all winter, and certainly did have some success. He killed a couple of grey Wolves, said to be the last of their race, and several Coyotes, some of which, no doubt, were of the Bobtailed pack, which thereby lost those members which were lacking in wisdom.

Yet that winter was marked by a series of Coyote raids and exploits; and usually the track in the snow or the testimony of eye-witnesses told that the master spirit of it all was a little Bobtailed Coyote.

One of these adventures was the cause of much talk. The Coyote challenge sounded close to the Chimney-pot Ranch after sundown. A dozen Dogs responded with the usual clamour. But only the Bull-terrier dashed away toward the place whence the Coyotes had called, for the reason that he only was loose. His chase was fruitless, and he came back growling. Twenty minutes later there was another Coyote yell close at hand. Off dashed the Terrier as before. In a minute his excited yapping told that he had sighted his game and was in full chase. Away he went, furiously barking, until his voice was lost afar, and nevermore was heard. In the morning the men read in the snow the tale of the night. The first cry of the Coyotes was to find out if all the Dogs were loose; then, having found that only one was free, they laid a plan. Five Coyotes hid along the side of the trail; one went forward and called till it had decoyed the rash Terrier, and then led him right into the ambush. What chance had he with six? They tore him limb from limb, and devoured him, too, at the very spot where once he had worried Coyotito. And next morning, when the men came, they saw by the signs that the whole thing had been planned, and that the leader whose cunning had made it a success was a little Bobtailed Coyote.

The men were angry, and Lincoln was furious; but Jake remarked: 'Well, I guess that Bobtail came back and got even with that Terrier.'

•

VI

When spring was near, the annual love-season of the Coyotes came on. Saddleback and Tito had been together merely as companions all winter, but now a new feeling was born. There was not much courting. Saddleback simply showed his teeth to possible rivals. There was no ceremony. They had been friends for months, and now, in the light of the new feeling, they naturally took to each other and were mated. Coyotes do not give each other names as do mankind, but have one sound like a growl and short howl, which stands for 'mate' or 'husband' or 'wife'. This they use in calling to each other, and it is by recognizing the tone of the voice that they know who is calling.

The loose rambling brotherhood of the Coyotes was broken up now, for the others also paired off, and since the returning warm weather was bringing out the Prairie-dogs and small game, there was less need to combine for hunting. Ordinarily Coyotes do not sleep in dens or in any fixed place. They move about all night while it is cool, then during the daytime they get a few hours' sleep in the sun, on some quiet hillside that also gives a chance to watch out. But the mating season changes this habit somewhat.

As the weather grew warm Tito and Saddleback set about preparing a den for the expected family. In a warm little hollow, an old Badger abode was cleaned out, enlarged, and deepened. A quantity of leaves and grass was carried into it and arranged in a comfortable nest. The place selected for it was a dry, sunny nook among the hills, half a mile west of the Little Missouri. Thirty yards from it was a ridge which commanded a wide view of the grassy slopes and cottonwood groves by the river. Men would have called the spot very beautiful, but it is tolerably certain that that side of it never touched the Coyotes at all.

Tito began to be much preoccupied with her impending duties. She stayed quietly in the neighbourhood of the den, and lived on such food as Saddleback brought her, or she herself could easily catch, and also on the little stores that she had buried at other times. She knew every Prairie-dog town in the region, as well as all the best places for Mice and Rabbits.

Not far from the den was the very Dog-town that first she had crossed the day she had gained her liberty and lost her tail. If she were capable of such retrospect, she must have laughed to herself to think what a fool she was then. The change in her methods was now shown. Somewhat removed from the others, a Prairie-dog had made his den in the most approved style, and now when Tito peered over he was feeding on the grass ten yards from his own door. A Prairie-dog away from the others is, of course, easier to catch than one in the middle of the town, for he has but one pair of eyes to guard him; so Tito set about stalking this one. How was she to do it when there was no cover, nothing but short grass and a few low weeds? The White-bear knows how to approach the Seal on the flat ice, and the Indian how to get within striking distance of the grazing Deer. Tito knew how to do the same trick, and although one of the town Owls flew over with a warning chuckle, Tito set about her plan. A Prairie-dog cannot see well unless he is sitting up on his hind legs; his eyes are of little use when he is nosing in the grass; and Tito knew this. Further, a yellowish-grey animal on a yellowish-grey landscape is invisible till it moves. Tito seemed to know that. So, without any attempt to crawl or hide, she walked gently up-wind toward the Prairie-dog. Up-wind, not in order to prevent the Prairie-dog smelling her, but so that she could smell him, which came to the same thing. As soon as the Prairie-dog sat up with some food in his hand she froze into a statue. As soon as he dropped again to nose in the grass, she walked steadily nearer, watching his every move so that she might be motionless each time he sat up to see what his distant brothers were barking at. Once or twice he seemed alarmed by the calls of his friends, but he saw nothing and resumed his feeding. She soon cut the fifty yards down to ten, and the ten to five, and still was undiscovered. Then, when again the Prairie-dog dropped down to seek more fodder, she made a quick dash, and bore him off kicking and squealing. Thus does the angel of the pruning-knife lop off those that are heedless and foolishly indifferent to the advantages of society.

VII

Tito had many adventures in which she did not come out so well. Once she nearly caught an Antelope fawn, but the hunt was spoiled by the sudden appearance of the mother, who gave Tito a stinging blow on the side of the head and ended her hunt for that day. She never again made that mistake she had sense. Once or twice she had to jump to escape the strike of a Rattlesnake. Several times she had been fired at by hunters with long-range rifles. And more and more she had to look out for the terrible Grey Wolves. The Grey Wolf, of course, is much larger and stronger than the Coyote, but the Coyote has the advantage of speed, and can always escape in the open. All it must beware of is being caught in a corner. Usually when a Grey Wolf howls the Coyotes go quietly about their business elsewhere.

Tito had a curious fad, occasionally seen among the Wolves and Coyotes, of carrying in her mouth, for miles, such things as seemed to be interesting and yet were not tempting as eatables. Many a time had she trotted a mile or two with an old Buffalo-horn or a cast-off shoe, only to drop it when something else attracted her attention. The cow-boys who remark these things have various odd explanations to offer: one, that it is done to stretch the jaws, or keep them in practice, just as a man in training carries weights. Coyotes have, in common with Dogs and Wolves, the habit of calling at certain stations along their line of travel, to leave a record of their visit. These stations may be a stone, a tree, a post, or an old Buffalo-skull, and the Coyote calling there can learn, by the odour and track of the last comer, just who the caller was, whence he came, and whither he went. The whole country is marked out by these intelligence depots. Now it often happens that a Coyote that has not much else to do will carry a dry bone or some other useless object in its mouth, but sighting the signal-post, will go toward it to get the news, lay down the bone, and afterward forget to take it along, so that the signal-posts in time become further marked with a curious collection of odds and ends.

This singular habit was the cause of a disaster to the Chimney-pot Wolf-hounds, and a corresponding advantage to the Coyotes in the war. Jake had laid a line of poison baits on the western bluffs. Tito knew what they were, and spurned them as usual; but finding more later, she gathered up three or four and crossed the Little Missouri toward the ranch-house. This she circled at a safe distance; but when something made the pack of Dogs break out into clamour, Tito dropped the baits, and next day, when the Dogs were taken out for exercise, they found and devoured these scraps of meat, so that in ten minutes there were four hundred dollars' worth of Greyhounds lying dead. This led to an edict against poisoning in that district, and thus was a great boon to the Coyotes.

Tito quickly learned that not only each kind of game must be hunted in a special way, but different ones of each kind may require quite different treatment. The Prairie-dog with the outlying den was really an easy prey, but the town was quite compact now that he was gone. Near the centre of it was a fine, big, fat Prairie-dog, a perfect alderman, that she had made several vain attempts to capture. On one occasion she had crawled almost within leaping distance, when the angry *bizz* of a Rattlesnake just ahead warned her that she was in danger. Not that the Rattler cared anything about the Prairie-dog, but he did not wish to be disturbed; and Tito, who had an instinctive fear of the Snake, was forced to abandon the hunt. The open stalk proved an utter failure with the Aderman, for the situation of his den made every Dog in the town his sentinel; but he was too good to lose, and Tito waited until circumstances made a new plan.

All Coyotes have a trick of watching from a high lookout whatever passes along the roads. After it has passed they go down and examine its track. Tito had this habit, except that she was always careful to keep out of sight herself.

One day a waggon passed from the town to the southward. Tito lay low and watched it. Something dropped on the road. When the waggon was out of sight Tito sneaked down, first to smell the trail as a matter of habit, second to see what it was that had dropped. The object was really an apple, but Tito saw only an unattractive round green thing like a cactus-leaf without spines, and of a peculiar smell. She snuffed it, spurned it, and was about to pass on; but the sun shone on it so brightly, and it rolled so curiously when she pawed, that she picked it up in a mechanical way and trotted back over the rise, where she found herself at the Dog-town. Just then two great Prairie-hawks came skimming like pirates over the plain. As soon as they were in sight the Prairie-dogs all barked, jerking their tails at each bark, and hid below. When all were gone Tito walked on toward the hole of the big fat fellow whose body she coveted, and dropping the apple on the ground a couple of feet from the rim of the crater that formed his home, she put her nose down to enjoy the delicious smell of Dog-fat. Even his den smelled more fragrant than those of the rest. Then she went quietly behind a greasewood-bush, in a lower place some twenty yards away, and lay flat. After a few seconds some venturesome Prairie-dog looked out, and seeing nothing, gave the 'all's well' bark. One by one they came out, and in twenty minutes the town was alive as before. One of the last to come out was the fat old Alderman. He always took good care of his own precious self. He peered out cautiously a few times, then climbed to the top of his lookout. A Prairie-dog hole is shaped like a funnel, going straight down. Around the top of this is built a high ridge which serves as a lookout, and also makes sure that, no matter how they may slip in their hurry, they are certain to drop into the funnel and be swallowed up by the all-protecting earth. On the outside the ground slopes away gently from the funnel. Now, when the Alderman saw that strange round thing at his threshold he was afraid. Second inspection led him to believe that it was not dangerous, but was probably interesting. He went cautiously toward it, smelled it, and tried to nibble it; but the apple rolled away, for it was round, and the ground was smooth as well as sloping. The Prairie-dog followed and gave it a nip which satisfied him that the strange object would make good eating. But each time he nibbled, it rolled farther away. The coast seemed clear, all the other Prairie-dogs were out, so the fat Alderman did not hesitate to follow up the dodging, shifting apple.

This way and that it wriggled, and he followed. Of course it worked toward the low place where grew the greasewood-bush. The little tastes of apple that he got only whetted his appetite. The Alderman was more and more interested. Foot by foot he was led from his hole toward that old, familiar bush, and had no thought of anything but the joy of eating. And Tito curled herself and braced her sinewy legs, and measured the distance between, until it dwindled to not more than three good jumps; then up and like an arrow she went, and grabbed and bore him off at last.

Now it will never be known whether it was accident or design that led to the placing of that apple, but it proved important, and if such a thing were to happen once or twice to a smart Coyote – and it is usually clever ones that get such chances – it might easily grow into a new trick of hunting.

After a hearty meal Tito buried the rest in a cold place, not to get rid of it, but to hide it for future use; and a little later, when she was too weak to hunt much, her various hoards of this sort came in very useful. True, the meat had turned very strong; but Tito was not critical, and she had no fears or theories of microbes, so suffered no ill effects.

VIII

The lovely Hiawathan spring was touching all things in the fairy Badlands. Oh, why are they called Badlands ? If Nature sat down deliberately on the eighth day of creation and said, ' Now work is done, let's play; let's make a place that shall combine everything that is finished and wonderful and beautiful a paradise for man and bird and beast,' it was surely then that she made these wild, fantastic hills, teeming with life, radiant with gayest flowers, varied with sylvan groves, bright with prairie sweeps and brimming lakes and streams. In foreground, offing, and distant hills that change at every step, we find some proof that Nature squandered here the riches that in other lands she used as sparingly as gold, with colourful sky above and colourful land below, and the distance blocked by sculptured buttes that are built of precious stones and ores, and tinged as by a lasting and unspeakable sunset. And yet, for all this ten times gorgeous wonderland enchanted, blind man has found no better name than one which says, *the road to it is hard*.

The little hollow west of Chimney Butte was freshly grassed. The dangerous-looking Spanish bayonets, that through the bygone winter had waged war with all things, now sent out their contribution to the peaceful triumph of the spring, in flowers that have stirred even the chilly scientists to name them *Gloriosa*; and the cactus, poisonous, most reptilian of herbs, surprised the world with a splendid bloom as little like itself as the pearl is like its mother shell-fish. The sage and the greasewood lent their gold, and the sand-anemone tinged the Badland hills like bluish snow; and in the air and earth and hills on every hand was felt the fecund promise of the spring. This was the end of the winter famine, the beginning of the summer feast, and this was the time by the All-mother ordained when first the little Coyotes should see the light of day.

A mother does not have to learn to love her helpless, squirming brood. They bring the love with them – not much or little, not measurable, but perfect love. And in that dimly lighted warm abode she fondled them and licked them and cuddled them with heartful warmth of tenderness that was as much a new epoch in her life as in theirs.

But the pleasure of loving them was measured in the same measure as anxiety for their safety. In bygone days her care had been mainly for herself. All she had learned in her strange puppyhood, all she had picked up since, was bent to the main idea of self-preservation. Now she was ousted from her own affections by her brood. Her chief care was to keep their home concealed, and this was not very hard at first, for she left them only when she must, to supply her own wants.

She came and went with great care, and only after spying well the land so that none should see and find the place of her treasure. If it were possible for the little ones' idea of their mother and the cowboys' idea to be set side by side they would be found to have nothing in common, though both were right in their point of view. The ranchmen knew the Coyote only as a pair of despicable, cruel jaws, borne around on tireless legs, steered by incredible cunning, and leaving behind a track of destruction. The little ones knew her as a loving, gentle, all-powerful guardian. For them her breast was soft and warm and infinitely tender. She fed and warmed them, she was their wise and watchful keeper. She was always at hand with food when they hungered, with wisdom to foil the cunning of their foes, and with a heart of courage tried to crown her well-laid plans for them with uniform success.

A baby Coyote is a shapeless, senseless, wriggling, – and to every one but its mother – a most uninteresting little lump. But after its eyes are open, after it has developed its legs, after it has learned to play in the sun with its brothers, or run at the gentle call of its mother when she brings home game for it to feed on, the baby Coyote becomes one of the cutest, dearest little rascals on earth. And when the nine that made up Coyotito's brood had reached this stage, it did not require the glamour of motherhood to make them objects of the greatest interest.

The summer was now on. The little ones were beginning to eat flesh-meat, and Tito, with some assistance from Saddleback, was kept busy to supply both themselves and the brood. Sometimes she brought them a Prairie-dog, at other times she would come home with a whole bunch of Gophers and Mice in her jaws; and once or twice, by the clever trick of relay-chasing, she succeeded in getting one of the big Northern Jack-rabbits for the little folks at home.

After they had feasted they would lie around in the sun for a time. Tito would mount guard on a bank and scan the earth and air with her keen, brassy eye, lest any dangerous foe should find their happy valley; and the merry pups played little games of tag, or chased the Butter-flies, or had apparently desperate encounters with each other, or tore and worried the bones and feathers that now lay about the threshold of the home. One, the least, for there is usually a runt, stayed near the mother and climbed on her back or pulled at her tail. They made a lovely picture as they played, and the wrestling group in the middle seemed the focus of it all at first; but a keener, later look would have rested on the mother, quiet, watchful, not without anxiety, but, above all, with a face full of motherly  tenderness. Oh, she was so proud and happy, and she would sit there and watch them and silently love them till it was time to go home, or until some sign of distant danger showed. Then, with a low growl, she gave the signal, and all disappeared from sight in a twinkling, after which she would set off to meet and turn the danger, or go on a fresh hunt for food.

Wolver Jake had several plans for making a fortune, but each in turn was abandoned as soon as he found that it meant work. At one time or other most men of this kind see the chance of their lives in a poultry-farm. They cherish the idea that somehow the poultry do all the work. And without troubling himself about the details, Jake devoted an unexpected windfall to the purchase of a dozen Turkeys for his latest scheme. The Turkeys were duly housed in one end of Jake's shanty, so as to be well guarded, and for a couple of days were the object of absorbing interest, and had the best of care – too much, really. But Jake's ardor waned about the third day; then the recurrent necessity for long celebrations at Medora, and the ancient allurements of idle hours spent lying on the tops of sunny buttes and of days spent sponging on the hospitality of distant ranches, swept away the last pretence of attention to his poultry-farm. The Turkeys were utterly neglected – left to forage for themselves; and each time that Jake returned to his uninviting shanty, after a few days' absence, he found fewer birds, till at last none but the old Gobbler was left.

Jake cared little about the loss, but was filled with indignation against the thief.

He was now installed as wolver to the Broad-arrow outfit. That is, he was supplied with poison, traps, and Horses, and was also entitled to all he could make out of Wolf bounties. A reliable man would have gotten pay in addition, for the ranchmen are generous, but Jake was not reliable. Every wolver knows, of course, that his business naturally drops into several well-marked periods.

In the late winter and early spring – the love-season – the Hounds will not hunt a She-wolf. They will quit the trail of a He-wolf at this time to take up that of a She-wolf, but when they do overtake her, they, for some sentimental reason, invariably let her go in peace. In August and September the young Coyotes and Wolves are just beginning to run alone, and they are then easily trapped and poisoned. A month or so later the survivors have learned how to take care of themselves, but in the early summer the wolver knows that there are dens full of little ones all through the hills. Each den has from five to fifteen pups, and the only difficulty is to know the whereabouts of these family homes.

One way of finding the dens is to watch from some tall butte for a Coyote carrying food to its brood. As this kind of wolving involved much lying still, it suited Jake very well. So, equipped with a Broad-arrow Horse and the boss's field-glasses, he put in week after week at den-hunting – that is, lying asleep in some possible lookout, with an occasional glance over the country when it seemed easier to do that than to lie still.

The Coyotes had learned to avoid the open. They generally went homeward along the sheltered hollows; but this was not always possible, and one day, while exercising his arduous profession in the country west of Chimney Butte, Jake's glasses and glance fell by chance on a dark spot which moved along an open hillside. It was grey, and it looked like 'A', and even Jake knew that that meant Coyote. If it had been a grey Wolf it would have been like 'B', with tail up. A Fox would have looked like 'C', the large ears and tail and the yellow colour would have marked it. And a Deer would have looked like 'D'. That dark shade from the front end meant something in his mouth, probably something being carried home, and that would mean a den of little ones.

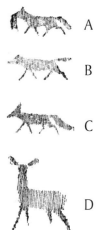

He made careful note of the place, and returned there next day to watch, selecting a high butte near where he had seen the Coyote carrying the food. But all day passed, and he saw nothing. Next day, however, he descried -a dark Coyote, old Saddleback, carrying a large Bird, and by the help of the glasses he made out that it was a Turkey, and then he knew that the yard at home was quite empty, and he also knew where the rest of them had gone, and vowed terrible venger.nce when he should find the den. He followed Saddleback with his eyes as far as possible, and that was no great way, then went to the place to see if he could track him any farther; but he found no guiding signs, and he did not chance on the little hollow that was the playground of Tito's brood.

Meanwhile Saddleback came to the little hollow and gave the low call that always conjured from the earth the unruly procession of the nine riotous little pups, and they dashed at the Turkey and pulled and worried till it was torn up, and each that got a piece ran to one side alone and silently proceeded to eat, seizing his portion in his jaws when another came near, and growling his tiny growl as he showed the brownish whites of his eyes in his effort to watch the intruder. Those that got the softer parts to feed on were well fed. But the three that did not turned all their energies on the frame of the Gobbler, and over that there waged a battle royal. This way and that they tugged and tussled, getting off occasional scraps, but really hindering each other feeding, till Tito glided in and deftly cut the Turkey into three or four, when each dashed off with a prize, over which he sat and chewed and smacked his lips and jammed his head down sideways to bring the backmost teeth to bear, while the baby runt scrambled into the home den, carrying in triumph his share – the Gobbler's grotesque head and neck.

X

Jake felt that he had been grievously wronged, indeed ruined, by that Coyote that stole his Turkeys. He vowed he would skin them alive when he found the pups, and took pleasure in thinking about how he would do it. His attempt to follow Saddleback by trailing was a failure, and all his searching for the den was useless, but he had come prepared for any emergency. In case he found the den he had brought a pick and shovel; in case he did not he had brought a living white Hen.

The Hen he now took to a broad open place near where he had seen Saddleback, and there he tethered her to a stick of wood that she could barely drag. Then he made himself comfortable on a lookout that was near, and lay still to watch. The Hen, of course, ran to the end of the string, and then lay on the ground flopping stupidly. Presently the clog gave enough to ease the strain, she turned by mere chance in another direction, and so, for a time, stood up to look around.

The day went slowly by, and Jake lazily stretched himself on the blanket in his spying-place. Toward evening Tito came by on a hunt. This was not surprising, for the den was only half a mile away. Tito had learned, among other rules, this, 'Never show yourself on the sky-line.' In former days the Coyotes used to trot along the tops of the ridges for the sake of the chance to watch both sides. But men and guns had taught Tito that in this way you are sure to be seen. She therefore made a practice of running along near the top, and once in a while peeping over.

This was what she did that evening as she went out to hunt for the children's supper, and her keen eyes fell on the white Hen, stupidly stalking about and turning up its eyes in a wise way each time a harmless Turkey-buzzard came in sight against a huge white cloud.

Tito was puzzled. This was something new. It *looked* like game, but she feared to take any chances. She circled all around without showing herself, then decided that, whatever it might be, it was better let alone. As she passed on, a faint whiff of smoke caught her attention. She followed cautiously, and under a butte far from the Hen she found Jake's camp. His bed was there, his Horse was picketed, and on the remains of the fire was a pot which gave out a smell which she well knew about men's camps – the smell of coffee. Tito felt uneasy at this proof that a man was staying so near her home, but she went off quietly on her hunt, keeping out of sight, and Jake knew nothing of her visit.

About sundown he took in his decoy Hen, as Owls were abundant, and went back to his camp.

XI

Next day the Hen was again put out, and late that afternoon Saddleback came trotting by. As soon as his eye fell on the white Hen he stopped short, his head on one side, and gazed. Then he circled to get the wind, and went cautiously sneaking nearer, very cautiously, somewhat puzzled, till he got a whiff that reminded him of the place where he had found those Turkeys. The Hen took alarm, and tried to run away; but Saddleback made a rush, seized the Hen so fiercely that the string was broken, and away he dashed toward the home valley.

Jake had fallen asleep, but the squawk of the Hen happened to awaken him, and he sat up in time to see her borne away in old Saddleback's jaws.

As soon as they were out of sight Jake took up the white-feather trail. At first it was easily followed, for the Hen had shed plenty of plumes in her struggles; but once she was dead in Saddleback's jaws, very few feathers were dropped except where she was carried through the brush. But Jake was following quietly and certainly, for Saddleback had gone nearly in a straight line home to the little ones with the dangerous tell-tale prize. Once or twice there was a puzzling delay when the Coyote had changed his course or gone over an open place; but one white feather was good for fifty yards, and when the daylight was gone, Jake was not two hundred yards from the hollow, in which at that very moment were the nine little pups, having a perfectly delightful time with the Hen, pulling it to pieces, feasting and growling, sneezing the white feathers from their noses or coughing them from their throats.

If a puff of wind had now blown from them toward Jake, it might have carried a flurry of snowy plumes or even the merry cries of the little revellers, and the den would have been discovered at once. But, as luck would have it, the evening lull was on, and all distant sounds were hidden by the crashing that Jake made in trying to trace his feather guides through the last thicket.

About this time Tito was returning home with a Magpie that she had captured by watching till it went to feed within the ribs of a dead Horse, when she ran across Jake's trail. Now, a man on foot is always a suspicious character in this country. She followed the trail for a little to see where he was going, and that she knew at once from the scent. How it tells her no one can say, yet all hunters know that it does. And Tito marked that it was going straight toward her home. Thrilled with new fear, she hid the Bird she was carrying, then followed the trail of the man. Within a few minutes she could hear him in the thicket, and Tito realized the terrible danger that was threatening. She went swiftly, quietly around to the den hollow, came on the heedless little roisterers, after giving the signal-call, which prevented them taking alarm at her approach; but she must have had a shock when she saw how marked the hollow and the den were now, all drifted over with feathers white as snow. Then she gave the danger-call that sent them all to earth, and the little glade was still.

Her own nose was so thoroughly and always her guide that it was not likely she thought of the white feathers being the telltale. But now she realized that a man, one she knew of old as a treacherous charac-ter, one whose scent had always meant mischief to her, that had been associated with all her own troubles and the cause of nearly all her desperate danger, was close to her darlings; was tracking them down; in a few minutes would surely have them in his merciless power.

Oh, the wrench to the mother's heart at the thought of what she could foresee! But the warmth of the mother-love lent life to the mother-wit. Having sent the little ones out of sight, and by a sign conveyed to Saddleback her alarm, she swiftly came back to the man, then she crossed before him, thinking, in her half-reasoning way, that the man must be following a foot-scent just as she herself would do, but would, of course, take the stronger line of tracks she was now laying. She did not realize that the failing daylight made any difference. Then she trotted to one side, and to make doubly sure of being followed, she uttered the fiercest challenge she could, just as many a time she had done to make the Dogs pursue her:

Grrr-wow-wow-wa-a-a-h,

and stood still; then ran a little nearer and did it again, and then again much nearer, and repeated her bark, she was so determined that the wolver should follow her.

Of course the wolver could see nothing of the Coyote, for the shades were falling. He had to give up the hunt anyway. His understanding of the details was as different as possible from that the Mother Coyote had, and yet it came to the same thing. He recognized that the Coyote's bark was the voice of the distressed mother trying to call him away. So he knew the brood must be close at hand, and all he now had to do was return in the morning and complete his search. So he made his way back to his camp.

XII

Saaddleback thought they had won the victory. He felt secure, because the foot-scent that he might have supposed the man to be following would be stale by morning. Tito did not feel so safe. That two-legged beast was close to her home and her little ones; had barely been turned aside; might come back yet.

The wolver watered and repicketed his Horse, kindled the fire anew, made his coffee and ate his evening meal, then smoked awhile before lying down to sleep, thinking occasionally of the little woolly scalps he expected to gather in the morning.

He was about to roll up in his blanket when, out of the dark distance, there sounded the evening cry of the Coyote, the rolling challenge of more than one voice. Jake grinned in fiendish glee, and said: 'There you are all right. Howl some more. I'll see you in the morning.'

It was the ordinary, or rather *one* of the ordinary, camp-calls of the Coyote. It was sounded once, and then all was still. Jake soon forgot it in his loggish slumber.

The callers were Tito and Saddleback. The challenge was not an empty bluff. It had a distinct purpose behind it – to know for sure whether the enemy had any dogs with him; and because there was no responsive bark Tito knew that he had none.

Then Tito waited for an hour or so till the flickering fire had gone dead, and the only sound of life about the camp was the cropping of the grass by the picketed Horse. Tito crept near softly, so softly that the Horse did not see her till she was within twenty feet; then he gave a start that swung the tightened picket-rope up into the air, and snorted gently. Tito went quietly forward, and opening her wide gape, took the rope in, almost under her ears, between the great scissor-like back teeth, then chewed it for a few seconds.

The fibres quickly frayed, and, aided by the strain the nervous Horse still kept up, the last of the strands gave way, and the Horse was free. He was not much alarmed; he knew the smell of Coyote; and after jumping three steps and walking six, he stopped.

The sounding thumps of his hoofs on the ground awoke the sleeper. He looked up, but, seeing the Horse standing there, he went calmly off to sleep again, supposing that all went well.

Tito had sneaked away, but she now returned like a shadow, avoided the sleeper, but came around, sniffed doubtfully at the coffee, and then puzzled over a tin can, while Saddleback examined the frying-pan full of 'camp-sinkers' and then defiled both cakes and pan with dirt. The bridle hung on a low bush; the Coyotes did not know what it was, but just for luck they cut it into several pieces, then, taking the sacks that held Jake's bacon and flour, they carried them far away and buried them in the sand.

Having done all the mischief she could, Tito, followed by her mate, now set off for a wooded gully some miles away, where was a hole that had been made first by a Chipmunk, but enlarged by several other animals, including a Fox that had tried to dig out its occupants. Tito stopped and looked at many possible places before she settled on this. Then she set to work to dig. Saddleback had followed in a half-comprehending way, till he saw what she was doing. Then when she, tired with digging, came out, he went into the hole, and after snuffing about went on with the work, throwing out the earth between his hind legs; and when it was piled up behind he would come out and push it yet farther away.

And so they worked for hours, not a word said, and yet with a sufficient comprehension of the object in view to work in relief of each other. And by the time the morning came they had a den big enough to do for their home, in case they must move, though it would not compare with the one in the grassy hollow.

XIII

It was nearly sunrise before the wolver awoke. With the true instinct of a plainsman he turned to look for the Horse. *It was gone*. What his ship is to the sailor, what wings are to the Bird, what money is to the merchant, the Horse is to the plainsman. Without it he is helpless, lost at sea, wing broken, crippled in business. A foot on the plains is the sum of earthly terrors. Even Jake realized this, and ere his foggy wits had fully felt the shock he sighted the steed afar on a flat, grazing and stepping ever farther from the camp. At a second glance Jake noticed that the Horse was trailing the rope. If the rope had been left behind Jake would have known that it was hopeless to try to catch him; he would have finished his den-hunt and found the little Coyotes. But, with the trailing rope, there was a good chance of catching the Horse; so Jake set out to try.

Of all maddening things there is nothing worse than to be almost, but not quite, able to catch your Horse. Do what he might, Jake could not get quite near enough to seize that short rope, and the Horse led him on and on, until at last they were well on the homeward trail.

Now Jake was afoot anyhow, so seeing no better plan, he set out to follow that Horse right back to the Ranch.

But when about seven miles were covered Jake succeeded in catching him. He rigged up a rough *jaquima* with the rope and rode bare-backed in fifteen minutes over the three miles that lay between him and the Sheep-ranch, giving vent all the way to his pent-up feelings in cruel abuse of that Horse. Of course it did not do any good, and he knew that, but he considered it was heaps of satisfaction.

Here Jake got a meal and borrowed a saddle and a mongrel Hound that could run a trail, and returned late in the afternoon to finish his den-hunt. Had he known it, he now could have found it without the aid of the cur, for it was really close at hand when he took up the feather-trail where last he had left it. Within one hundred yards he rose to the top of the little ridge; then just over it, almost face to face, he came on a Coyote, carrying in its mouth a large Rabbit. The Coyote leaped just at the same moment that Jake fired his revolver, and the Dog broke into a fierce yelling and dashed off in pursuit, while Jake blazed and blazed away, without effect, and wondered why the Coyote should still hang on to that Rabbit as she ran for her life with the Dog yelling at her heels. Jake followed as far as he could and fired at each chance, but scored no hit. So when they had vanished among the buttes he left the Dog to follow or come back as he pleased, while he returned to the den, which, of course, was plain enough now. Jake knew that the pups were there yet. Had he not seen the mother bringing a Rabbit for them?

So he set to work with pick and shovel all the rest of that day. There were plenty of signs that the den had inhabitants, and, duly encouraged, he dug on, and after several hours of the hardest work he had ever done, he came to the end of the den – *only to find it empty*. After cursing his luck at the first shock of disgust, he put on his strong leather glove and groped about in the nest. He felt something firm and drew it out. It was the head and neck of his own Turkey Gobbler, and that was all he got for his pains.

XIV

Tito had not been idle during the time that the enemy was Horse-hunting. Whatever Saddleback might have done, Tito would live in no fool's paradise. Having finished the new den, she trotted back to the little valley of feathers, and the first young one that came to meet her at the door of this home was a broad-headed one much like herself. She seized him by the neck and set off, carrying him across country toward the new den, a couple of miles away. Every little while she had to put her offspring down to rest and give it a chance to breathe. This made the moving slow, and the labour of transporting the pups occupied all that day, for Saddleback was not allowed to carry any of them, probably because he was too rough.

Beginning with the biggest and brightest, they were carried away one at a time, and late in the afternoon only the runt was left. Tito had not only worked at digging all night, she had also trotted over thirty miles, half of it with a heavy baby to carry. But she did not rest. She was just coming out of the den, carrying her youngest in her mouth, when over the very edge of this hollow appeared the mongrel Hound, and a little way behind him Wolver Jake.

Away went Tito, holding the baby tight, and away went the Dog behind her.

Bang! bang! bang! said the revolver.

But not a shot touched her. Then over the ridge they dashed, where the revolver could not reach her, and sped across a flat, the tired Coyote and her baby, and the big fierce Hound behind her, bounding his hardest. Had she been fresh and unweighted she could soon have left the clumsy cur that now was barking furiously on her track and rather gaining than losing in the race. But she put forth all her strength, careered along a slope, where she gained a little, then down across a brushy flat where the cruel bushes robbed her of all she had gained. But again into the open they came, and the wolver, labouring far behind, got sight of them and fired again and again with his revolver, and only stirred the dust, but still it made her dodge and lose time, and it also spurred the Dog. The hunter saw the Coyote, his old acquaintance of the bobtail, carrying still, as he thought, the Jack-rabbit she had been bringing to her brood, and wondered at her strange persistence. 'Why doesn't she drop that weight when flying for her life?' But on she went and gamely bore her load over the hills, the man cursing his luck that he had not brought his Horse, and the mongrel bounding in deadly earnest but thirty feet behind her. Then suddenly in front of Tito yawned a little cut-bank gully. Tired and weighted, she dared not try the leap; she skirted around. But the Dog was fresh; he cleared it easily, and the mother's start was cut down by half. But on she went, straining to hold the little one high above the scratching brush and the dangerous bayonet-spikes; but straining too much, for the helpless cub was choking in his mother's grip. She must lay him down or strangle him; with such a weight she could not much longer keep out of reach. She tried to give the howl for help, but her voice was muffled by the cub, now struggling for breath, and as she tried to ease her grip on him a sudden wrench jerked him from her mouth into the grass into the power of the merciless Hound. Tito was far smaller than the Dog; ordinarily she would have held him in fear; but her little one, her baby, was the only thought now, and as the brute sprang forward to tear it in his wicked jaws, she leaped between and stood facing him with all her mane erect, her teeth exposed, and plainly showed her resolve to save her young one at any price. The Dog was not brave, only confident that he was bigger and had the man behind him. But the man was far away, and balked in his first rush at the trembling little Coyote, that tried to hide in the grass, the cur hesitated a moment, and Tito howled the long howl for help the muster-call:

Yap-yap-yap-yah-yah-yah-h-h-h-h
Yap-yap-yap-yah-yah-yah-h-h-h-h,

and made the buttes around reecho so that Jake could not tell where it came from; but some one else there was that heard and did know whence it came. The Dog's courage revived on hearing something like a far-away shout. Again he sprang at the little one, but again the mother balked him with her own body, and then they closed in deadly struggle. 'Oh, if Saddleback would only come! ' But no one came, and now she had no further chance to call. Weight is everything in a closing fight, and Tito soon went down, bravely fighting to the last, but clearly worsted; and the Hound's courage grew with the sight of victory, and all he thought of now was to finish her and then kill her helpless baby in its turn. He had no ears or eyes for any other thing, till out of the nearest sage there flashed a streak of grey, and in a trice the big-voiced coward was hurled back by a foe almost as heavy as himself hurled back with a crippled shoulder. Dash, chop, and staunch old Saddleback sprang on him again. Tito struggled to her feet, and they closed on him together. His courage fled at once when he saw the odds, and all he wanted now was safe escape escape from Saddleback, whose speed was like the wind, escape from Tito, whose baby's life was at stake. Not twenty jumps away did he get; not breath enough had he to howl for help to his master in the distant hills; not fifteen yards away from her little one that he meant to tear, they tore him all to bits.

And Tito lifted the rescued young one, and travelling as slowly as she wished, they reached the new-made den. There the family safely reunited, far away from danger of further attack by Wolver Jake or his kind.

And there they lived in peace till their mother had finished their training, and every one of them grew up wise in the ancient learning of the plains, wise in the later wisdom that the ranchers' war has forced upon them, and not only they, but their children's children, too.

The Buffalo herds have gone; they have succumbed to the rifles of the hunters. The Antetope droves are nearly gone; Hound and lead were too much for them. The Blacktail bands have dwindled before axe and fence. The ancient dwellers of the Badlands have faded like snow under the new conditions, but the Coyotes are no more in fear of extinction. Their morning and evening song still sounds from the level buttes, as it did long years ago when every plain was a teeming land of game. They have learned the deadly secrets of traps and poisons, they know how to baffle the gunner and Hound, they have matched their wits with the hunter's wits. They have learned how to prosper in a land of man-made plenty, in spite of the worst that man can do, and it was Tito that taught them how.

JOHNNY BEAR

I

Johnny was a queer little Bear cub that lived with Grumpy, his mother, in the Yellowstone Park. They were among the many Bears that found a desirable home in the country about the Fountain Hotel.

The steward of the Hotel had ordered the kitchen garbage to be dumped in an open glade of the surrounding forest, thus providing, throughout the season, a daily feast for the Bears, and their numbers have increased each year since the law of the land has made the Park a haven of refuge where no wild thing may be harmed. They have accepted man's peace-offering, and many of them have become so well known to the Hotel men that they have received names suggested by their looks or ways. Slim Jim was a very long-legged thin Blackbear; Snuffy was a Blackbear that looked as though he had been singed; Fatty was a very fat, lazy Bear that always lay down to eat; the Twins were two half-grown, ragged specimens that always came and went together. But Grumpy and Little Johnny were the best known of them all.

Grumpy was the biggest and fiercest of the Blackbears, and Johnny, apparently her only son, was a peculiarly tiresome little cub, for he seemed never to cease either grumbling or whining. This probably meant that he was sick, for a healthy little Bear does not grumble all the time, any more than a healthy child. And indeed Johnny looked sick; he was the most miserable specimen in the Park. His whole appearance suggested dyspepsia; and this I quite understood when I saw the awful mixtures he would eat at that garbage-heap. Anything at all that he fancied he would try. And his mother allowed him to do as he pleased; so, after all, it was chiefly her fault, for she should not have permitted such things.

– 159 –

Johnny had only three good legs, his coat was faded and mangy, his limbs were thin, and his ears and paunch were disproportionately large. Yet his mother thought the world of him. She was evidently convinced that he was a little beauty and the Prince of all Bears, so, of course, she quite spoiled him. She was always ready to get into trouble on his account, and he was always delighted to lead her there. Although such a wretched little failure, Johnny was far from being a fool, for he usually knew just what he wanted and how to get it, if teasing his mother could carry the point.

II

IT was in the summer of 1897 that I made their acquaintance. I was in the Park to study the home life of the animals, and had been told that in the woods, near the Fountain Hotel, I could see Bears at any time, which, of course, I scarcely believed. But on stepping out of the back door five minutes after arriving, I came face to face with a large Black-bear and her two cubs.

I stopped short, not a little startled. The Bears also stopped and sat up to look at me. Then Mother Bear made a curious short *Koff Koff*, and looked toward a near pine-tree. The cubs seemed to know what she meant, for they ran to this tree and scrambled up like two little monkeys, and when safely aloft they sat like small boys, holding on with their hands, while their little black legs dangled in the air, and waited to see what was to happen down below.

The Mother Bear, still on her hind legs, came slowly toward me, and I began to feel very uncomfortable indeed, for she stood about six feet high in her stockings and had apparently never heard of the magical power of the human eye.

I had not even a stick to defend myself with, and when she gave a low growl, I was about to retreat to the Hotel, although previously assured that the Bears have always kept their truce with man. However, just at this turning-point the old one stopped, now but thirty feet away, and continued to survey me calmly. She seemed in doubt for a minute, but evidently made up her mind that, 'although that human thing might be all right, she would take no chances for her little ones.'

She looked up to her two hopefuls, and gave a peculiar whining *Er-r-r Er-r*, whereupon they, like obedient children, jumped, as at the word of command. There was nothing about them heavy or bear-like as commonly understood; lightly they swung from bough to bough till they dropped to the ground, and all went off together into the woods. I was much tickled by the prompt obedience of the little Bears. As soon as their mother told them to do something they did it. They did not even offer a suggestion. But I also found out that there was a good reason for it, for had they not done as she had told them they would have got such a spanking as would have made them howl.

This was a delightful peep into Bear home life, and would have been well worth coming for, if the insight had ended there. But my friends in the Hotel said that that was not the best place for Bears. I should go to the garbage-heap, a quarter-mile off in the forest. There, they said, I surely could see as many Bears as I wished (which was absurd of them).

Early the next morning I went to this Bears' Banqueting Hall in the pines, and hid in the nearest bushes.

Before very long a large Blackbear came quietly out of the woods to the pile, and began turning over the garbage and feeding. He was very nervous, sitting up and looking about at each slight sound, or running away a few yards when startled by some trifle. At length he cocked his ears and galloped off into the pines, as another Blackbear appeared. He also behaved in the same timid manner, and at last ran away when I shook the bushes in trying to get a better view.

At the outset I myself had been very nervous, for of course no man is allowed to carry weapons in the Park; but the timidity of these Bears reassured me, and thenceforth I forgot everything in the interest of seeing the great, shaggy creatures in their home life.

Soon I realized I could not get the close insight I wished from that bush, as it was seventy-five yards from the garbage-pile. There was none nearer; so I did the only thing left to do: I went to the garbage-pile itself, and, digging a hole big enough to hide in, remained there all day long, with cabbage-stalks, old potato-peelings, tomato-cans, and carrion piled up in odourous heaps around me. Notwithstanding the opinions of countless flies, it was not an attractive place. Indeed, it was so unfragrant that at night, when I returned to the Hotel, I was not allowed to come in until after I had changed my clothes in the woods.

It had been a trying ordeal, but I surely did see Bears that day. If I may reckon it a new Bear each time one came, I must have seen over forty. But of course it was not, for the Bears were coming and going. And yet I am certain of this: there were at least thirteen Bears, for I had thirteen about me at one time.

All that day I used my sketch-book and journal. Every Bear that came was duly noted; and this process soon began to give the desired insight into their ways and personalities.

Many unobservant persons think and say that all Negroes, or all Chinamen, as well as all animals of a kind, look alike. But just as surely as each human being differs from the next, so surely each animal is different from its fellow; otherwise how would the old ones know their mates or the little ones their mother, as they certainly do? These feasting Bears gave a good illustration of this, for each had its individuality; no two were quite alike in appearance or in character.

This curious fact also appeared: I could hear the Wood-peckers pecking over one hundred yards away in the woods, as well as the Chickadees chickadeeing, the Blue-jays blue-jaying, and even the Squirrels scampering across the leafy forest floor; and yet I *did not hear one of these Bears come*. Their huge, padded feet always went down in exactly the right spot to break no stick, to rustle no leaf, showing how perfectly they had learned the art of going in silence through the woods.

III

ALL morning the Bears came and went or wandered near my hiding-place without discovering me; and, except for one or two brief quarrels, there was nothing very exciting to note. But about three in the afternoon it became more lively.

There were then four large Bears feeding on the heap. In the middle was Fatty, sprawling at full length as he feasted, a picture of placid ursine content, puffing just a little at times as he strove to save himself the trouble of moving by darting out his tongue like a long red serpent, farther and farther, in quest of the tidbits just beyond claw reach.

Behind him Slim Jim was puzzling over the anatomy and attributes of an ancient lobster. It was something outside his experience, but the principle, 'In case of doubt take the trick,' is well known in Bearland, and settled the difficulty.

The other two were clearing out fruit-tins with marvellous dexterity. One supple paw would hold the tin while the long tongue would dart again and again through the narrow opening, avoiding the sharp edges, yet cleaning out the can to the last taste of its sweetness.

This pastoral scene lasted long enough to be sketched, but was ended abruptly. My eye caught a movement on the hilltop whence all the Bears had come, and out stalked a very large Blackbear with a tiny cub. It was Grumpy and Little Johnny.

The old Bear stalked down the slope toward the feast, and Johnny hitched alongside, grumbling as he came, his mother watching him as solicitously as ever a hen did her single chick. When they were within thirty yards of the garbage-heap, Grumpy turned to her son and said something which, judging from its effect, must have meant: 'Johnny, my child, I think you had better stay here while I go and chase those fellows away.'

Johnny obediently waited; but he wanted to see, so he sat up on his hind legs with eyes agog and ears acock.

Grumpy came striding along with dignity, uttering warning growls as she approached the four Bears. They were too much engrossed to pay any heed to the fact that yet another one of them was coming, till Grumpy, now within fifteen feet, let out a succession of loud coughing sounds, and charged into them. Strange to say, they did not pretend to face her, but, as soon as they saw who it was, scattered and all fled for the woods.

Slim Jim could safely trust his heels, and the other two were not far behind; but poor Fatty, puffing hard and waddling like any other very fat creature, got along but slowly, and, unluckily for him, he fled in the direction of Johnny, so that Grumpy overtook him in a few bounds and gave him a couple of sound slaps in the rear which, if they did not accelerate his pace, at least made him bawl, and saved him by changing his direction. Grumpy, now left alone in possession of the feast, turned toward her son and uttered the whining *Er-r-r Er-r-r Er-r-r-r*. Johnny responded eagerly. He came 'hopity-hop' on his three good legs as fast as he could, and, joining her on the garbage, they began to have such a good time that Johnny actually ceased grumbling.

He had evidently been there before now, for he seemed to know quite well the staple kinds of canned goods. One might almost have supposed that he had learned the brands, for a lobster-tin had no charm for him as long as he could find those that once were filled with jam. Some of the tins gave him much trouble, as he was too greedy or too clumsy to escape being scratched by the sharp edges. One seductive fruit-tin had a hole so large that he found he could force his head into it, and for a few minutes his joy was full as he licked into all the farthest corners. But when he tried to draw his head out, his sorrows began, for he found himself caught. He could not get out, and he scratched and screamed like any other spoiled child, giving his mother no end of concern, although she seemed not to know how to help him. When at length he got the tin off his head, he revenged himself by hammering it with his paws till it was perfectly flat.

A large syrup-can made him happy for a long time. It had had a lid, so that the hole was round and smooth; but it was not big enough to admit his head, and he could not touch its riches with his tongue stretched out its longest. He soon hit on a plan, however. Putting in his little black arm, he churned it around, then drew out and licked it clean; and while he licked one he got the other one ready; and he did this again and again, until the can was as clean inside as when first it had left the factory.

A broken mouse-trap seemed to puzzle him. He clutched it between his fore paws their strong inturn being sympathetically reflected in his hind feet, and held it firmly for study. The cheesy smell about it was decidedly good, but the thing responded in such an uncanny way, when he slapped it, that he kept back a cry for help only by the exercise of unusual self-control. After gravely inspecting it, with his head first on this side and then on that, and his lips puckered into a little tube, he submitted it to the same punishment as that meted out to the refractory fruit-tin, and was rewarded by discovering a nice little bit of cheese in the very heart of the culprit.

Johnny had evidently never heard of ptomaine-poisoning, for nothing came amiss. After the jams and fruits gave out he turned his attention to the lobster-and sardine-cans, and was not appalled by even the army beef. His paunch grew quite balloon-like, and from much licking his arms looked thin and shiny, as though he was wearing black silk gloves.

IV

IT occurred to me that I might now be in a really dangerous place. For it is one thing surprising a Bear that has no family responsibilities, and another stirring up a bad-tempered old mother by frightening her cub.

'Supposing,' I thought, 'that cranky Little Johnny should wander over to this end of the garbage and find me in the hole; he will at once set up a squall, and his mother, of course, will think I am hurting him, and, without giving me a chance to explain, may forget the rules of the Park and make things very unpleasant.'

Luckily, all the jam-pots were at Johnny's end; he stayed by them, and Grumpy stayed by him. At length he noticed that his mother had a better tin than any he could find, and as he ran whining to take it from her he chanced to glance away up the slope. There he saw something that made him sit up and utter a curious little *Koff Koff Koff Koff*.

His mother turned quickly, and sat up to see 'what the child was looking at'. I followed their gaze, and there, oh, horrors! was an enormous Grizzly Bear. He was a monster; he looked like a fur-clad omnibus coming through the trees.

Johnny set up a whine at once and got behind his mother. She uttered a deep growl, and all her back hair stood on end. Mine did too, but I kept as still as possible.

With stately tread the Grizzly came on. His vast shoulders sliding along his sides, and his silvery robe swaying at each tread, like the trappings on an elephant, gave an impression of power that was appalling. Johnny began to whine more loudly, and I fully sympathized with him now, though I did not join in. After a moment's hesitation Grumpy turned to her noisy cub and said something that sounded to me like two or three short coughs – *Koff Koff Koff*. But I imagine that she really said: 'My child, I think you had better get up that tree, while I go and drive the brute away.'

At any rate, that was what Johnny did, and this what she set out to do. But Johnny had no notion of missing any fun. He wanted to see what was going to happen. So he did not rest contented where he was hidden in the thick branches of the pine, but combined safety with view by climbing to the topmost branch that would bear him, and there, sharp against the sky, he squirmed about and squealed aloud in his excitement. The branch was so small that it bent under his weight, swaying this way and that as he shifted about, and every moment I expected to see it snap off. If it had been broken when swaying my way, Johnny would certainly have fallen on me, and this would probably have resulted in bad feelings between myself and his mother; but the limb was tougher than it looked, or perhaps Johnny had had plenty of experience, for he neither lost his hold nor broke the branch.

Meanwhile, Grumpy stalked out to meet the Grizzly. She stood as high as she could and set all her bristles on end; then, growling and chopping her teeth, she faced him.

The Grizzly, so far as I could see, took no notice of her. He came striding toward the feast as though alone. But when Grumpy got within twelve feet of him she uttered a succession of short, coughy roars, and, charging, gave him a tremendous blow on the ear. The Grizzly was surprised; but he replied with a left-hander that knocked her over like a sack of hay.

Nothing daunted, but doubly furious, she jumped up and rushed at him. Then they clinched and rolled over and over, whacking and pounding, snorting and growling, and making no end of dust and rumpus. But above all their noise I could clearly hear Little Johnny, yelling at the top of his voice, and evidently encouraging his mother to go right in and finish the Grizzly at once.

Why the Grizzly did not break her in two I could not understand. After a few minutes' struggle, during which I could see nothing but dust and dim flying legs, the two separated as by mutual consent – perhaps the regulation time was up – and for a while they stood glaring at each other, Grumpy at least much winded.

The Grizzly would have dropped the matter right there. He did not wish to fight. He had no idea of troubling himself about Johnny. All he wanted was a quiet meal. But no! The moment he took one step toward the garbage-pile, that is, as Grumpy thought, toward Johnny, she went at him again. But this time the Grizzly was ready for her. With one blow he knocked her off her feet and sent her crashing on to a huge upturned pine-root. She was fairly staggered this time. The force of the blow, and the rude reception of the rooty antlers, seemed to take all the fight out of her. She scrambled over and tried to escape. But the Grizzly was mad now. He meant to punish her, and dashed around the root. For a minute they kept up a dodging chase about it; but Grumpy was quicker of foot, and somehow always managed to keep the root between herself and her foe, while Johnny, safe in the tree, continued to take an intense and uproarious interest.

At length, seeing he could not catch her that way, the Grizzly sat up on his haunches; and while he doubtless was planning a new move, old Grumpy saw her chance, and making a dash, got away from the root and up to the top of the tree where Johnny was perched.

Johnny came down a little way to meet her, or perhaps so that the tree might not break off with the additional weight. Having photographed this interesting group from my hiding-place, I thought I must get a closer picture at any price, and for the first time in the day's proceedings. I jumped out of the hole and ran under the tree. This move-

proved a great mistake, for here the thick lower boughs came between, and I could see nothing at all of the Bears at the top.

I was close to the trunk, and was peering about and seeking for a chance to use the camera, when old Grumpy began to come down, chopping her teeth and uttering her threatening cough at me. While I stood in doubt, I heard a voice far behind me calling: 'Say, Mister! You better look out; that ole B'ar is liable to hurt you.'

I turned to see the cowboy of the Hotel on his Horse. He had been riding after the cattle, and chanced to pass near just as events were moving quickly.'

'Do you know these Bears?' said I, as he rode up.

'Wall, I reckon I do,' said he. 'That there little one up top is Johnny; he's a little crank. An' the big un is Grumpy; she's a big crank. She's mighty onreliable gen'relly, but she's always strictly ugly when Johnny hollers like that.'

'I should much like to get her picture when she comes down,' said I.

'Tell ye what I'll do: I'll stay by on the pony, an' if she goes to bother you I reckon I can keep her off,' said the man.

He accordingly stood by as Grumpy slowly came down from branch to branch, growling and threatening. But when she neared the ground she kept on the far side of the trunk, and finally slipped down and ran into the woods, without the slightest pretence of carrying out any of her dreadful threats. Thus Johnny was again left alone. He climbed up to his old perch and resumed his monotonous whining:

Wah! Wah! Wah! ('Oh, dear! Oh, dear! Oh, dear!')

I got the camera ready, and was arranging deliberately to take his picture in his favourite and peculiar attitude for threnodic song, when all at once he began craning his neck and yelling, as he had done during the fight.

I looked where his nose pointed, and here was the Grizzly coming on straight toward me – not charging, but striding along, as though he meant to come the whole distance.

I said to my cowboy friend: 'Do you know this Bear?'

He replied: 'Wall! I reckon I do. That's the ole Grizzly. He's the biggest B'ar in the Park. He gen'relly minds his own business, but he ain't scared o' nothin'; an' today, ye see, he's been scrappin', so he's liable to be ugly.'

'I would like to take his picture,' said I 'and if you will help me, I am willing to take some chances on it.'

'All right,' said he, with a grin. 'I'll stand by on the Horse, an' if he charges you I'll charge him; an' I kin knock him down once, but I can't do it twice. You better have your tree picked out.'

As there was only one tree to pick out, and that was the one that Johnny was in, the prospect was not alluring. I imagined myself scrambling up there next to Johnny, and then Johnny's mother coming up after me, with the Grizzly below to catch me when Grumpy should throw me down.

The Grizzly came on, and I snapped him at forty yards, then again at twenty yards; and still he came quietly toward me. I sat down on the garbage and made ready. Eighteen yards – sixteen yards – twelve yards – eight yards, and still he came, while the pitch of Johnny's protests kept rising proportionately. Finally at five yards he stopped, and swung his huge bearded head to one side, to see what was making that aggravating row in the tree-top, giving me a profile view, and I snapped the camera. At the click he turned on me with a thunderous

G – R – O – W – L !

and I sat still and trembling, wondering if my last moment had come. For a second he glared at me, and I could note the little green electric lamp in each of his eyes. Then he slowly turned and picked up – a large tomato-can.

'Goodness!' I thought, 'is he going to throw that at me? ' But he deliberately licked it out, dropped it, and took another, paying thenceforth no heed whatever either to me or to Johnny, evidently considering us equally beneath his notice.

I backed slowly and respectfully out of his royal presence, leaving him in possession of the garbage, while Johnny kept on caterwauling from his safety-perch.

What became of Grumpy the rest of that day I do not know. Johnny, after bewailing for a time, realized that there was no sympathetic hearer of his cries, and therefore very sagaciously stopped them. Having no mother now to plan for him, he began to plan for himself, and at once proved that he was better stuff than he seemed. After watching, with a look of profound cunning on his little black face, and waiting till the Grizzly was some distance away, he silently slipped down behind the trunk, and, despite his three-leggedness, ran like a hare to the next tree, never stopping to breathe till he was on its topmost bough. For he was thoroughly convinced that the only object that the Grizzly had in life was to kill him, and he seemed quite aware that his enemy could not climb a tree.

Another long and safe survey of the Grizzly, who really paid no heed to him whatever, was followed by another dash for the next tree, varied occasionally by a cunning feint to mislead the foe. So he went dashing from tree to tree and climbing each to its very top, although it might be but ten feet from the last, till he disappeared in the woods. After, perhaps, ten minutes, his voice again came floating on the breeze, the habitual querulous whining which told me he had found his mother and had resumed his customary appeal to her sympathy.

VI

IT is quite a common thing for Bears to spank their cubs when they need it, and if Grumpy had disciplined Johnny this way, it would have saved them both a deal of worry.

Perhaps not a day passed, that summer, without Grumpy getting into trouble on Johnny's account. But of all these numerous occasions the most ignominious was shortly after the affair with the Grizzly.

I first heard the story from three bronzed mountaineers. As they were very sensitive about having their word doubted, and very good shots with the revolver, I believed every word they told me, especially when afterward fully indorsed by the Park authorities.

It seemed that of all the tinned goods on the pile the nearest to Johnny's taste were marked with a large purple plum. This conclusion he had arrived at only after most exhaustive study. The very odour of those plums in Johnny's nostrils was the equivalent of ecstasy. So when it came about one day that the cook of the Hotel baked a huge batch of plum-tarts, the telltale wind took the story afar into the woods, where it was wafted by way of Johnny's nostrils to his very soul.

Of course Johnny was whimpering at the time. His mother was busy 'washing his face and combing his hair, so he had double cause for whimpering. But the smell of the tarts thrilled him; he jumped up, and when his mother tried to hold him he squalled, and I am afraid – he bit her. She should have cuffed him, but she did not. She only gave a disapproving growl, and followed to see that he came to no harm.

With his little black nose in the wind, Johnny led straight for the kitchen. He took the precaution, however, of climbing from time to time to the very top of a pine-tree lookout to take an observation, while Grumpy stayed below.

Thus they came close to the kitchen, and there, in the last tree, Johnny's courage as a leader gave out, so he remained aloft and expressed his hankering for tarts in a woe-begone wail.

It is not likely that Grumpy knew exactly what her son was crying for. But it is sure that as soon as she showed an inclination to go back into the pines, Johnny protested in such an outrageous and heartrending screeching that his mother simply could not leave him, and he showed no sign of coming down to be led away.

Grumpy herself was fond of plum-jam. The odour was now, of course, very strong and proportionately alluring; so Grumpy followed it somewhat cautiously up to the kitchen door.

There was nothing surprising about this. The rule of 'live and let live' is so strictly enforced in the Park that the Bears often come to the kitchen door for pickings, and on getting something, they go quietly back to the woods. Doubtless Johnny and Grumpy would each have gotten their tart but that a new factor appeared in the case.

That week the Hotel people had brought a new Cat from the East. She was not much more than a kitten, but still had a litter of her own, and at the moment that Grumpy reached the door, the Cat and her family were sunning themselves on the top step. Pussy opened her eyes to see this huge, shaggy monster towering above her. The Cat had never before seen a Bear – she had not been there long enough; she did not know even what a Bear was. She knew what a Dog was, and here was a bigger, more awful bobtailed black dog than ever she had dreamed of coming right at her. Her first thought was to fly for her life. But her next was for the kittens. She must take care of them. She must at least cover their retreat. So, like a brave little mother, she braced herself on that door-step, and spreading her back, her claws, her tail, and everything she had to spread, she screamed out at that Bear an unmistakable order to

STOP!

The language must have been 'Cat', but the meaning was clear to the Bear; for those who saw it maintain stoutly that Grumpy not only stopped, but she also conformed to the custom of the country and in token of surrender held up her hands. However, the position she thus took made her so high that the Cat seemed tiny in the distance below.

Old Grumpy had faced a Grizzly once, and was she now to be held up by a miserable little spike-tailed skunk no bigger than a mouthful? She was ashamed of herself, especially when a wail from Johnny smote on her ear and reminded her of her plain duty, as well as supplied his usual moral support.

So she dropped down on her front feet to proceed.

Again the Cat shrieked, 'STOP!'

But Grumpy ignored the command. A scared mew from a kitten nerved the Cat, and she launched her ultimatum, which ultimatum was herself. Eighteen sharp claws, a mouthful of keen teeth, had Pussy, and she worked them all with a desperate will when she landed on Grumpy's bare, bald, sensitive nose, just the spot of all where the Bear could not stand it, and then worked backward to a point outside the sweep of Grumpy's claws. After one or two vain attempts to shake the spotted fury off, old Grumpy did just as most creatures would have done under the circumstances: she turned tail and bolted out of the enemy's country into her own woods.

But Puss's fighting blood was up. She was not content with repelling the enemy; she wanted to inflict a crushing defeat, to achieve an absolute and final rout. And however fast old Grumpy might go, it did not count, for the Cat was still on top, working her teeth and claws like a little demon. Grumpy, always erratic, now became panic-stricken.

The trail of the pair was flecked with tufts of long black hair, and there was even bloodshed (in the fiftieth degree). Honour surely was satisfied, but Pussy was not. Round and round they had gone in the mad race. Grumpy was frantic, absolutely humiliated, and ready to make any terms; but Pussy seemed deaf to her cough-like yelps, and no one knows how far the Cat might have ridden that day had not Johnny unwittingly put a new idea into his mother's head by bawling in his best style from the top of his last tree, which tree Grumpy made for and scrambled up.

This was so clearly the enemy's country and in view of his reinforcements that the Cat wisely decided to follow no farther. She jumped from the climbing Bear to the ground, and then mounted sentry-guard below, marching around with tail in the air, daring that Bear to come down. Then the kittens came out and sat around, and enjoyed it all hugely. And the mountaineers assured me that the Bears would have been kept up the tree till they were starved, had not the cook of the Hotel come out and called off his Cat – although this statement was not among those vouched for by the officers of the Park.

VII

THE last time I saw Johnny he was in the top of a tree, bewailing his unhappy lot as usual, while his mother was dashing about among the pines, 'with a chip on her shoulder', seeking for some one – anyone – that she could punish for Johnny's sake, provided, of course, that it was not a big Grizzly or a Mother Cat.

This was early in August, but there were not lacking symptoms of change in old Grumpy. She was always reckoned 'onsartain', and her devotion to Johnny seemed subject to her characteristic. This perhaps accounted for the fact that when the end of the month was near,

Johnny would sometimes spend half a day in the top of some tree, alone, miserable, and utterly unheeded.

The last chapter of his history came to pass after I had left the region. One day at grey dawn he was tagging along behind his mother as she prowled in the rear of the Hotel. A newly hired Irish girl was already astir in the kitchen. On looking out, she saw, as she thought, a Calf where it should not be, and ran to shoo it away. That open kitchen door still held unmeasured terrors for Grumpy, and she ran in such alarm that Johnny caught the infection, and not being able to keep up with her, he made for the nearest tree, which unfortunately turned out to be a post, and soon – too soon – he arrived at its top, some seven feet from the ground, and there poured forth his woes on the chilly morning air, while Grumpy apparently felt justified in continuing her flight alone. When the girl came near and saw that she had treed some wild animal, she was as much frightened as her victim. But others of the kitchen staff appeared, and recognizing the vociferous Johnny, they decided to make him a prisoner.

A collar and chain were brought, and after a struggle, during which several of the men got well scratched, the collar was buckled on Johnny's neck and the chain made fast to the post.

When he found that he was held, Johnny was simply too mad to scream. He bit and scratched and tore till he was tired out. Then he lifted up his voice again to call his mother. She did appear once or twice in the distance, but could not make up her mind to face that Cat, so disappeared, and Johnny was left to his fate.

He put in the most of that day in alternate struggling and crying. Toward evening he was worn out, and glad to accept the meal that was brought by Norah, who felt herself called on to play mother, since she had chased his own mother away.

When night came it was very cold; but Johnny nearly froze at the top of the post before he would come down and accept the warm bed provided at the bottom.

During the days that followed, Grumpy came often to the garbage-heap, but soon apparently succeeded in forgetting all about her son. He was daily tended by Norah, and received all his meals from her. He also received something else; for one day he scratched her when she brought his food, and she very properly spanked him till he squealed. For a few hours he sulked; he was not used to such treatment. But hunger subdued him, and thenceforth he held his new guardian in wholesome respect. She, too, began to take an interest in the poor motherless little wretch, and within a fortnight Johnny showed signs of developing a new character. He was much less noisy. He still expressed his hunger in a whining *Er-r-r Er-r-r Er-r-r*, but he rarely squealed now, and his unruly outbursts entirely ceased.

By the third week of September the change was still more marked. Utterly abandoned by his own mother, all his interest had centred in Norah, and she had fed and spanked him into an exceedingly well-behaved little Bear. Sometimes she would allow him a taste of freedom, and he then showed his bias by making, not for the woods, but for the kitchen where she was, and following her around on his hind legs. Here also he made the acquaintance of that dreadful Cat; but Johnny had a powerful friend now, and Pussy finally became reconciled to the black, woolly interloper.

As the Hotel was to be closed in October, there was talk of turning Johnny loose or of sending him to the Washington Zoo; but Norah had claims that she would not forego.

When the frosty nights of late September came, Johnny had greatly improved in his manners, but he had also developed a bad cough. An examination of his lame leg had shown that the weakness was not in the foot, but much more deeply seated, perhaps in the hip, and that meant a feeble and tottering constitution.

He did not get fat, as do most Bears in fall; indeed, he continued to fail. His little round belly shrank in, his cough became worse, and one morning he was found very sick and shivering in his bed by the post. Norah brought him indoors, where the warmth helped him so much that thenceforth he lived in the kitchen.

For a few days he seemed better, and his old-time pleasure in *seeing things* revived. The great blazing fire in the range particularly appealed to him, and made him sit up in his old attitude when the opening of the door brought the wonder to view. After a week he lost interest even in that, and drooped more and more each day. Finally not the most exciting noises or scenes around him could stir up his old fondness for seeing what was going on.

He coughed a good deal, too, and seemed wretched, except when in Norah's lap. Here he would cuddle up contentedly, and whine most miserably when she had to set him down again in his basket.

A few days before the closing of the Hotel, he refused his usual breakfast, and whined softly till Norah took him in her lap; then he feebly snuggled up to her, and his soft *Er-r-r Er-r-r* grew fainter, till it ceased. Half an hour later, when she laid him down to go about her work, Little Johnny had lost the last trace of his anxiety to see and know what was going on.

THE PACING MUSTANG

I

Jo Calone threw down his saddle on the dusty ground, turned his horses loose, and went clanking into the ranchhouse.

'Nigh about chuck time?' he asked.

'Seventeen minutes,' said the cook glancing at the Waterbury, with the air of a train-starter, though this show of precision had never yet been justified by events.

'How's things on the Perico?' said Jo's pard.

'Hotter'n hinges,' said Jo. 'Cattle seem O.K.; lots of calves.'

'I seen that bunch o' mustangs that waters at Antelope Springs; couple o' colts along; one little dark one, a fair dandy; a born pacer. I run them a mile or two, and be led the bunch, an' never broke his pace. Cut loose, an' pushed them jest for fun, an' darned if I could make him break.'

'You didn't have no reefreshments along?' said Scarth, incredulously.

'That's all right, Scarth. You had to crawl on our last bet, an' you'll get another chance soon as you're man enough.'

'Chuck,' shouted the cook, and the subject was dropped.

Next day the scene of the roundup was changed, and he mustangs were forgotten.

A year later the same corner of New Mexico was worked over by the roundup, and again the mustang bunch was seen. The dark colt was now a black yearling, with thin, clean legs and glossy flanks; and more than one of the boys saw with his own eyes this oddity – the mustang was a born pacer.

Jo was along, and the idea now struck him that that colt was worth having. To an Easterner this thought may not seem startling or original, but in the West, where an unbroken horse is worth $5, and where an ordinary saddlehorse is worth $15 or $20, the idea of a wild mustang being desirable property does not occur to the average cowboy, for mustangs are hard to catch, and when caught are merely wild animal prisoners, perfectly useless and untamable to the last, Not a few of the cattle-owners make a point of shooting all mustangs at sight, they are not only useless cumberers of the feeding-grounds, but commonly lead away domestic horses, which soon take to wild life and are thenceforth lost.

Wild Jo Calone knew a 'bronk right down to sub-soil'. 'I never seen a white that wasn't soft, nor a chestnut that wasn't nervous, nor a bay that wasn't good if broke right, nor a black that wasn't hard as nails, an' full of the old Harry. All a black bronk wants is claws to be wus'n Daniel's hull outfit of lions.'

Since, then, a mustang is worthless vermin, and a black mustang ten times worse than worthless, Jo's pard 'didn't see no sense in Jo's wantin' to corral the yearling', as he now seemed intent on doing. But Jo got no chance to try that year.

He was only a cow-puncher on $25 a month, and tied to hours. Like most of the boys, he always looked forward to having a ranch and an outfit of his own. His brand, the hogpen, of sinister suggestion, was already registered at Santa Fe, but of horned stock it was borne by a single old cow, so as to give him a legal right to put his brand on any maverick (or unbranded animal) he might chance to find.

Yet each fall, when paid off, Jo could not resist the temptation to go to town with the boys and have a good time 'while the stuff held out'. So that his property consisted of little more than his saddle, his bed, and his old cow. He kept on hoping to make a strike that would leave him well fixed with a fair start, and when the thought came that the Black Mustang was his mascot, he only needed a chance to 'make the try'.

The roundup circled down to the Canadian River, and back in the fall by the Don Carlos Hills, and Jo saw no more of the Pacer, though he heard of him from many quarters, for the colt, now a vigourous, young horse, rising three, was beginning to be talked of.

Antelope Springs is in the middle of a great level plain. When the water is high it spreads into a small lake with a belt of sedge around it; when it is low there is a wide flat of black mud, glistening white with alkali in places, and the spring a water-hole in the middle. It has no flow or outlet and is fairly good water, the only drinking-place for many miles.

This flat, or prairie as it would be called farther north, was the favourite feeding-ground of the Black Stallion, but it was also the pasture of many herds of range horses and cattle. Chiefly interested was the 'L cross F' outfit. Foster, the manager and part owner, was a man of enterprise. He believed it would pay to handle a better class of cattle and horses on the range, and one of his ventures was ten half-blooded mares, tall, clean-limbed, deer-eyed creatures that made the scrub cow-ponies look like pitiful starvelings of some degenerate and quite different species.   Lf

One of these was kept stabled for use, but the nine, after the weaning of their colts, managed to get away and wandered off on the range.

A horse has a fine instinct for the road to the best feed, and the nine mares drifted, of course, to the prairie of Antelope Springs, twenty miles to the southward, And when, later that summer Foster went to round them up, he found the nine indeed, but with them and guarding them with an air of more than mere comradeship was a coal-black stallion, prancing around and rounding up the bunch like an expert, his jet-black coat a vivid contrast to the golden hides of his harem.

The mares were gentle, and would have been easily driven homeward but for a new and unexpected thing. The Black Stallion became greatly aroused. He seemed to inspire them too with his wildness, and flying this way and that way drove the whole band at full gallop where he would. Away they went, and the little cow-ponies that carried the men were easily left behind.

This was maddening, and both men at last drew their guns and sought a chance to drop that 'blasted stallion'. But no chance came that was not 9 to 1 of dropping one of the mares. A long day of manoeuvring made no change. The Pacer, for it was he, kept his family together and disappeared among the southern sand-hills. The cattlemen on their jaded ponies set out for home with the poor satisfaction of vowing vengeance for their failure on the superb cause of it.

One of the most aggravating parts of it was that one or two experiences like this would surely make the mares as wild as the Mustang, and there seemed to be no way of saving them from it.

Scientists differ on the power of beauty and prowess to attract female admiration among the lower animals, but whether it is admiration or the prowess itself, it is certain that a wild animal of uncommon gifts soon wins a large following from the harems of his rivals. And the great Black Horse, with his inky mane and tail and his green-lighted eyes, ranged through all that region and added to his following from many bands till not less than a score of mares were in his 'bunch'. Most were merely humble cow-ponies turned out to range, but the nine great mares were there, a striking group by themselves. According to all reports, this bunch was always kept rounded up and guarded with such energy and jealously that a mare, once in it, was a lost animal so far as man was concerned, and the ranchmen realised soon that they had gotten on the range a mustang that was doing them more harm than all other sources of loss put together.

II

It was December, 1893. I was new in the country, and was setting out from the ranch-house on the Pinavetitos, to go with a waggon to the Canadian River. As I was leaving, Foster finished his remark by: 'And if you get a chance to draw a bead on that accursed mustang, don't fail to drop him in his tracks.'

This was the first I had heard of him, and as I rode along I gathered from Burns, my guide, the history that has been given. I was full of curiosity to see the famous three-year-old, and was not a little disappointed on the second day when we came to the prairie on Antelope Springs and saw no sign of the Pacer or his band.

But on the next day, as we crossed the Alamosa Arroyo, and were rising to the rolling prairie again, Jack Burns, who was riding on ahead, suddenly dropped flat on the neck of his horse, and swung back to me in the waggon, saying:

'Get out your rifle, here's that – stallion.'

I seized my rifle, and hurried forward to a view over the prairie ridge. In the hollow below was a band of horses, and there at one end was the Great Black Mustang. He had heard some sound of our approach, and was not unsuspicious of danger. There he stood with head and tail erect, and nostrils wide, an image of horse perfection and beauty, as noble an animal as ever ranged the plains, and the mere notion of turning that magnificent creature into a mass of carrion was horrible. In spite of Jack's exhortation to 'shoot quick', I delayed, and threw open the breach, whereupon he, always hot and hasty, swore at my slowness, growled, 'Gi' me that gun,' and as he seized it I turned the muzzle up, and *accidentally* the gun went off.

Instantly the herd below was all alarm, the great black leader snorted and neighed and dashed about. And the mares bunched, and away all went in a rumble of hoofs, and a cloud of dust.

The Stallion careered now on this side, now on that, and kept his eye on all and led and drove them far away. As long as I could see I watched, and never once did he break his pace.

Jack made Western remarks about me and my gun, as well as that mustang, but I rejoiced in the Pacer's strength and beauty, and not for all the mares in the bunch would I have harmed his glossy hide.

III

There are several ways of capturing wild horses. One is by creasing – that is, grazing the animal's nape with a rifle-ball so that he is stunned long enough for hobbling.

'Yest I seen about a hundred necks broke trying it, but I never seen a mustang creased yet,' was Wild Jo's critical remark.

Sometimes, if the shape of the country abets it, the herd can be driven into a corral; sometimes with extra fine mounts they can be run down, but by far the commonest way, paradoxical as it may seem, is to *walk* them down.

The fame of the Stallion that never was known to gallop was spreading. Extraordinary stories were told of his gait, his speed, and his wind, and when old Montgomery of the 'triangle-bar' outfit came out plump at Well's Hotel in Clayton, and in presence of witnesses said he'd give one thousand dollars cash for him safe in a box-car, providing the stories were true, a dozen young cow-punchers were eager to cut loose and win the purse, as soon as present engagements were up. But Wild Jo had had his eye on this very deal for quite a while; there was no time to lose, so ignoring present contracts he rustled all night to raise the necessary equipment for the game.

By straining his already overstrained credit, and taxing the already overtaxed generosity of his friends, he got together an expedition consisting of twenty good saddle-horses, a mess-waggon, and a fortnight's stuff for three men – himself, his 'pard', Charley, and the cook.

Then they set out from Clayton, with the avowed intention of walking down the wonderfully swift wild horse. The third day they arrived at Antelope Springs, and as it was about noon they were not surprised to see the black Pacer marching down to drink with all his band behind him. Jo kept out of sight until the wild horses each and all had drunk their fill, for a thirsty animal always travels better than one laden with water.

Jo then rode quietly forward. The Pacer took alarm at half a mile, and led his band away out of sight on the soapweed mesa to the southeast. Jo followed at a gallop till he once more sighted them, then came back and instructed the cook, who was also teamster, to make for Alamosa Arroyo in the south. Then away to the southeast he went after the mustangs. After a mile or two he once more sighted them, and walked his horse quietly till so near that they again took alarm and circled away to the south. An hour's trot, not on the trail, but cutting across to where they ought to go, brought Jo again in close sight. Again he walked quietly toward the herd, and again there was the alarm and fright. And so they passed the afternoon, but circled ever more and more to the south, so that when the sun was low they were, as Jo had expected, not far from Alamosa Arroyo. The band was again close at hand, and Jo, after starting them off, rode to the waggon, while his pard, who had been taking it easy, took up the slow chase on a fresh horse.

After supper the waggon moved on to the upper ford of the Alamosa, as arranged, and there camped for the night.

Meanwhile, Charley followed the herd. They had not run so far as at first, for their pursuer made no sign of attack, and they were getting used to his company. They were more easily found, as the shadows fell, on account of a snow-white mare that was in the bunch. A young moon in the sky now gave some help, and relying on his horse to choose the path, Charley kept him quietly walking after the herd, represented by that ghost-white mare, till they were lost in the night. He then got off, unsaddled and picketed his horse, and in his blanket quickly went to sleep.

At the first streak of dawn he was up, and within a short half-mile, thanks to the snowy mare, he found the band. At his approach, the shrill neigh of the Pacer bugled his troop into a flying squad. But on the first mesa they stopped, and faced about to see what this persistent follower was, and what he wanted. For a moment or so they stood against the sky to gaze, and then deciding that he knew him as well as he wished to, that black meteor flung his mane on the wind, and led off at his tireless, even swing, while the mares came streaming after.

Away they went, circling now to the west, and after several repetitions of this same play, flying, following, and overtaking, and flying again, they passed, near noon, the old Apache look-out, Buffalo Bluff. And here, on watch, was Jo. A long thin column of smoke told Charley to come to camp, and with a flashing pocket-mirror he made response. Jo, freshly mounted, rode across, and again took up the chase, and back came Chancy to camp to eat and rest, and then move on up stream.

All that day Jo followed, and managed, when it was needed, that the herd should keep the great circle, of which the waggon cut a small chord. At sundown he came to Verde Crossing, and there was Charley with a fresh horse and food, and Jo went on in the same calm, dogged way. All the evening he followed, and far into the night, for the wild herd was now getting somewhat used to the presence of the harmless strangers, and were more easily followed; moreover, they were thing out with perpetual traveling. They were no longer in the good grass country, they were not grain-fed like the horses on their track, and above all, the slight but continuous nervous tension was surely telling. It spoiled their appetites, but made them very thirsty. They were allowed, and as far as possible encouraged, to drink deeply at every chance. The effect of large quantities of water on a running animal is well known; it tends to stiffen the limbs and spoil the wind. Jo carefully guarded his own horse against such excess, and both he and his horse were fresh when they camped that night on the trail of the jaded mustangs.

At dawn he found them easily close at hand, and though they ran at first they did not go far before they dropped into a walk. The battle seemed nearly won now, for the chief difficulty in the 'walk-down' is to keep track of the herd the first two or three days when they are fresh.

All that morning Jo kept in sight, generally in close sight, of the band. About ten o'clock, Charley relieved him near Jose. Peak and that day the mustangs walked only a quarter of a mile ahead with much less spirit than the day before and circled now more north again. At night Charley was supplied with a fresh horse and followed as before.

Next day the mustangs walked with heads held low, and in spite of the efforts of the Black Pacer at times they were less than a hundred yards ahead of their pursuer.

The fourth and fifth days passed the same way, and now the herd was nearly back to Antelope Springs. So far all had come out as expected. The chase had been in a great circle with the waggon following a lesser circle. The wild herd was back to its starting-point, worn out; and the hunters were back, fresh and on fresh horses. The herd was kept from drinking till late in the afternoon and then driven to the Springs to swell themselves with a perfect water gorge. Now was the chance for the skilful ropers on the grain-fed horses to close in, for the sudden heavy drink was ruination, almost paralysis, of wind and limb, and it would be easy to rope and hobble them one by one.

There was only one weak spot in the programme, the Black Stallion, the cause of the hunt, seemed made of iron, that ceaseless swinging pace seemed as swift and vigourous now as on the morning when the chase began. Up and down he went rounding up the herd and urging them on by voice and example to escape. But they were played out. The old white mare that had been such help in sighting them at night, had dropped out hours ago, dead beat. The half-bloods seemed to be losing all fear of the horsemen, the band was clearly in Jo's power. But the one who was the prize of all the hunt seemed just as far as ever out of reach.

Here was a puzzle. Jo's comrades knew him well and would not have been surprised to see him in a sudden rage attempt to shoot the Stallion down. But Jo had no such mind. During that long week of following he had watched the horse all day at speed and never once had he seen him gallop.

The horseman's adoration of a noble horse had grown and grown, till now he would as soon have thought of shooting his best mount as firing on that splendid beast.

Jo even asked himself whether he would take the handsome sum that was offered for the prize. Such an animal would be a fortune in himself to sire a race of pacers for the track.

But the prize was still at large – the time had come to finish up the hunt. Jo's finest mount was caught. She was a mare of Eastern blood, but raised on the plains. She never would have come into Jo's possession but for a curious weakness. The loco is a poisonous weed that grows in these regions. Most stock will not touch it; but sometimes an animal tries it and becomes addicted to it.

It acts somewhat like morphine, but the animal, though sane for long intervals, has always a passion for the herb and finally dies mad. A beast with the craze is said to be locoed. And Jo's best mount had a wild gleam in her eye that to an expert told the tale.

But she was swift and strong and Jo chose her for the grand finish of the chase. It would have been an easy matter now to rope the mares, but was no longer necessary. They could be separated from their black leader and driven home to the corral. But that leader still had the look of untamed strength. Jo, rejoicing in a worthy foe, went bounding forth to try the odds. The lasso was flung on the ground and trailed to take out every kink, and gathered as he rode into neatest coils across his left palm. Then putting on the spur the first time in that chase he rode straight for the Stallion a quarter of a mile beyond. Away he went, and away went Jo, each at his best, while the fagged-out mares scattered right and left and let them pass.

Straight across the open plain the fresh horse went at its hardest gallop, and the Stallion, leading off, still kept his start and kept his famous swing.

It was incredible, and Jo put on more spur and shouted to his horse, which fairly flew, but shortened up the space between by not a single inch. For the Black One whirled across the flat and up and passed a soap-weed mesa and down across a sandy treacherous plain, then over a grassy stretch where prairie dogs barked, then hid below, and on came Jo, but there to see, could he believe his eyes, the Stallion's start grown longer still, and Jo began to curse his luck, and urge and spur his horse until the poor uncertain brute got into such a state of nervous fright, her eyes began to roll, she wildly shook her head from side to side, no longer picked her ground – a badger-hole received her foot and down she went, and Jo went flying to the earth. Though badly bruised, he gained his feet and tried to mount his crazy beast. But she, poor brute, was done for – her off foreleg hung loose.

There was but one thing to do. Jo loosed the cinch, put Lightfoot out of pain, and carried back the saddle to the camp. While the Pacer steamed away till lost to view.

This was not quite defeat, for all the mares were manageable now, and Jo and Charley drove them carefully to the 'L cross F' corral and claimed a good reward. But Jo was more than ever bound to own the Stallion. He had seen what stuff he was made of, he prized him more and more, and only sought to strike some better plan to catch him.

IV

The cook on that trip was Bates – Mr. Thomas Bates, he called himself at the post-office where he regularly went for the letters and remittance which never came. Old Tom Turkeytrack, the boys called him, from his cattle-brand, which he said was on record at Denver, and which, according to his story, was also borne by countless beef and saddle stock on the plains of the unknown North.

When asked to join the trip as a partner, Bates made some sarcastic remarks about horses not fetching $12 a dozen, which had been literally true within the year, and he preferred to go on a very meagre salary. But no one who once saw the Pacer going had failed to catch the craze. Turkeytrack experienced the usual change of heart. He now wanted to own that mustang. How this was to be brought about he did not clearly see till one day there called at the ranch that had 'secured his services', as he put it, one, Bill Smith, more usually known as Horseshoe Billy, from his cattle-brand. While the excellent fresh beef and bread and the vile coffee, dried peaches and molasses were being consumed, he of the horseshoe remarked, in tones which percolated through a huge stop-gap of bread:

'Wall, I seen that thar Pacer today, nigh enough to put a plait in his tail.'

'What, you didn't shoot?'

'No, but I come mighty near it.'

'Don't you be led into no sich foolishness,' said a 'double-bar H' cowpuncher at the other end of the table. 'I calc'late that maverick 'ill carry my brand before the moon changes.'

'You'll have to be pretty spry or you'll find a 'triangle dot' on his weather side when you get there.'

'Where did you run across him?'

'Wail, it was like this; I was riding the flat by Antelope Springs and I sees a lump on the dry mud inside the rush belt. I knowed I never seen that before, so I rides up, thinking it might be some of our stock, an' seen it was a horse lying plumb flat. The wind was blowing like – from him to me, so I rides up close and seen it was the Pacer, dead as a mackerel. Still, he didn't look swelled or cut, and there wa'n't no smell, an' I didn't know what to think till I seen his ear twitch off a fly and then I knowed he was sleeping. I gits down me rope and coils it, and seen it was old and pretty shaky in spots, and me saddle a single cinch, an' me pony about 700 again a 1,200 lbs. stallion, an' I sez to meself, sez I: "Tain't no use, I'll only break me cinch and git throwed an' lose me saddle.' So I hits the saddle-horn a crack with the hondu, and I wish't you'd a seen that mustang. He lept six foot in the air an' snorted like he was shunting cars. His eyes fairly bugged out an' he lighted out lickety split for California, and he orter be there about now if he kep' on like he started – and I swear he never made a break the hull trip.'

The story was not quite so consecutive as given here. It was much punctuated by present engrossments, and from first to last was more or less infiltrated through the necessaries of life, for Bill was a healthy young man without a trace of false shame. But the account was complete and everyone believed it, for Billy was known to be reliable. Of all those who heard, old Turkeytrack talked the least and probably thought the most, for it gave him a new idea.

During his after-dinner pipe he studied it out and deciding that he could not go it alone, he took Horseshoe Billy into his council and the result was a partnership in a new venture to capture the Pacer; that is, the $5,000 that was now said to be the offer for him safe in a box-car.

Antelope Springs was still the usual watering-place of the Pacer. The water being low left a broad belt of dry black mud between the sedge and the spring. At two places this belt was broken by a well-marked trail made by the animals coming to drink. Horses and wild animals usually kept to these trails, though the horned cattle had no hesitation in taking a short cut through the sedge.

In the most used of these trails the two men set to work with shovels and dug a pit 15 feet long, 6 feet wide and 7 feet deep. It was a hard twenty hours work for them as it had to be completed between the Mustang's drinks, and it began to be very damp work before it was finished. With poles, brush, and earth it was then cleverly covered over and concealed. And the men went to a distance and bid in pits made for the purpose.

About noon the Pacer came, alone now since the capture of his band. The trail on the opposite side of the mud belt was little used, and old Tom, by throwing some fresh rushes across it, expected to make sure that the Stallion would enter by the other, if indeed he should by any caprice try to come by the unusual path.

What sleepless angel is it watches over and cares for the wild animals? In spite of all reasons to take the usual path, the Pacer came along the other. The suspicious-looking rushes did not stop him; he walked calmly to the water and drank. There was only one way now to prevent utter failure; when he lowered his head for the second draft which horses always take, Bates and Smith quit their holes and ran swiftly toward the trail behind him, and when he raised his proud head Smith sent a revolver shot into the ground behind him.

Away went the Pacer at his famous gait straight to the trap. Another second and he would be into it. Already he is on the trail, and already they feel they have him, but the Angel of the wild things is with him, that incomprehensible warning comes, and with one mighty bound he clears the fifteen feet of treacherous ground and spurns the earth as he fades away unharmed, never again to visit Antelope Springs by either of the beaten paths.

V

Wild Jo never lacked energy. He meant to catch that Mustang, and when he learned that others were be stirring themselves for the same purpose he at once set about trying the best untried plan he knew – the plan by which the coyote catches the fleeter jackrabbit, and the mounted Indian the far swifter antelope – the old plan of the relay chase.

The Canadian River on the south, its affluent, the Pinavetitos Arroyo, on the northeast, and the Don Carlos Hills with the Ute Creek Canyon on the west, formed a sixty-mile triangle that was the range of the Pacer. It was believed that he never went outside this, and at all times Antelope Springs was his headquarters. Jo knew this country well, all the water-holes and canon crossings as well as the ways of the Pacer.

If he could have gotten fifty good horses he could have posted them to advantage so as to cover all points, but twenty mounts and five good riders were all that proved available.

The horses, grain-fed for two weeks before, were sent on ahead; each man was instructed how to play his part and sent to his post the day before the race. On the day of the start Jo with his waggon drove to the plain of Antelope Springs and, camping far off in a little draw, waited.

At last he came, that coal-black Horse, out from the sand-hills at the south, alone as always now, and walked calmly down to the Springs and circled quite around it to sniff for any hidden foe. Then he approached where there was no trail at all and drank.

Jo watched and wished that he would drink a hogs-head. But the moment that he turned and sought the grass Jo spurred his steed. The Pacer heard the hoofs, then saw the running horse, and did not want a nearer view but led away. Across the flat he went down to the south, and kept the famous swinging gait that made his start grow longer.

Now through the sandy dunes he went, and steadying to an even pace he gained considerably and Jo's too-laden horse plunged through the sand and sinking fetlock deep, he lost at every bound. Then came a level stretch where the runner seemed to gain, and then a long decline where Jo's horse dared not run his best, so lost again at every step.

But on they went, and Jo spared neither spur nor quirt. A mile – a mile – and another mile, and the far-off rock at Arriba loomed up ahead.

And there Jo knew fresh mounts were held, and on they dashed. But the night-black mane out level on the breeze ahead was gaining more and more.

Arriba Canyon reached at last, the watcher stood aside, for it was not wished to turn the race, and the Stallion passed – dashed down, across and up the slope, with that unbroken pace, the only one he knew. And Jo came bounding on his foaming steed, and on the waiting mount, then urged him down the slope and up upon the track, and on the upland once more drove in the spurs, and raced and raced, and raced, but not a single inch he gained.

Ga-lump, ga-lump, ga-lump, with measured beat he went – an hour – an hour, and another hour – Arroyo Alamosa just ahead with fresh relays, and Jo yelled at his horse and pushed him on and on. Straight for the place the Black One made, but on the last two miles some strange foreboding turned him to the left, and Jo foresaw escape in this, and pushed his jaded mount at any cost to head him off, and hard as they had raced this was the hardest race of all, with gasps for breath and leather squeaks at every straining bound. Then cutting right across, Jo seemed to gain, and drawing his gun he fired shot after shot to toss the dust, and so turned the Stallion's head and forced him back to take the crossing to the right.

Down they went. The Stallion crossed and Jo sprang to the ground. His horse was done, for thirty miles had passed in the last stretch, and Jo himself was worn out. His eyes were burnt with flying alkali dust. He was half blind so he motioned to his 'pard' to 'go ahead and keep him straight for Alamosa ford.'

Out shot the rider on a strong, fresh steed, and away they went – up and down on the rolling plain – the Black Horse flecked with snowy foam. His heaving ribs and noisy breath showed what he felt – but on and on he Went.

And Tom on Ginger seemed to gain, then lose and lose, when in an hour the long decline of Alamosa came. And there a freshly mounted lad took up the chase and turned it west, and on they went past towns of prairie dogs, through soapweed tracts and cactus brakes by scores, and pricked and wrenched rode on. With dust and sweat the Black was now a dappled brown, but still he stepped the same. Young Carrington, who followed, bad hurt his steed by pushing at the very start, and spurred and urged him now to cut across a gulch at which the Pacer shied. Just one misstep and down they went.

The boy escaped, but the pony lies there yet, and the wild Black Horse kept on.

This was close to old Gallego's ranch where Jo himself had cut across refreshed to push the chase. Within thirty minutes he was again scorching the Pacer's trail.

Far in the west the Carlos Hills were seen, and there Jo knew fresh men and mounts were waiting, and that way the indomitable rider tried to turn, the race, but by a sudden whim, of the inner warning born perhaps – the Pacer turned. Sharp to the north he went, and Jo, the skilful wrangler, rode and rode and yelled and tossed the dust with shots, but down on a gulch the wild black meteor streamed and Jo could only follow. Then came the hardest race of all; Jo, cruel to the Mustang, was crueller to his mount and to himself. The sun was hot, the scorching plain was dim in shimmering heat, his eyes and lips were burnt with sand and salt, and yet the chase sped on. The only chance to win would be if he could drive the Mustang back to the Big Arroyo Crossing. Now almost for the first time he saw signs of weakening in the Black. His mane and tail were not just quite so high, and his short half mile of start was down by more than half, but still he stayed ahead and paced and paced and paced.

An hour and another hour, and still they went the same. But they turned again, and night was near when Big Arroyo ford was reached – fully twenty miles. But Jo was game, he seized the waiting horse. The one he left went gasping to the stream and gorged himself with water till he died.

Then Jo held back in hopes the foaming Black would drink. But he was wise; he gulped a single gulp, splashed through the stream and then passed on with Jo at speed behind him. And when they last were seen the Black was on ahead just out of reach and Jo's horse bounding on.

It was morning when Jo came to camp on foot. His tale was briefly told: – eight horses dead – five men worn out – the matchless Pacer safe and free.

'Tain't possible; it can't be done. Sorry I didn't bore his hellish carcass through when I had the chance,' said Jo, and gave it up.

VI

Old Turkeytrack was cook on this trip. He had watched the chase with as much interest as anyone, and when it failed he grinned into the pot and said: 'That mustang's mine unless I'm a darned fool.' Then falling back on Scripture for a precedent, as was his habit, he still addressed the pot:

'Reckon the Philistines tried to run Samson down and they got done up, an' would a stayed don only for a nat'ral weakness on his part. An' Adam would a loafed in Eden yit it ony for a leetle failing, which we all onder stand. An' it aint $5,000 I'll take for him nuther.'

Much persecution had made the Pacer wilder than ever. But it did not drive him away from Antelope Springs. That was the only drinking-place with absolutely no shelter for a mile on every side to hide an enemy. Here he came almost every day about noon, and after thoroughly spying the land approached to drink.

His had been a lonely life all winter since the capture of his harem, and of this old Turkeytrack was fully aware. The old cook's chum had a nice little brown mare which he judged would serve his ends, and taking a pair of the strongest hobbles, a spade, a spare lasso, and a stout post he mounted the mare and rode away to the famous Springs.

A few antelope skimmed over the plain before him in the early freshness of the day. Cattle were lying about in groups, and the loud, sweet song of the prairie lark was' heard on every side. For the bright snowless winter of the mesas was gone and the springtime was at hand. The grass was greening and all nature seemed turning to thoughts of love.

It was in the air, and when the little brown mare was picketed out to graze she raised her nose from time to time to pour forth a long shrill whinny that surely was her song, if song she had, of love.

Old Turkeytrack studied the wind and the lay of the land. There was the pit he had laboured at, now opened and filled with water that was rank with drowned prairie dogs and mice. Here was the new trail the animals were forced to make by the pit. He selected a sedgy clump near some smooth, grassy ground, and first firmly sunk the post, then dug a hole large enough to hide in, and spread his blanket in it. He shortened up the little mare's tether, till she could scarcely move; then on the ground between he spread his open lasso, tying the long end to the post, then covered the rope with dust and grass, and went into his hiding-place.

About noon, after long waiting, the amorous whinny of the mare was answered from the high ground, away to the west, and there, black against the sky, was the famous Mustang.

Down he came at that long swinging gait, but grown crafty with much pursuit, he often stopped to gaze and whinny, and got answer that surely touched his heart. Nearer he came again to call, then took alarm, and paced all round in a great circle to try the wind for his foes, and seemed in doubt. The Angel whispered 'Don't go.' But the brown mare called again. He circled nearer still, and neighed once more, and got reply that seemed to quell all fears, and set his heart aglow.

Nearer still he pranced, till he touched Solly's nose with his own, and finding her as responsive as he well could wish, thrust aside all thoughts of danger, and abandoned himself to the delight of conquest, until, as he pranced around, his hind legs for a moment stood within the evil circle of the rope. One deft sharp twitch, the noose flew tight, and he was caught.

A snort of terror and a bound in the air gave Tom the chance to add the double hitch. The loop flashed up the line, and snake-like bound those mighty hoofs.

Terror lent speed and double strength for a moment, but the end of the rope was reached, and down he went a captive, a hopeless prisoner at last. Old Tom's ugly, little crooked form sprang from the pit to complete the mastering of the great glorious creature whose mighty strength had proved as nothing when matched with the wits of a little old man. With snorts and desperate bounds of awful force the great beast dashed and struggled to be free; but all in vain. The rope was strong.

The second lasso was deftly swung, and the forefeet caught, and then with a skilful move the feet were drawn together, and down went the raging Pacer to lie a moment later 'hog-tied' and helpless on the ground. There he struggled till worn out, sobbing great convulsive sobs while tears ran down his cheeks.

Tom stood by and watched, but a strange revulsion of feeling came over the old cow-puncher. He trembled nervously from head to foot, as he had not done since he roped his first steer, and for a while could do nothing but gaze on his tremendous prisoner. But the feeling soon passed away. He saddled Delilah, and taking the second lasso, roped the great horse about the neck, and left the mare to hold the Stallion's head, while he put on the hobbles. This was soon done, and sure of him now old Bates was about to loose the ropes, but on a sudden thought he stopped. He had quite forgotten, and had come unprepared for something of importance. In Western law the Mustang was the property of the first man to mark him with his brand; how was this to be done with the nearest branding-iron twenty miles away?

Old Tom went to his mare, took up her hoofs one at a time, and examined each shoe. Yes! one was a little loose; he pushed and pried it with the spade, and got it off. Buffalo chips and kindred fuel were plentiful about the plain, so a fire was quickly made, and he soon had one arm of the horse-shoe red hot, then holding the other wrapped in his sock he rudely sketched on the left shoulder of the helpless mustang a turkeytrack, his brand, the first time really that it had ever been used.

The Pacer shuddered as the hot iron seared his flesh, but it was quickly done, and the famous Mustang Stallion was a maverick no more.

Now all there was to do was to take him home. The ropes were loosed, the Mustang felt himself freed, thought he was free, and sprang to his feet only to fall as soon as he tried to take a stride. His forefeet were strongly tied together, his only possible gait a shuffling walk, or else a desperate laboured bounding with feet so unnaturally held that within a few yards he was inevitably thrown each time he tired to break away. Tom on the light pony headed him off again and again, and by dint of driving, threatening, and manoeuvering, contrived to force his foaming, crazy captive northward toward the Pinavetitos Canyon. But the wild horse would not drive, would not give in. With snorts of terror or of rage and maddest bounds, he tried and tried to get away. It was one long cruel fight; his glossy sides were thick with dark foam, and the foam was stained with blood. Countless hard falls and exhaustion that a long day's chase was powerless to produce were telling on him; his straining bounds first this way and then that, were not now quite so strong, and the spray he snorted as he gasped was half a spray of blood. But his captor, relentless, masterful and cool, still forced him on. Down the slope toward the canyon they had come, every yard a fight, and now they were at the head of the draw that took the trail down to the only crossing of the canon, the northmost limit of the Pacer's ancient range.

From this the first corral and ranch-house were in sight. The man rejoiced, but the Mustang gathered his remaining strength for one more desperate dash. Up, up the grassy slope from the trail he went, defied the swinging, slashing rope and the gunshot fired in air, in vain attempt to turn his frenzied course. Up, up and on, above the sheerest cliff he dashed then sprang away into the vacant air, down – down – two hundred downward feet to fall, and land upon the rocks below, a lifeless wreck – but free.

THE WINNIPEG WOLF

I

It was during the great blizzard of 1882 that I first met the Winnipeg Wolf. I had left St. Paul in the middle of March to cross the prairies to Winnipeg, expecting to be there in twenty-four hours, but the Storm King had planned it otherwise and sent a heavy-laden eastern blast. The snow came down in a furious, steady torrent, hour after hour. Never before had I seen such a storm. All the world was lost in snow – snow, snow, snow – whirling, biting, stinging, drifting snow – and the puffing, monstrous engine was compelled to stop at the command of those tiny feathery crystals of spotless purity.

 Many strong hands with shovels came to the delicately curled snowdrifts that barred our way, and in an hour the engine could pass – only to stick in another drift yet farther on. It was dreary work – day after day, night after night, sticking in the drifts, digging ourselves out, and still the snow went whirling and playing about us.

'Twenty-two hours to Emerson,' said the official; but nearly two weeks of digging passed before we did reach Emerson, and the poplar country where the thickets stop all drifting of the snow. Thenceforth the train went swiftly, the poplar woods grew more thickly – we passed for miles through solid forests, then perhaps through an open space. As we neared St. Boniface, the eastern outskirts of Winnipeg, we dashed across a little glade fifty yards wide, and there in the middle was a group that stirred me to the very soul.

In plain view was a great rabble of Dogs, large and small, black, white, and yellow, wriggling and heaving this way and that way in a rude ring; to one side was a little yellow Dog stretched and quiet in the snow; on the outer part of the ring was a huge black Dog bounding about and barking, but keeping ever behind the moving mob. And in the midst, the centre and cause of it all, was a great, grim, Wolf.

Wolf? He looked like a Lion. There he stood, all alone – resolute-calm – with bristling mane, and legs braced firmly, glancing this way and that, to be ready for an attack in any direction. There was a curl on his lips – it looked like scorn, but I suppose it was really the fighting snarl of tooth display. Led by a wolfish-looking Dog that should have been ashamed, the pack dashed in, for the twentieth time no doubt. But the great grey form leaped here and there, and chop, chop, chop went those fearful jaws, no other sound from the lonely warrior; but a death yelp from more than one of his foes, as those that were able again sprang back, and left him statuesque as before, untamed, unmaimed, and contemptuous of them all.

How I wished for the train to stick in a snowdrift now, as so often before, for all my heart went out to that Grey-wolf; I longed to go and help him. But the snow-deep glade flashed by, the poplar trunks shut out the view, and we went on to our journey's end.

This was all I saw, and it seemed little; but before many days had passed I knew surely that I had been favoured with a view, in broad daylight, of a rare and wonderful creature, none less than the Winnipeg Wolf.

His was a strange history – a Wolf that preferred the city to the country, that passed by the Sheep to kill the Dogs, and that always hunted alone.

In telling the story of *le Garou*, as he was called by some, although I speak of these things as locally familiar, it is very sure that to many citizens of the town they were quite unknown. The smug shopkeeper on the main street had scarcely heard of him until the day after the final scene at the slaughter-house, when his great carcass was carried to Hine's taxidermist shop and there mounted, to be exhibited later at the Chicago World's Fair, and to be destroyed, alas! in the fire that reduced the Mulvey Grammar School to ashes in 1896.

II

It seems that Fiddler Paul, the handsome ne'er-do-well of the half-breed world, readier to hunt than to work, was prowling with his gun along the wooded banks of the Red River by Kildonan, one day in the June of 1880. He saw a Grey-wolf come out of a hole in a bank and fired a chance shot that killed it. Having made sure, by sending in his Dog, that no other large Wolf was there, he crawled into the den, and found, to his utter amazement and delight, eight young Wolves – nine bounties of ten dollars each. How much is that? A fortune surely. He used a stick vigourously, and with the assistance of the yellow Cur, all the little ones were killed but one. There is a superstition about the last of a brood – it is not lucky to kill it. So Paul set out for town with the scalp of the old Wolf, the scalps of the seven young, and the last Cub alive.

The saloon-keeper, who got the dollars for which the scalps were exchanged, soon got the living Cub. He grew up at the end of a chain, but developed a chest and jaws that no Hound in town could match. He was kept in the yard for the amusement of customers, and this amusement usually took the form of baiting the captive with Dogs. The young Wolf was bitten and mauled nearly to death on several occasions, but he recovered, and each month there were fewer Dogs willing to face him. His life was as hard as it could be. There was but one gleam of gentleness in it all, and that was the friendship that grew up between himself and Little Jim, the son of the saloonkeeper.

Jim was a wilful little rascal with a mind of his own. He took to the Wolf because it had killed a Dog that had bitten him. He thenceforth fed the Wolf and made a pet of it, and the Wolf responded by allowing him to take liberties which no one else dared venture.

Jim's father was not a model parent. He usually spoiled his son, but at times would get in a rage and beat him cruelly for some trifle. The child was quick to learn that he was beaten, not because he had done wrong, but because he had made his father angry. If, therefore, he could keep out of the way until that anger had cooled, he had no further cause for worry. One day, seeking safety in flight with his father behind him, he dashed into the Wolf's kennel, and his grizzly chum thus unceremoniously awakened turned to the door, displayed a double row of ivories, and plainly said to the father: 'Don't you dare to touch him.'

If Hogan could have shot the Wolf then and there he would have done so, but the chances were about equal of killing his son, so he let them alone and, half an hour later, laughed at the whole affair. Thenceforth Little Jim made for the Wolf's den whenever he was in danger, and sometimes the only notice any one had that the boy had been in mischief was seeing him sneak in behind the savage captive.

Economy in hired help was a first principle with Hogan. Therefore his 'barkeep' was a Chinaman. He was a timid, harmless creature, so Paul des Roches did not hesitate to bully him. One day, finding Hogan out, and the Chinaman alone in charge, Paul, already tipsy, demanded a drink on credit, and Tung Ling, acting on standing orders, refused. His artless explanation, 'No good, neber pay,' so far from clearing up the difficulty, brought Paul staggering back of the bar to avenge the insult. The Celestial might have suffered grievous bodily hurt, but that Little Jim was at hand and had a long stick, with which he adroitly tripped up the Fiddler and sent him sprawling. He staggered to his feet swearing he would have Jim's life. But the child was near the back door and soon found refuge in the Wolf's kennel.

Seeing that the boy had a protector, Paul got the long stick, and from a safe distance began to belabour the Wolf, The grizzly creature raged at the end of the chain, but, though he parried many cruel blows by seizing the stick in his teeth, he was suffering severely, when Paul realised that Jim, whose tongue had not been idle, was fumbling away with nervous fingers to set the Wolf loose, and soon would succeed. Indeed, it would have been done already but for the strain that the Wolf kept on the chain.

The thought of being in the yard at the mercy of the huge animal that he had so enraged, gave the brave Paul a thrill of terror.

Jim's wheedling voice was heard – 'Hold on now, Wolfie; back up just a little, and you shall have him. Now do; there's a good Wolfie' – that was enough; the Fiddler fled and carefully closed all doors behind him.

Thus the friendship between Jim and his pet grew stronger, and the Wolf, as he developed his splendid natural powers, gave daily evidence also of the mortal hatred he bore to men that smelt of whiskey and to all Dogs, the causes of his sufferings. This peculiarity, coupled with his love for the child – and all children seemed to be included to some extent – grew with his growth and seemed to prove the ruling force of his life.

•

III

At this time – that is, the fall of 1881 – there were great complaints among the Qu'Appelle ranchmen that the Wolves were increasing in their country and committing great depredations among the stock. Poisoning and trapping had proved failures, and when a distinguished German visitor appeared at the Club in Winnipeg and announced that he was bringing some Dogs that could easily rid the country of Wolves, he was listened to with unusual interest. For the cattle-men are fond of sport, and the idea of helping their business by establishing a kennel of Wolfhounds was very alluring.

The German soon produced as samples of his Dogs, two magnificent Danes, one white, the other blue with black spots and a singular white eye that completed an expression of unusual ferocity. Each of these great creatures weighed nearly two hundred pounds. They were muscled like Tigers, and the German was readily believed when he claimed that these two alone were more than a match for the biggest Wolf. He thus described their method of hunting: 'All you have to do is show them the trail and, even if it is a day old, away they go on it. They cannot be shaken off. They will soon find that Wolf, no matter how he doubles and hides. Then they close on him. He turns to run, the blue Dog takes him by the haunch and throws him like this,' and the German jerked a roll of bread into the air; 'then before he touches the ground the white Dog has his head, the other his tail, and they pull him apart like that.'

It sounded all right; at any rate every one was eager to put it to the proof. Several of the residents said there was a fair chance of finding a Grey-wolf along the Assiniboine, so a hunt was organized. But they searched in vain for three days and were giving it up when some one suggested that down at Hogan's saloon was a Wolf chained up, that they could get for the value of the bounty, and though little more than a year old he would serve to show what the Dogs could do.

The value of Hogan's Wolf went up at once when he knew the importance of the occasion; besides, 'he had conscientious scruples'. All his scruples vanished, however, when his views as to price were met.

His first care was to get Little Jim out of the way by sending him on an errand to his grandma's; then the Wolf was driven into his box and nailed in. The box was put in a waggon and taken to the open prairie along the Portage trail.

The Dogs could scarcely be held back, they were so eager for the fray, as soon as they smelt the Wolf. But several strong men held their leash, the waggon was drawn half a mile farther, and the Wolf was turned out with some difficulty. At first he looked scared and sullen. He tried to get out of sight, but made no attempt to bite. However, on finding himself free, as well as hissed and hooted at, he started off at a slinking trot toward the south, where the land seemed broken. The Dogs were released at that moment, and, baying furiously, they bounded away after the young Wolf. The men cheered loudly and rode behind them. From the very first it was clear that he had no chance. The Dogs were much swifter; the white one could run like a Greyhound. The German was wildly enthusiastic as she flew across the prairie, gaining visibly on the Wolf at every second. Many bets were offered on the Dogs, but there were no takers. The only bets accepted were Dog against Dog. The young Wolf went at speed now, but within a mile the white Dog was right behind him – was closing in.

The German shouted: 'Now watch and see that Wolf go up in the air.'

In a moment the runners were together. Both recoiled, neither went up in the air, but the white Dog rolled over with a fearful gash in her shoulder – out of the fight, if not killed. Ten seconds later the Bluespot arrived, open-mouthed. This meeting was as quick and almost as mysterious as the first. The animals barely touched each other. The grey one bounded aside, his head out of sight for a moment in the flash of quick movement. Spot reeled and showed a bleeding flank. Urged on by the men, he assaulted again, but only to get another wound that taught him to keep off.

Now came the keeper with four more huge Dogs. They turned these loose, and the men armed with clubs and lassos were closing to help in finishing the Wolf, when a small boy came charging over the plain on a Pony. He leaped to the ground and wriggling through the ring flung his arms around the Wolf's neck. He called him his 'Wolfie pet', his 'dear Wolfie' – the Wolf licked his face and wagged its tail – then the child turned on the crowd and through his streaming tears, he –

Well! It would not do to print what he said. He was only nine, but he was very old-fashioned, as well as a rude little boy. He had been  brought up in a low saloon, and had been an apt pupil at picking up the vile talk of the place. He cursed them one and all and for generations back; he did not spare even his own father.

If a man had used such shocking and insulting language he might have been lynched, but coming from a baby, the hunters did not know what to do, so finally did the best thing. They laughed aloud – not at themselves, that is not considered good form – but they all laughed at the German whose wonderful Dogs had been worsted by a half-grown Wolf.

Jimmie now thrust his dirty, tear-stained little fist down into his very-much-of-a-boy's pocket, and from among marbles and chewing-gum, as well as tobacco, matches, pistol cartridges, and other contraband, he fished out a flimsy bit of grocer's twine and fastened it around the Wolf's neck. Then, still blubbering a little, he set out for home on the Pony, leading the Wolf and hurling a final threat and anathema at the German nobleman: 'Fur two cents I'd sic him on *you*, gol darn ye.'

IV

Early that winter Jimmie was taken down with a fever. The Wolf howled miserably in the yard when he missed his little friend, and finally on the boy's demand was admitted to the sick-room, and there this great wild Dog – for that is all a Wolf is – continued faithfully watching by his friend's bedside.

The fever had seemed slight at first, so that every one was shocked when there came suddenly a turn for the worse, and three days before Christmas Jimmie died. He had no more sincere mourner than his 'Wolfie'. The great grey creature howled in miserable answer to the

church-bell tolling when he followed the body on Christmas Eve to the graveyard at St. Boniface. He soon came back to the premises behind the saloon, but when an attempt was made to chain him again, he leaped a board fence and was finally lost sight of.

Later that same winter old Renaud, the trapper, with his pretty half-breed daughter, Ninette, came to live in a little log-cabin on the river bank. He knew nothing about Jimmie Hogan, and he was not a little puzzled to find Wolf tracks and signs along the river on both sides between St. Boniface and Fort Garry. He listened with interest and doubt to tales that the Hudson Bay Company's men told of a great Grey-wolf that had come to live in the region about, and even to enter the town at night, and that was in particular attached to the woods about St. Boniface Church.

On Christmas Eve of that year when the bell tolled again as it had done for Jimmie, a lone and melancholy howling from the woods almost convinced Renaud that the stories were true. He knew the wolf-cries – the howl for help, the love song, the lonely wail, and the sharp defiance of the Wolves. This was the lonely wail.

The trapper went to the riverside and gave an answering howl. A shadowy form left the far woods and crossed on the ice to where the man sat, log-still, on a log. It came up near him, circled past and sniffed, then its eye glowed; it growled like a Dog that is a little angry, and glided back into the night.

Thus Renaud knew, and before long many townfolk began to learn, that a huge Grey-wolf was living in their streets, 'a Wolf three times as big as the one that used to be chained at Hogan's gin-mill'. He was the terror of Dogs, killing them on all possible occasions, and some said, though it was never proven, that he had devoured more than one half-breed who was out on a spree.

And this was the Winnipeg Wolf that I had seen that day in the wintry woods. I had longed to go to his help, thinking the odds so hopelessly against him, but later knowledge changed the thought. I do not know how that fight ended, but I do know that he was seen many times afterward and some of the Dogs were not.

Thus his was the strangest life that ever his kind had known. Free of all the woods and plains, he elected rather to lead a life of daily hazard in the town – each week at least some close escape, and every day a day of daring deeds; finding momentary shelter at times under the

very boardwalk crossings. Hating the m
fought his daily way and held the hord
when he found them few or single; ha
with guns, learned traps – learned p
tell, but learn it he did, for he passe
only with a Wolf's contempt.

Not a street in Winnipeg that h
Winnipeg that had not seen his
dawn as he passed where he wo
not cower and bristle when the
Garou was crouching near. His
world his foes. But throughout
one recurring pleasant thoug
child.

Ninette was a desert-bor
like her Normandy fath
She might have marri
men of the country, b

the grey
knew it fo
said he ra
climbed th
the ice to
the tree, t
branch and
The savage,
distance, th
came down.
and he went
Fiddler Pau
would to any o
lessly ill with
as he should re
Company, as do
three great Hus
but fierce and la
drive to Fort Ale
tant packets. He
lessly cruel. He se
several necessary
and would then co
ing thus provided t
ment. Away they w
swiftly but sulkily as
marchez.' They pass
Paul, cracking his w
to Ninette as she sto
Dogs and drunken dr
the last ever seen of

That evening the Huski
spattered with frozen b
strange to tell they were

Runners went on the back trail and recovered the packages. They were lying on the ice unharmed. Fragments of the sled were strewn for a mile or more up the river; not far from the packages were shreds of clothing that had belonged to the Fiddler.

It was quite clear, the Dogs had murdered and eaten their driver.

The Factor was terribly wrought up over the matter. It might cost him his Dogs. He refused to believe the report and set off to sift the evidence for himself. Renaud was chosen to go with him, and before they were within three miles of the fatal place Renaud pointed to a very large track crossing from the east to the west bank of the river, just after the Dog sled. He ran it backward for a mile or more on the eastern bank, noted how it had walked when the Dogs walked and run when they ran, before he turned to the Factor and said: 'A beeg Voolf – he come after ze cariole all ze time.'

Now they followed the track where it had crossed to the west shore. Two miles above Kildonan woods the Wolf had stopped his gallop to walk over to the sled trail, had followed it a few yards, then had returned to the woods.

'Paul he drop somesin' here, ze packet maybe; ze Voolf he come for smell. He follow so – now he know zat eez ze drunken Paul vot slash heem on ze head.'

A mile farther the Wolf track came galloping on the ice behind the cariole. The man track disappeared now, for the driver had leaped on the sled and lashed the Dogs. Here is where he cut adrift the bundles. That is why things were scattered over the ice. See how the Dogs were bounding under the lash. Here was the Fiddler's knife in the snow. He must have dropped it in trying to use it on the Wolf. And here-what! the Wolf track disappears, but the sled track speeds along. The Wolf has leaped on the sled. The Dogs, in terror, added to their speed; but on the sleigh behind them there is a deed of vengeance done. In a moment it is over; both roll off the sled; the Wolf track reappears on the east side to seek the woods. The sled swerves to the west bank, where, after half a mile, it is caught and wrecked on a root.

The snow also told Renaud how the Dogs, entangled in the harness, had fought with each other, had cut themselves loose, and trotting homeward by various ways up the river, had gathered at the body of their late tyrant and devoured him at a meal.

Bad enough for the Dogs, still they were cleared of the murder. That certainly was done by the Wolf, and Renaud, after the shock of horror was past, gave a sigh of relief and added, 'Eet is le Garou. He hab save my leel girl from zat Paul. He always was good to children.'

VI

This was the cause of the great final hunt that they fixed for Christmas Day just two years after the scene at the grave of Little Jim. It seemed as though all the Dogs in the country were brought together. The three Huskies were there – the Factor considered them essential – there were Danes and trailers and a rabble of farm Dogs and nondescripts. They spent the morning beating all the woods east of St. Boniface and had no success. But a telephone message came that the trail they sought had been seen near the Assiniboine woods west of the city, and an hour later the hunt was yelling on the hot scent of the Winnipeg Wolf.

Away they went, a rabble of Dogs, a motley rout of horsemen, a mob of men and boys on foot. Garou had no fear of the Dogs, but men he knew had guns and were dangerous. He led off for the dark timber line of the Assiniboine, but the horsemen had open country and they headed him back. He coursed along the Colony Creek hollow and so eluded the bullets already flying. He made for a barb-wire fence, and passing that he got rid of the horsemen for a time, but still must keep the hollow that baffled the bullets. The Dogs were now closing on him. All he might have asked would probably have been to be left alone with them – forty or fifty to one as they were – he would have taken the odds. The Dogs were all round him now, but none dared to close in, A lanky Hound, trusting to his speed, ran alongside at length and got a side chop from Garou that laid him low. The horsemen were forced to take a distant way around, but now the chase was toward the town, and more men and Dogs came running out to join the fray.

The Wolf turned toward the slaughter-house, a familiar resort, and the shooting ceased on account of the houses, as well as the Dogs, being so near. These were indeed now close enough to encircle him and hinder all further flight. He looked for a place to guard his rear for a final stand, and seeing a wooden foot-bridge over a gutter he sprang in, there faced about and held the pack at bay. The men got bars and demolished the bridge. He leaped out, knowing now that he had to die, but ready, wishing only to make a worthy fight, and then for the first time in broad day view of all his foes he stood – the shadowy Dog-killer, the disembodied voice of St. Boniface woods, the wonderful Winnipeg Wolf.

VII

At last after three long years of fight he stood before them alone, con-fronting twoscore Dogs, and men with guns to back them – but facing them just as resolutely as I saw him that day in the wintry woods. The same old curl was on his lips – the hard-knit flanks heaved just a little, but his green and yellow eye glowed steadily. The Dogs closed in, led not by the huge Huskies from the woods – they evidently knew too much for that – but by a Bulldog from the town; there was scuffling of many feet; a low rumbling for a time replaced the yapping of the pack; a flashing of those red and grizzled jaws, a momentary hurl back of the onset, and again he stood alone and braced, the grim and grand old bandit that he was. Three times they tried and suffered. Their boldest were lying about him. The first to go down was the Bull-dog. Learning wisdom now, the Dogs held back, less sure; but his square-built chest showed never a sign of weakness yet, and after waiting impatiently he advanced a few steps, and thus, alas! gave to the gunners their long-expected chance. Three rifles rang, and in the snow Garou went down at last, his life of combat done.

He had made his choice. His days were short and crammed with quick events. His tale of many peaceful years was spent in three of daily brunt. He picked his trail, a new trail, high and short. He chose to drink his cup at a single gulp, and break the glass-but he left a death-less name.

Who can look into the mind of the Wolf? Who can show us his well-spring of motive? Why should he still cling to a place of endless tribu-lation? It could not be because he knew no other country, for the region is limitless, food is everywhere, and he was known at least as far as Selkirk. Nor could his motive be revenge. No animal will give up its whole life to seeking revenge; that evil kind of mind is found in man alone. The brute creation seeks for peace.

There is then but one remaining bond to chain him, and that the strongest claim that anything can own – the mightiest force on earth.

The Wolf is gone. The last relic of him was lost in the burning Grammar School, but to this day the sexton of St. Boniface Church avers that the tolling bell on Christmas Eve never fails to provoke that weird and melancholy Wolf-cry from the wooded graveyard a hundred steps away, where they laid his Little Jim, the only being on earth that ever met him with the touch of love.

BINGO

The Story of My Dog

I

It was early in November, 1882, and the Manitoba winter had just set in. I was tilting back in my chair for a few lazy moments after breakfast, idly alternating my gaze from the one window-pane of our shanty, through which was framed a bit of the prairie and the end of our cowshed, to the old rhyme of the 'Franckelyn's dogge' pinned on the logs near by. But the dreamy mixture of rhyme and view was quickly dispelled by the sight of a large grey animal dashing across the prairie into the cowshed, with a smaller black and white animal in hot pursuit.

'A wolf,' I exclaimed, and seizing a rifle dashed out to help the dog. But before I could get there they had left the stable, and after a short run over the snow the wolf again turned at bay, and the dog, our neighbour's collie, circled about watching his chance to snap.

I fired a couple of long shots, which had the effect only of setting them off again over the prairie. After another run this matchless dog closed and seized the wolf by the haunch, but again retreated to avoid the fierce return chop. Then there was another stand at bay, and again a race over the snow. Every few hundred yards this scene was repeated, the dog managing so that each fresh rush should be toward the settlement, while the wolf vainly tried to break back toward the dark belt of trees in the east. At last after a mile of this fighting and running I overtook them, and the dog, seeing that he now had good backing, closed in for the finish.

After a few seconds the whirl of struggling animals resolved itself into a wolf, on his back, with a bleeding collie gripping his throat, and it was now easy for me to step up and end the fight by putting a ball through the wolf's head.

Then, when this dog of marvellous wind saw that his foe was dead, he gave him no second glance, but set out at a lope for a farm four miles across the snow where he had left his master when first the wolf was started. He was a wonderful dog, and even if I had not come he undoubtedly would have killed the wolf alone, as I learned he had already done with others of the kind, in spite of the fact that the wolf, though of the smaller or prairie race, was much large than himself. I was filled with admiration for the dog's prowess and at once sought to buy him at any price. The scornful reply of his owner was, 'Why don't you try to buy one of the children?'

Since Frank was not in the market I was obliged to content myself with the next best thing, one of his alleged progeny. That is, a son of his wife. This probable offspring of an illustrious sire was a roly-poly ball of black fur that looked more like a long-tailed bearcub than a puppy. But he had some tan markings like those on Frank's coat, that were, I hoped, guarantees of future greatness, and also a very characteristic ring of white that he always wore on his muzzle.

Having got possession of his person, the next thing was to find him a name. Surely this puzzle was already solved. The rhyme of the 'Franckelyn's dogge' was in-built with the foundation of our acquaintance, so with adequate pomp we yclept him little Bingo.'

called

II

The rest of that winter Bingo spent in our shanty, living the life of a blubbery, fat, well-meaning, ill-doing puppy; gorging himself with food and growing bigger and clumsier each day. Even sad experience failed to teach him that he must keep his nose out of the rat trap. His most friendly overtures to the cat were wholly misunderstood and resulted only in an armed neutrality that varied by occasional reigns of terror, continued to the end; which came when Bingo, who early showed a mind of his own, got a notion for sleeping at the barn and avoiding the shanty altogether.

When the spring came I set about his serious education. After much pains on my behalf and many pains on his, he learned to go at the word in quest of our old yellow cow, that pastured at will on the unfenced prairie.

Once he had learned his business, he became very fond of it and nothing pleased him more than an order to go and fetch the cow. Away he would dash, barking with pleasure and leaping high in the air that he might better scan the plain for his victim. In a short time he would return driving her at full gallop before him, and gave her no peace until, puffing and blowing, she was safely driven into the farthest corner of her stable.

Less energy on his part would have been more satisfactory, but we bore with him until he grew so fond of this semi-daily hunt that he began to bring 'old Dunne' without being told. And at length not once or twice but a dozen times a day this energetic cowherd would sally forth on his own responsibility and drive the cow home to the stable.

At last things came to such a pass that whenever he felt like taking a little exercise, or had a few minutes of spare time, or even happened to think of it, Bingo would sally forth at racing speed over the plain and a few minutes later return, driving the unhappy yellow cow at full gallop before him.

At first this did not seem very bad, as it kept the cow from straying too far; but soon it was seen that it hindered her feeding. She became thin and gave less milk; it seemed to weigh on her mind too, as she was always watching nervously for that hateful dog, and in the mornings would hang around the stable as though afraid to venture off and subject herself at once to an onset.

This was going too far. All attempts to make Bingo more moderate in his pleasure were failures, so he was compelled to give it up altogether. After this, though he dared not bring her home, he continued to show his interest by lying at her stable door while she was being milked.

As the summer came on the mosquitoes became a dreadful plague, and the consequent vicious switching of Dunne's tail at milking-time was even more annoying than the mosquitoes.

Fred, the brother who did the milking, was of an inventive as well as an impatient turn of mind, and he devised a simple plan to stop the switching. He fastened a brick to the cow's tail, then set blithely about his work assured of unusual comfort while the rest of us looked on in doubt.

Suddenly through the mist of mosquitoes came a dull whack and an outburst of 'language'. The cow went on placidly chewing till Fred got on his feet and furiously attacked her with the milking-stool. It was bad enough to be whacked on the ear with a brick by a stupid old cow, but the uproarious enjoyment and ridicule of the bystanders made it unendurable.

Bingo, hearing the uproar, and divining that he was needed, rushed in and attacked Dunne on the other side. Before the affair quieted down the milk was spilt, the pail and stool were broken, and the cow and the dog severely beaten.

Poor Bingo could not understand it at all. He had long ago learned to despise that cow, and now in utter disgust he decided to forsake even her stable door, and from that time be attached himself exclusively to the horses and their stable.

The cattle were mine, the horses were my brother's, and in transferring his allegiance from the cow-stable to the horse-stable Bingo seemed to give me up too, and anything like daily companionship ceased, and yet, whenever any emergency arose Bingo turned to me and I to him, and both seemed to feel that the bond between man and dog is one that lasts as long as life.

The only other occasion on which Bingo acted as cowherd was in the autumn of the same year at the annual Carberry Fair, Among the dazzling inducements to enter one's stock there was, in addition to a prospect of glory, a cash prize of 'two dollars' for the 'best collie in training'.

Misled by a false friend, I entered Bingo, and early on the day fixed, the cow was driven to the prairie just outside of the village. When the time came she was pointed out to Bingo and the word given – 'Go fetch the cow.' It was the intention, of course, that he should bring her to me at the judge's stand.

But the animals knew better. They hadn't rehearsed all summer for nothing. When Dunne saw Bingo's careering form she knew that her only hope for safety was to get into her stable, and Bingo was equally sure that his sole mission in life was to quicken her pace in that direction. So off they raced over the prairie, like a wolf after a deer, and heading straight toward their home two miles way, they disappeared from view.

That was the last that judge or jury ever saw of dog or cow. The prize was awarded to the only other entry.

III

Bingo's loyalty to the horses was quite remarkable; by day he trotted beside them, and by night he slept at the stable door. Where the team went Bingo went, and nothing kept him away from them. This interesting assumption of ownership lent the greater significance to the following circumstance.

I was not superstitious, and up to this time had had no faith in omens, but was now deeply impressed by a strange occurrence in which Bingo took a leading part. There were but two of us now living on the De Winton Farm. One morning my brother set out for Boggy Creek for a load of hay. It was a long day's journey there and back, and he made an early start. Strange to tell, Bingo for once in his life did not follow the team. My brother called to him, but still he stood at a safe distance, and eyeing the team askance, refused to stir. Suddenly he raised his nose in the air and gave vent to a long, melancholy howl. He watched the waggon out of sight, and even followed for a hundred yards or so, raising his voice from time to time in the most doleful howlings.

All that day he stayed about the barn, the only time that he was willingly separated from the horses, and at intervals howled a very death dirge. I was alone, and the dog's behaviour inspired me with an awful foreboding of calamity, that weighed upon use more and more as the hours passed away.

About six o'clock Bingo's howlings became unbearable, so that for lack of a better thought I threw something at him, and ordered him away. But oh, the feeling of horror that filled me. Why did I let my brother go away alone? Should I ever again see him alive? I might have known from the dog's actions that something dreadful was about to happen.

At length the hour for his return arrived, and there was John on his load. I took charge of the horses, vastly relieved, and with an air of assumed unconcern, asked, 'All right?'

'Right,' was the laconic answer.

Who now can say that there is nothing in omens.

And yet when, long afterward, I told this to one skilled in the occult, he looked grave, and said, 'Bingo always turned to you in a crisis?'

'Yes.'

'Then do not smile. It was you that were in danger that day; he stayed and saved your life, though you never knew from what.'

IV

Early in the spring I bad begun Bingo's education. Very shortly afterward he began mine.

Midway on the two-mile stretch of prairie that lay between our shanty and the village of Carberry, was the corner-stake of the farm; it was a stout post in a low mound of earth, and was visible from afar.

I soon noticed that Bingo never passed without minutely examining this mysterious post. Next I learned that it was also visited by the prairie wolves as well as by all the dogs in the neighbourhood, and at length, with the aid of a telescope, I made a number of observations that helped me to an understanding of the matter and enabled me to enter more fully into Bingo's private life.

The post was by common agreement a registry of the canine tribes. Their exquisite sense of smell enabled each individual to tell at once by the track and trace what other had recently been at the post. When the snow came much more was revealed. I then discovered that this post was but one of a system that covered the country; that, in short, the entire region was laid out in signal stations at convenient intervals. These were marked by any conspicuous post, stone, buffalo skull, or other object that chanced to be in the desired locality, and extensive observation showed that it was a very complete system for getting and giving the news.

Each dog or wolf makes a point of calling at those stations that are near his line of travel to learn who has recently been there, just as a man calls at his club on returning to town and looks up the register.

I have seen Bingo approach the post, sniff, examine the ground about, then growl, and with bristling mane and glowing eyes, scratch fiercely and contemptuously with his hind feet, finally walking off very stiffly, glancing back from time to time. All of which, being interpreted, said:

'*Grrrh!* woof! there's that dirty cur of McCarthy's. *Woof!* I'll tend to him tonight. *Woof! woof!*' On another occasion, after the preliminaries, he became keenly interested and studied a coyote's track that came and went, saying to himself, as I afterward learned:

'A coyote track coming from the north, smelling of dead cow. Indeed? Pollworth's old Brindle must be dead at last. This is worth looking into.'

At other times he would wag his tail, trot about the vicinity and come again and again to make his own visit more evident, perhaps for the benefit of his brother Bill just back from Brandon! So that it was not by chance that one night Bill turned up at Bingo's home and was taken to the hills, where a delicious dead horse afforded a chance to suitably celebrate the reunion.

At other times he would be suddenly aroused by the news, take up the trail, and race to the next station for later information.

Sometimes his inspection produced only an air of grave attention, as though he said to himself, 'Dear me, who the deuce is this?' or 'It

who the deuce is this?

seems to me I met that fellow at the Portage last summer.'

One morning on approaching the post Bingo's every hair stood on end, his tail dropped and quivered, and he gave proof that he was suddenly sick at the stomach, sure signs of terror. He showed no desire to follow up or know more of the matter, but returned to the house, and half an hour afterward his mane was still bristling and his expression one of hate or fear.

I studied the dreaded track and learned that in Bingo's language the half-terrified, deep-gurgled '*grr-wff*' means '*timber wolf*'.

These were among the things that Bingo taught me. And in the after time when I might chance to see him arouse from his frosty nest by the stable door, and after stretching himself and shaking the snow from his shaggy coat, disappear into the gloom at a steady trot, trot, trot, I used to think:

'Ahh! old dog, I know where you are off to, and why you eschew the shelter of the shanty. Now I know why your nightly trips over the country are so well timed, and how you know just where to go for what you want, and when and how to seek it.'

V

In the autumn of 1884, the shanty at De Winton farm was closed and Bingo changed his home to the establishment, that is, to the stable, not the house, of Gordon Wright, our most intimate neighbour.

Since the winter of his puppyhood he had declined to enter a house at any time excepting during a thunderstorm. Of thunder and guns he had a deep dread – no doubt the fear of the first originated in the second, and that arose from some unpleasant shot-gun experiences, the cause of which will be seen. His nightly couch was outside the stable, even during the coldest weather, and it was easy to see he enjoyed to the full the complete nocturnal liberty entailed. Bingo's midnight wanderings extended across the plains for miles. There was plenty of proof of this. Some farmers at very remote points sent word to old Gordon that if he did not keep his dog home nights, they would use the shot-gun, and Bingo's terror of firearms would indicate that the threats were not idle. A man living as far away as Petrel said he saw a large black wolf kill a coyote on the snow one winter evening, but afterward he changed his opinion and 'reckoned it must 'a' been Wright's dog.' Whenever the body of a winter-killed ox or horse was exposed, Bingo was sure to repair to it nightly, and driving away the prairie wolves, feast to repletion.

Sometimes the object of a night foray was merely to maul some distant neighbour's dog, and notwithstanding vengeful threats, there seemed no reason to fear that the Bingo breed would die out. One man even avowed that he had seen a prairie wolf accompanied by three young ones which resembled the mother, excepting that they were very large and black and had a ring of white around the muzzle.

True or not as that may be, I know that late in March, while we were out in the sleigh with Bingo trotting behind, a prairie wolf was started from a hollow. Away it went with Bingo in full chase, but the wolf did not greatly exert itself to escape, and within a short distance Bingo was close up, yet strange to tell, there was no grappling, no fight!

Bingo trotted amiably alongside and licked the wolf's nose.

We were astounded, and shouted to urge Bingo on. Our shouting and approach several times started the wolf off at speed and Bingo again pursued until he had overtaken it, but his gentleness was too obvious.

'It is a she-wolf, he won't harm her,' I exclaimed as the truth dawned on me. And Gordon said: 'Well, I be darned.'

So we called our unwilling dog and drove on.

For weeks after this we were annoyed by the depredations of a prairie wolf who killed our chickens, stale pieces of pork from the end of the house, and several times terrified the children by looking into the window of the shanty while the men were away.

Against this animal Bingo seemed to be no safeguard. At length the wolf, a female, was killed, and then Bingo plainly showed his hand by his lasting enmity toward Oliver, the man who did the deed.

VI

It is wonderful and beautiful how a man and his dog will stick to one another, through thick and thin. Butler tells of an undivided Indian tribe, in the Far North which was all but exterminated by an internecine feud over a dog that belonged to one man and was killed by his neighbour; and among ourselves we have lawsuits, fights, and deadly feuds, all pointing the same old moral, 'Love me, love my dog'.

One of our neighbours had a very fine hound that he thought the best and dearest dog in the world. I loved him, so I loved his dog, and when one day poor Tan crawled home terribly mangled and died by the door, I joined my threats of vengeance with those of his master and thenceforth lost no opportunity of tracing the miscreant, both by offering rewards and by collecting scraps of evidence. At length it was clear that one of three men to the southward had had a hand in the cruel affair. The scent was warming up, and soon we should have been in a position to exact rigorous justice, at least, from the wretch who had murdered poor old Tan.

Then something took place which at once changed my mind and led me to believe that the mangling of the old hound was not by any means an unpardonable crime, but indeed on second thoughts was rather commendable than otherwise.

Gordon Wright's farm lay to the south of us, and while there one day, Gordon Jr, knowing that I was tracking the murderer, took me aside and looking about furtively, he whispered, in tragic tones:

'It was Bing done it.'

And the matter dropped right there. For I confess that from that moment I did all in my power to baffle the justice I had previously striven so hard to further. I had given Bingo away long before, but the feeling of ownership did not die; and of this indissoluble fellowship of dog and man he was soon to take part in another important illustration.

Old Gordon and Oliver were close neighbours and friends; they joined in a contract to cut wood, and worked together harmoniously till late on in winter. Then Oliver's old horse died, and he, determining to profit as far as possible, dragged it out on the plain and laid poison baits for wolves around it. Alas for poor Bingo! He would lead a wolfish life, though again and again it brought him into wolfish misfortunes.

He was as fond of dead horse as any of his wild kindred. That very night, with Wright's own dog Curley, he visited the carcass. It seemed as though Bing had busied himself chiefly keeping off the wolves, but Curley feasted immoderately. The tracks in the snow told the story of the banquet; the interruption as the poison began to work, and of the dreadful spasms of pain during the erratic course back home where Curley, falling in convulsions at Gordon's feet, died in the greatest agony.

'Love me, love my dog,' No explanations or apology were acceptable; it was useless to urge that it was accidental; the long-standing feud between Bingo and Oliver was now remembered as an important sidelight. The wood-contract was thrown up, all friendly relations ceased, and to this day there is no county big enough to hold the rival factions which were called at once into existence and to arms by Curley's dying yell.

It was months before Bingo really recovered from the poison. We believed indeed that he never again would be the sturdy old-time Bingo. But when the spring came he began to gain strength, and bettering as the grass grew, he was within a few weeks once more in full health and vigour to be a pride to his friends and a nuisance to his neighbours.

VII

Changes took me far away from Manitoba, and on my return in 1886 Bingo was still a member of Wright's household. I thought he would have forgotten me after two years' absence, but not so. One day early in the winter, after having been lost for forty-eight hours, he crawled home to Wright's with a wolf-trap and a heavy log fast to one foot, and the foot frozen to stony hardness. No one had been able to ap-

proach to help him, he was so savage, when I, the stranger now, stooped down and laid hold of the trap with one hand and his leg with the other. Instantly he seized my wrist in his teeth.

Without stirring I said, 'Bing, don't you know me?'

He had not broken the skin and at once released his hold and offered no further resistance, although he whined a good deal during the removal of the trap. He still acknowledged me his master in spite of his change of residence and my long absence, and notwithstanding my surrender of ownership I still felt that he was my dog.

Bing was carried into the house much against his will and his frozen foot thawed out. During the rest of the winter he went lame and two of his toes eventually dropped off. But before the return of warm weather his health and strength were fully restored, and to a casual glance he bore no mark of his dreadful experience in the steel trap.

VIII

During that same winter I caught many wolves and foxes who did not have Bingo's good luck in escaping the traps, which I kept out right into the spring, for bounties are good even when fur is not.

Kennedy's Plain was always a good trapping ground because it was unfrequented by man and yet lay between the heavy woods and the settlement. I had been fortunate with the fur here, and late in April rode in on one of my regular rounds.

The wolf-traps are made of heavy steel and have two springs, each of one hundred pounds power. They are set in fours around a buried bait, and after being strongly fastened to concealed logs are carefully covered in cotton and in fine sand so as to be quite invisible.

A prairie wolf was caught in one of these. I killed him with a club and throwing him aside proceeded to reset the trap as I had done so many hundred times before. All was quickly done. I threw the trap-wrench over toward the pony, and seeing some fine sand nearby, I reached out for a handful of it to add a good finish to the setting.

Oh, unlucky thought! Oh, mad heedlessness born of long immunity! That fine sand was *on the next wolftrap* and in an instant I was a prisoner. Although not wounded, for the traps have no teeth, and my thick trapping gloves deadened the snap, I was firmly caught across the hand above the knuckles. Not greatly alarmed at this, I tried to reach the trap-wrench with my right foot. Stretching out at full length, face downward, I worked myself toward it, making my imprisoned arm as long and straight as possible. I could not see and reach at the same time, but counted on my toe telling me when I touched the little iron key to my fetters. My first effort was a failure; strain as I might at the chain my toe struck no metal. I swung slowly around my anchor, but still failed. Then a painfully taken observation showed I was much too far to the west. I set about working around, tapping blindly with my toe to discover the key. Thus wildly groping with my right foot I forgot about the other till there was a sharp 'clank' and the iron jaws of trap No. 5 closed tight on my left foot.

The terrors of the situation did not, at first, impress me, but I soon found that all my struggles were in vain. I could not get free from either trap or move the traps together, and there I lay stretched out and firmly staked to the ground.

What would become of me now? There was not much danger of freezing for the cold weather was over, but Kennedy's Plain was never visited by the winter wood-cutters. No one knew where I had gone, and unless I could manage to free myself there was no prospect ahead but to be devoured by wolves, or else die of cold and starvation.

As I lay there the red sun went down over the spruce swamp west of the plain, and a shorelark on a gopher mound a few yards off twittered his evening song, just as one had done the night before at our shanty door, and though the numb pains were creeping up my arm, and a deadly chill possessed me, I noticed how long his little ear-tufts were. Then my thoughts went to the comfortable supper-table at Wright's shanty, and I thought, now they are frying the pork for supper, or just sitting down. My pony still stood as I left him with his bridle on the ground patiently waiting to take me home. He did not understand the long delay, and when I called, he ceased nibbling the grass and looked at me in dumb, helpless inquiry. If he would only go home the empty saddle might tell the tale and bring help. But his very faithfulness kept him waiting hour after hour while I was perishing of cold and hunger.

Then I remembered how old Girou the trapper had been lost, and in the following spring his comrades found his skeleton held by the leg in a bear-trap. I wondered which part of my clothing would show my identity. Then a new thought came to me. This is how a wolf feels when he is trapped. Oh! what misery have I been responsible for! Now I'm to pay for it.

Night came slowly on. A prairie wolf howled, the pony pricked up his ears and, walking nearer to me, stood with his head down. Then another prairie wolf howled and another, and I could make out that they were gathering in the neighbourhood. There I lay prone and helpless, wondering if it would not be strictly just that they should come and tear me to pieces. I heard them calling for a long time before I realised that dim, shadowy forms were sneaking near. The horse saw them first, and his terrified snort drove them back at first, but they came nearer next time and sat around me on the prairie. Soon one bolder than the others crawled up and tugged at the body of his dead relative. I shouted and he retreated growling. The pony ran to a distance in terror. Presently the wolf returned, and after after two or three of these retreats and returns, the body was dragged off and devoured by the rest in a few minutes.

After this they gathered nearer and sat on their haunches to look at me, and the boldest one smelt the rifle and scratched dirt on it. He retreated when I kicked at him with my free foot and shouted, but growing bolder as I grew weaker he came and snarled right in my face. At this several others snarled and came up closer, and I realised that I was to be devoured by the foe that I most despised; when suddenly out of the gloom with a guttural roar sprang a great black wolf. The prairie wolves scattered like chaff except the bold one, which, seized by the black new-corner, was in a few moments a draggled corpse, and then, oh horrors! this mighty brute bounded at me and – Bingo – noble Bingo, rubbed his shaggy, panting sides against me and licked my cold face.

'Bingo – Bing – old – boy – Fetch me the trap wrench!' Away he went and returned dragging the rifle, for he knew only that I wanted something.

'No – Bing – the trap-wrench.' This time it was my sash, but at last he brought the wrench and wagged his tail in joy that it was right. Reaching out with my free hand, after much difficulty I unscrewed the pillar-nut. The trap fell apart and my hand was released, and a minute later I was free. Bing brought the pony up, and after slowly walking to restore the circulation I was able to mount. Then slowly at first but soon at a gallop, with Bingo as herald careering and barking ahead, we set out for home, there to learn that the night before, though never taken on the trapping rounds, the brave dog had acted strangely, whimpering and watching the timber-trail; and at last when night came on, in spite of attempts to detain him he had set out in the gloom and guided by a knowledge that is beyond us had reached the spot in time to avenge me as well as set me free.

Staunch old Bing – he was a strange dog. Though his heart was with me, he passed me next day with scarcely a look, but responded with alacrity when little Gordon called him to a gopher-hunt. And it was so to the end; and to the end also he lived the wolfish life that he loved, and never failed to seek the winter-killed horses and found one again with a poisoned bait, and wolfishly bolted that; then feeling the pang, set out, not for Wright's but to find me, and reached the door of my shanty where I should have been. Next day on returning I found him dead in the snow with his head on the sill of the door – the door of his puppyhood's days; my dog to the last in his heart of hearts – it was my help he sought, and vainly sought, in the hour of his bitter extremity.

The Ten Commandments

I   Thou shalt have no other gods before me.

II   Thou shalt not make unto thee any graven image, or any likeness of any thing that is in heaven above, or that is in the earth beneath, or that is in the water under the earth: Thou shalt not bow down thyself to them, nor serve them: for I the LORD thy God am a jealous God, visiting the iniquity of the fathers upon the children unto the third and fourth generation of them that hate me; And shewing mercy unto thousands of them that love me, and keep my commandments.

III   Thou shalt not take the name of the Lord thy God in vain; for the Lord will not hold him guiltless that taketh his name in vain.

IV   Remember the sabbath day to keep it holy. Six days shalt thou labour, and do all thy work: But the seventh day is the sabbath of the Lord thy God: in it thou shalt not do any work, thou, nor thy son, nor thy daughter, thy manservant, nor thy maidservant, nor thy cattle, nor thy stranger that is within thy gates: For in six days the LORD made heaven and earth, the sea, and all that in them is, and rested the seventh day: wherefore the Lord blessed the sabbath day, and hallowed it.

V   Honour thy father and thy mother: that thy days may be long upon the land which the LORD thy God giveth thee.

VI   Thou shalt not kill.

VII   Thou shalt not commit adultery.

VIII   Thou shalt not steal.

IX   Thou shalt not bear false witness against thy neighbour.

X   Thou shalt not covet thy neighbour's house, thou shalt not covet thy neighbour's wife, nor his manservant, nor his maidservant, nor his ox, nor his ass, nor any thing that is thy neighbour's.

THE NATURAL HISTORY
OF THE TEN COMMANDMENTS

More than one heathen philosopher conceived creation as a tree with its roots in the nether world, its fruit in the skies. Had these men been other than heathen, we today might have called them inspired. They outlined in advance the view of modern science, that the universe is an organic whole, a thing of growth, with ceaseless upward struggle.

Darwin and his school taught us the literal verity of this in material things.

Modern psychologists are daily discovering its truth in their own fields. Possibly we may go further and find it apply equally in the moral world.

A theory is a great aid to study.

It helps one to observe, provided always one does not cut the facts to fit the theory, but rather keeps changing the theory to fit the new facts.

Years ago I set for my theory that: The Ten Commandments are *not arbitrary laws given to man, but are fundamental laws of all highly developed animals.*

If this be true I shall be able to trace them through the animal world. We can learn an unwritten law only by breaking it and suffering the penalty. My task therefore was to discover among the animals disaster following breach of the ten great principles on which human society is founded. There are two disasters commonly discernible: the first is, direct punishment of the individual by those he wronged; the other, a slow and general visitation on the whole race of the criminal, as the working out of the law. The former, the objective, is more obvious; the latter, the subjective, more important. But they are fundamentally the same, since the agents in the first case were impelled by their own recognition that wrong had been done, that a law had been broken.

Most commentators divide the Commandments into two groups:

The first four on man's duty to a Supreme Being.

The last six on man's duty to man.

For many reasons I found it better to take the latter group first, beginning with No. V.

Commandment V

Against Disobedience

The law which imposes unreasoning acceptance of the benefits deriv-able from the experience of those over us. This is the foundation of all government, since the family is the social unit. Its force everywhere is so seen that it scarcely needs proof

A Hen sets out with her Chickens a-foraging; one loiters, does not hasten up at her 'cluck cluck' of invitation and command; consequently he gets lost and dies.

Another neglects to run to the spot when she calls in the established way that she has found 'good food'. He is not so well nourished as the others; he becomes a weakling, and in the first hard pinch he is the one that fails – he dies.

Again, she may call out 'Hawk!' and run for shelter; the obedient ones run with her, and are safe; the disobedient loiter – and die. They pay the penalty, their days are short in the land.

Yet again: A Black-bear in the Cincinnati Zoo produced a family of two cubs in January, 1879. When they were seventy-one days old, one of them left the den for the first time, and followed the mother in her quest for food. This in a wild state would have been a fatal mistake for

the young one. 'As soon as the mother found it out,' says Superintendent F. J. Thompson, 'she immedi-ately drove it gently back, and on the second attempt she cuffed it soundly, which put a stop to its wander-ing propensity. After a few days she allowed the cubs to wander about at will, provided no one was imme-diately in front of the den; but so soon as a visitor put in an appearance, they were driven back into the den, and not allowed to emerge until the strangers were out of sight.'

Under natural conditions this maternal rule was essential, and a breach of it meant death to the cul-prit.

When a mother Deer or Antelope sights, scents, or hears danger, she quickly communicates her warn-ing to her young.

How it is done, varies greatly with the species; some bleat or snort; others may merely spread the disk of white hair around the tail, but all give what is understood to be warning of danger. The young at once squat in the grass, and the mother goes forth to baffle the foe as best she may. But it is essential to the little one and to the race that the warning be acted on promptly and fully.

This action on the part of the young is purely instinctive – which means that the law of obedience has been a long, long time in successful operation.

It would be easy to fill a volume with incidents illustrating this rule. But it is well known among all naturalists that obedience to parents is vital, and disobedience on the part of the young means injury to themselves, and, if uncurbed, death to the race.

Commandment VI

Against Murder

That is, against taking the life of one of our own species. There is a deep-rooted feeling against murder in most animals. Their senses tell them that this individual is one of their own race, and their instinct tells them that therefore it is not lawful prey.

New-born Rattlesnakes will strike instantly at a stranger of any other species, but never at one of their own. I have seen a young Mink, still blind, suck at a mother Cat till fed, then try to take her life. Though a creature of such blood-thirst, it would never have attacked its own mother.

Wild animals often fight for the mastery, usually over a question of mates, but in practically all cases the fight is over when one yields. The vanquished can save himself either by submission or byflight. What is commoner than to see the weaker of two Dogs disarm his conqueror by grovelling on the ground?

The victor in a fight between two Cats is satisfied when the foe flies; he will not pursue him twenty yards. In either case had the enemy been of a different race the victor would have followed and killed him.

What makes the difference ? Obviously not a reasoned-out conclusion, but a deep instinctive feeling – the recognition of the un-written law against unnecessarily killing one's own kind.

There are doubtless exceptions to this. Cannibalism is recorded of many species; but investigation shows that it is rare except in the lowest forms, and among creatures demoralized by domestication or captivity. The higher the animals are, the more repugnant does cannibalism become. It is seldom indulged in except under dire stress of famine. Nothing but actual starvation induced Nansen's Dogs to eat the flesh of their comrades, although it was offered to them in a disguised form. Numberless experiences showed me that it is useless to bait a Wolf-trap with a part of a dead Wolf. His kinsmen shun it in disgust, unless absolutely famished.

Obviously, no race can live by cannibalism; and this is instinctively recognized by all the higher animals. In other words, the law against murder has been hammered into animals by natural selection, and so fully established that they will not only abstain from preying on one of their own tribe, but will rally to rescue one whose life is threatened.

The fact that there are exceptional cases does not disprove the law among beasts any more than among men.

Commandment VII

Against Impurity

Although on the face of it directed against the grossest form of misapplied reproductive instinct, most commentators agree that it is meant to cherish the general principle of purity.

Of what service is such a general principle to the race? A review of many creatures and their marriage customs shows that from the beginning they have been groping for an ideal form of marriage.

Promiscuity was doubtless the mode when first sex appeared in the animal world. It had the great advantage that it insures all finding mates with whom fruitful union is possible. But it has several disadvantages, the most obvious being that unlimited personal contact opens the way for epidemic diseases of all sorts. The less personal contact, the less disease.

The promiscuous animals today – the Northwestern Rabbit and the Voles – are high in the scale of fecundity, low in the scale of general development, and are periodically scourged by epidemic plagues.

The Chinaman who reduces personal contact to a minimum by refraining even from shaking the hand of a friend, has gone to the extreme, and without doubt has had his reward.

Another danger from this lawless reproduction is the evil called 'in-breeding', that is, the mating of near kin.

Promiscuity has been displaced by polyandry and polygamy, among certain animals. That the former has not been a success is shown by the fact that it is very rare among the higher kinds, and practised only under exceptional circumstances.

The few cases I can find are the European Cuckoo, and, possibly, the American Cowbirds. The extraordinary, hazardous and dishonest methods these are driven to for support of their young are well known.

The fact that these species are healthy and prospering is a puzzle to me. Nevertheless it must be observed that their parasitism is *on the other races, not on their own kind*.

Polygamy seems much more satisfactory: there are hundreds of species of polygamous animals in the world today that are prospering and growing with the world's growth.

On the face of it, polygamy might seem to be good, because it makes it possible for only the finest males to breed, and insures for them the greatest possible number of off-spring.

This sounds convincing, but some unexpected light has been shed by Caton's observation among the Wapiti, the most polygamous of all our Deer.

Referring to Sultan, the great bull Wapiti that for a longer time than any other was the monarch of the herd in his park, he says:* 'At first

* *Antelope and Deer of America*, pp. 294–5.

his progeny were reasonably numerous, but during the last few years of his life they gradually diminished from a dozen to a single fawn in 1875, with about twenty-five females, more than half of which had previously produced fawns.' He was removed, though yet able to hold the harem by force, and replaced by a younger buck; 'the result was that I had twelve fawns the next season, including one pair of twins.' It is probable that a far better result would have been secured had each female been paired off with a single male.

As the Wapiti is the most polygamous of the Deer in America, probably in the world, it is interesting to note that it is the first of the family to disappear before civilization. This may be due in part to its size; but it is further remarkable that the most successful of all our true Deer, that is, the common White-tail, is the least polygamous.

There is at least one strong and obvious objection to polygamy among animals: the offspring of such union have but one parent to care for them, and the weaker one at that.

It is commonly remarked that while the Mosaic law did not expressly forbid polygamy, it surrounded marriage with so many restrictions that by living up to the spirit of them the Hebrew was ultimately forced into pure monogamy.

It is extremely interesting to note that the animals in their blind groping for an ideal form of union have gone through the same stages and have arrived at exactly the same conclusion. Monogamy is their best solution of the marriage question, and is the rule among all the highest and most successful animals.

There are four degrees of monogamy:

One, in which the male stays with one female as long as she interests him or desires a mate, then changes to another; for his season may be many times as long as hers. Thus he may have several wives in the season, but only one at a time. This is convenient for both parties, but it is open to the same objection as frank polygamy. It is the way of the Moose.

A second kind, in which the male and one female are paired for that breeding season only, the male staying with the family, and sharing the care of the young till they are well grown; after which the parents may or may not resume their fellowship. This is admirable. It is seen in Hawks,

A third, in which the pair consort for life, but the death of one leaves the other free to mate again. This is ideal. It is the way of Wolves.

A fourth, in which they pair for life, and in case of death the survivor remains disconsolate and alone to the end. This seems absurd. It is the way of the wild Geese.

Upon the whole we find the animals succeeding, that is, avoiding disease and holding their own, spreading, and high in the scale, in proportion as they approach the ideal union.*

I confess, however, that monogamy in the fourth degree puzzles me.

In making observations, one is hampered by the fact that association with man has always been ruinous to the morals of animals.

There can be no doubt that the Dog, now so promiscuous, was originally a monogamous creature. One of the great difficulties besetting the growing of Blue-foxes for their fur, on the islands of the Behring Sea, is what has been called the obstinate and deplorable monogamy of those animals. The breeders are working hard to break down this high moral sentiment and produce a Blue-fox that does not object to polygamy, promiscuity, or any other combination, and so remove all sentimental obstacles to their experiments.

The wild Goose is a most exemplary bird; the tame Goose is little better than the Dog. Of Rabbits, wild or tame, the less said the better.

There is, however, one domestic bird that maintains its honourable wild tradition in spite of all that sinful man can do; that is the Pigeon. The breeder knows that the young in a given nest are unquestionably the offspring of their alleged parents, no matter how many hundreds of their kind may freely fly with them all day.

* Dr. Woods Hutchinson in *Animal Marriage* has pointed out that other things being equal, a monogamous race will beat a polygamous one in the long run.

What wonder that Gadow, the distinguished ornithologist, should proclaim the Pigeons the birds of the future, implying that when, under the relentless unwritten laws, all other species shall have paid the penalty and run themselves out, the Pigeons will be happily possessing the earth.

Similarly the most successful wild quadrupeds in American today are the Grey-wolves. Not only have they through strict monogamy eliminated much possibility of disease, and given their young the advantage of two wise protectors, but they have even developed a spirit of chivalry; that is, the male shows consideration for the female in the non-mating season on account of her sex. This is very high in the scale. And one result, at least partly due to these things, is that the Wolves defy all attempts to exterminate them, and are increasing today in exact ratio to the improved food supplies for which the settlers are responsible.

The proverbial exceptions undoubtedly occur, and they have their value as proof, not disproof.

Immorality in its broadest sense may be defined as the deflection of any natural power, member, or instinct from its proper purpose to one that works harm for the species.

Among animals we have recorded nearly every kind of abominable vice that was known among men, and forbidden by the Mosaic law.

In captivity and domestication we see such things all too often, but rarely in a state of nature, partly because the cases are scarce and difficult to observe, and partly because the creatures of vice soon destroy themselves; they pay the extreme penalty.

Incest is admittedly forbidden by the spirit of this ordinance. The numberless contrivances among plants to prevent any but cross-fertilization, evidence the importance of preventing the marriage of near kin. Among higher animals, strange to tell, observation of this law is not so marked, probably because their safeguard is not a mechanism, but a sentiment, which suffers in domestication and in captivity. It seems to exist, however.

Mr. L. H. Ohnimus, for years the director of Woodward's Garden

Menagerie at San Francisco, told me that often among higher animals they had great difficulty in mating brother and sister that were brought up together. The friendly feeling commonly overpowered the sex instinct. If, however, the pair were separated long enough to be brought together as practically strangers of opposite sexes, the difficulty disappeared.

But the penalty must be paid. The resultant young in most cases are feeble creatures, tending to die out in a generation or two, that is, paying with their death for the sin of their parents. This is physical law, and the fact that it was unwitting sin does not in any degree absolve the sinners from the consequences.

To sum up: There is evidence that in the animal world there has long been a groping after an ideal form of marriage. Beginning with promiscuity, they have worked through many stages into pure monogamy; and, other things being equal, the species, owing to natural laws, are successful in proportion as they have reached it, and therefore have developed an instinctive recognition of the seventh commandment.

Commandment VIII

Against Stealing

The whole property question is in this, and the high development of the property idea among animals must be a surprise to all who have not studied it This is the animal law:

The producer owns the product; unproduced property belongs to the first who discovers and possesses it.

Numberless instances in proof will occur to every naturalist Property among animals consists of food, nest, playground, range, and wives. Ownership is indicated in two ways: one by actual possession, the other by ownership marks. Of these there are two kinds, smell marks and visible marks; by far the more important are those of smell.

I once threw peanuts for an hour to the Fox-squirrels in City Hall Park, Madison, Wisconsin. In each case, the peanut, when thrown, was no one's property. All the near Squirrels rushed for it; the first one to get it securely in his mouth was admittedly the owner; his claim was never questioned after a few seconds' actual possession. If hungry he ate it at once; otherwise his first act was to turn it round in his mouth three or four times, as he licked it, marking it with his own smell, before burying it for future use.

This is paralleled in many tribes of men. Eskimo of Davis Strait, according to Franklin, lick each new acquisition by way of taking possession. Sailors commonly spit on a new-got article, and boys, in the north of England at least, indicate the beginning of their ownership in the same way. Many animals, as Rabbits and Bears, rub their bodies against trees in their range, to let other animals know that this place is already possessed. Some creatures, as the Weasels, have glands that secrete an odour which they use for an owner-mark. As this odour must vary with each individual it answers admirably. I have seen Martens, Wolves, and Foxes marking their property in this way. The Wolverine is commonly described as a monster of iniquity, that not only lugs off and hides the hunter's food, but defiles it with his abominable secretion, so that it is useless to the original owner. It is quite certain that malice of this kind is unusual; although Dogs and Wolves, high in mental development, have been observed to show scorn in this manner. The Wolverine eats what he can of the trapper's hoard, and hides the rest for future use, after taking care to mark it with his ownership smell-mark.

Foxes and Wolves are known to store up food, and after it is buried they defile the place in a characteristic way. Many harsh terms are applied to this practice. It is, or was formerly, ascribed to the inherent and abominable filthiness of all creation unregenerated in the particular manner specially advocated by the then critic. The fact is that the odour glands of the Fox and Wolf are so situated that their product is given out with the product of the kidneys. They do this, then, merely to put their mark on their cache.

Thus they have the property instinct in high development.

In the August of 1906, at Petoskey, Mich., I made the acquaintance of a team of Eskimo train Dogs – they were seven-eighths Wolf, and showed all the wild traits in force. The leader, a big savage creature, was easily master of the others. I gave the smallest one a bone after he was already fed. True to the wild instinct of his kind, he set off to hide this for future use. The bone was buried under a cedar bush some hundred yards away, and the place marked in Dog fashion. The owner then retired about fifty yards to a shady spot, where he could see his cache, and lay down.

The biggest Dog of all saw the hiding of the bone, but did not see the watcher. He walked quietly to the cache. When within twenty feet, there could no longer be any doubt of his purpose; the smaller Dog rushed from his covert and stood guard over his property, showing his teeth and clearly intimating that only over his dead body could the bully take his property. The big Dog, though he could have whipped the smaller in a minute, turned slowly and sullenly away, as though he knew his cause was weak.

What is the psychology of this situation? (And it was purely psychological.)

Can any one deny that the little Dog felt that he was right, the big Dog that he was wrong? In other words, they recognized the law of property, and that stealing was crime.

Many instances of this kind could be adduced. The principle is very old, and has, indeed, given rise to several proverbs: 'Any cock will fight on his own dung-hill'; 'He is a poor thing that won't fight for his own'; 'Thrice is he armed that hath his quarrel just', etc.

For how long are these caches made? In the case of domesticated Wolves they are opened and the contents eaten within a few hours or days at most But I found it the opinion of hunters, that among the truly wild animals the cache is made in time of plenty for a season of starvation, maybe months ahead.

There is good reason for believing, however, that the Wolf, Coyote and Fox have no compunction about stealing from each other. I found it a most alluring bait, if I buried a piece of meat, that is, formed a cache, and either made it fair game for Wolves by pattering the ground with an old Coyote foot, or leaving it with man tracks only around. Whether pattering it with a Wolf's foot would make other Wolves respect it, I am not prepared to say.

The food idea is probably the first property idea. Ownership of the home-place came later, but is now deeply rooted.

Many cases in line have been reported to me from among rookeries in England. Rooks are ordinarily moral birds, A stick found in the woods is the property of the Rook that discovers it, and doubly his when he has laboured to bring it to his nest. This is recognized law. Nevertheless there are degenerates or thieves that think it easier to steal sticks from their neighbour's nest than to fetch them from afar. The result is war.

In the autumn I put up opposite my window an artificial shelter hole for birds. A Flying-squirrel used it for a nest. In the spring I several times saw a pair of Chickadees peeping into the hole, but noting the nesting material, the evidence of a possessor, they withdrew without entering. If they knew that the occupant was a Squirrel, fear may have kept them back, and the incident means nothing; but all they could see were some shreds of bark which might have represented the nest of another Chickadee, in which case they were restrained by the un-written law.

To get without labour is theft; and the thief and his children must be the sufferers in the end.

How does this work out in our animal world ?

The Squirrel that will not store must starve or steal in winter. If he escapes being killed by his honest neighbours, the vice of stealing will spread, so that it will no longer be worth while to store up for winter, and the habit will be abandoned.

We must remember that the lives of animals are in a delicate balance; at times a featherweight easily turns the scales against them. A single hard winter among Squirrels that had been forced to abandon storage, might wipe out the whole race.

So also among Rooks. The thief taken red-handed may suffer griev-ous bodily punishment, or even death; this is the objective retribution. But the subjective is farther reaching, for a spread of the vice would prove ruinous to all the nests, and tend to exterminate the race.

Out of the food-property instinct has grown the territory-property instinct. Bears, Martens, Foxes, Wolves, and many other species mark their range by putting their signs on trees, stones, etc., scattered over the region claimed.

Bears not only Tub their backs on the trees, but claw them and tear them with their teeth. These things are familiar to all who have lived among Bears. The visible marks may appeal to the eyes of another Bear when he is far off, but the smell record is, I take it, of chief importance, and is the only one used by Wolves and Foxes.

These are the marks of ownership: to what extent are they re-spected ?

It is well known that each wild animal has a little home region or range that he considers his, and for which he will fight. But it is not so well known that others of his kind will respect his claim without any fight, without anything, apparently, but the little sign-boards or smell-marks already noted. Dr. F. W. True, writing of the Blue-foxes on the islands of the Behring Sea and their tameness, says one of them will follow a man for a long way, apparently hoping to be fed, will follow indeed 'to the boundary of his domain, for each Fox, like his neighbour, the bull Seal, seems to have a definite territory … which he regards as his own, and upon which he resents intrusion.' *

From these examples it will be seen that the operation of natural laws has produced in the animals ideas of property rights in materials and in places, and means of putting those rights on record. That is, has tended to give ever-growing force to the law against stealing.

Commandment IX

Against False Witness

Although the commandment forbids especially false witness against a neighbour, it is generally considered to have a broader meaning – to prohibit any falsification.

In Fox-hunting the character of every Hound becomes well known, not only to the men, but to the Hounds themselves. When they are scattered for a 'find', each Hound does his individual best and is keen to be first. Oftentimes a very young Hound will jump at a conclusion, think, or hope, he has the trail, then allowing his enthusiasm to carry him away, give the first tongue, shouting in Hound language, 'Trail!'

* 'Fox Propagation in Alaska', Rep. Sec. Int., 1903, p. 280.

The other Hounds run to this, but if a careful examination shows that he was wrong, the announcer suffers in. the opinion of the pack, and after a few such blunders, that individual is entirely discredited. Thenceforth he may bawl 'Trail!' as often as he likes, no one heeds him.

The spread of such a habit of false witness would be disastrous to the whole race of Dogs in a wild state. They would discredit each other. All the enormous benefits derivable from collaboration would be lost to them; and since it takes but a little thing long continued in the struggle for life to work great changes, it is easily conceivable that this vice of lying might exterminate the race that became addicted to it

The wild animals no doubt afford safer instances, but they are so difficult of observation that few are at hand. One of the most remarkable cases in point is among Wolves. I do not know that the incident is true, but it sounds true, and there is no inherent reason why it should not be so. The story appeared in the 'Leisure Hour' in the volume of 1892–3, and was written by E. L. Hickey.

It was many and many a league away
    from the place where now we are,
And many a year ago it happ'ed in the
    land of the Great White Czar.
It was morn – I remember how cold it felt –
    out under a low pale sky,
When we moored our boat on the river bank,
    my companion Leigh and I.

And the plunge in the water unwarmed of the sun
    was less for desire than pluck,
And we hurried on our clothes again and longed
    for our breakfast luck;
When all of a sudden he clutched my arm
    and pointed across, and there
We stood up side by side and watched,
    and as mute as the dead we were.

We saw the grey-wolfs fateful spring,
    and we saw the death of the deer.

And the grey-wolf left the body alone,
    and swift as the feet of fear
His feet sped over the brow of the hill,
    and we lost the sight of him
Who had left the dead deer there
    on the ground uneaten, body or limb.

So when he vanished out of our sight
    we rowed our boat across,
And lifted the carcass and rowed again
    to the other side. The loss
For you, good Master Wolf, much more
    than the gain for us will be.
'T were half a pity to spoil your sport,
    except that we fain would see

The reason why with hunger unstaunched
    you have left your quarry behind;
Red-toothed, red-mawed, foregone your meal;
    Sir Wolf, we'll know your mind.
Hungry and cold we waited and watched
    to see him return on his track;
At last we spied him atop of the hill,
    the same grey-wolf come back,

No longer alone, but a leader of wolves,
    the head of a grewsome pack.
He went right up to the very place
    where the dead deer's body had lain,
And he sniffed and looked for the prey of his claws,
    the beast that himself had slain.
The deer at our feet and the river between
    and the searching all in vain.

He threw up his muzzle and slunk his tail
    and whined so pitifully,
And the whole pack howled and fell on him –
    we hardly could bear to see.

Breaker of civic law, or pact,
   or whatever they deemed of him.
He knew his fate and he met his fate,
   for they tore him limb from limb.

I tell you we felt as we ne'er felt since
   ever our days began –
Less like men that had cozened a brute
   than men that had murdered a man.

This, of course, was a tragic miscarriage of justice, but the principle is well known. All the higher animals profit by each other's knowledge through methods of intercommunication. Falsification would certainly work dire disaster.

Commandment X

Against Coveting

The broad principle of this commandment is against unduly hankering for a neighbour's property, against scheming to dispossess him.

A remarkable case has occurred many times of late in the country around Yellowstone Park. It may have present application.

A band of Wapiti drifting southward to their winter range came on the haystack of a pioneer. It was so fenced in that they could not get near, but it smelt so desirable that the band lingered about it, hoping some time to get possession. Thus the days passed, the Deer grew weaker, winter came down, and the whole band perished; whereas, had they moved on or worked to find their proper food they would, as often before, have come safely through to the spring.

In this case I am by no means sure of the principle involved, and cite the incident with much hesitancy. A weak spot in the illustration is the circumstance that the possessor of the stack was *not another Elk*.

A more nearly pertinent circumstance was recently told me by a friend.*

Under the barn eaves at his home a colony of Swallows had for long been established. In the spring of 1885 a pair of Bluebirds came and took forcible possession of one of the nests. The owners first tried to oust the invaders, next the whole Swallow colony joined in the attempt, without success. The Bluebird inside was entrenched behind hard mud walls, and defied them. At length the Swallows came in a body, each with a pellet of mud, and walled up the entrance to the nest. The Bluebird in possession starved to death, and was found there ten days later.

In this case the retribution came direct from the Swallows, in obedience to the inner impulse. But it is clear that Bluebirds adopting habitually these methods of nesting would become parasites dependent on the Swallows; this additional burden might easily turn the balance of nature against the Swallows, ending in their death as a species and, of course, the death of their dependents.

A still more obvious episode I have seen many times in the barnyard. A Hen had made a nest in a certain place, and was already sitting. Later another Hen, desiring the same nest, took possession several times during the owner's brief absence, adding some of her own eggs, and endeavouring to sit. The result was a state of war, and the eggs of both Hens were destroyed.

It is not easy to say whether this was coveting or stealing, but I find it equally difficult to discriminate between the two laws that forbid these things.

This was the last of the lower group of commandments, and here my pathway seemed to end. If the next in order merely enforced a period of rest among toilers, then could I find illustrations among all toilers. But this would be a physical interpretation, and would take it out of

* Mr. H. Dallas, of Morristown, Ohio.

the superior class of ordinances, where commentators generally agree that it belongs. They maintain that its purpose is to set apart a time for spiritual matters, and of this there was no discernible recognition in my field. I could find nothing in the animal world that seemed to suggest any relation to a Supreme Being.

Therefore I reformed my theory to fit the new facts, and presented it thus:

The first four commandments have a purely spiritual bearing; the last six are physical. Man is concerned with all, the animals only with the last six.

I was also struck by the thought that in all cases the ultimate penalty is death.

There was another, a disappointing conclusion forced on me. It seems that law exists only between members of the same species. Wolf and Wolf have law, Crow and Crow, Weasel and Weasel, Mouse and Mouse even, but never so far as I can see. Wolf and Mouse, or Crow and Weasel. There is nothing but bitter war between them; their might is their right.

We should not marvel at this, however, since it was ever thus with man until the latest light came. Ask any savage which is worse, to steal some trifling article, the property of his tribesman, or to massacre a family of the neighbouring tribe. He will as surely answer the former as we should the latter.

Only in his highest development is man capable of the broad love and sympathy that take in all the human race, and extend even to the beasts of the field.

With this conclusion then I was forced to halt the investigation: That we may find in the animals the beginnings of man's physical and . mental attributes, but not a vestige of foundation for his spiritual nature. And the conclusion seemed the end. Because the trail became obscured I thought it went no further. But a faint glimmering of light came unexpectedly.

My twenty-five years of journals had been copied and the copies cut up so that incidents referring to each subject might easily be filed. I found several new subjects well represented, such as the evolution of sanitation, amusement, intercommunication, etc, and a final department of *unexplained strange instances*; when I got many of these together I found that they began to explain each other. To make this clear I give several of them now:

1st Dr. G. B. Grinnell tells me that when out shooting with General Custer's party near the Black Hills in 1874, they observed a Falcon in pursuit of a wild Pigeon; when the latter saw that it could not escape its winged foe, it took refuge among the men, resting on one of the saddles.

2d. Mr. Geo. F. Guernsey, of Fort Qu'Appelle, Saskatchewan, writes me that some years ago a neighbour and his wife standing in their cattle yard saw a pack of five Coyotes chasing a Fox. The Fox was pretty nearly spent; it ran finally right up to the woman, and crouched for protection at her feet.

3d. In the December of 1886, I was hunting Snow-shoe Rabbits in a little grove near Carberry. The one I was pursuing escaped. It was an exceedingly cold day, some 35 degrees below zero. I laid my gun on my sleigh and busied myself lighting a fire to make some tea. As I cowered over this trying to think I was getting warm, I saw a Rabbit running through the little grove. It ran past me some forty yards away; then I noticed some twenty-five feet behind it another Rabbit running very fast in pursuit The first circled round, came nearer. Now I saw that the smaller Rabbit was not a Rabbit at all, but a white Weasel, an Ermine, that was running the Rabbit down. The chase continued around me, but ever nearer. Though so much swifter the Rabbit was losing because the paralysis of terror was setting in.

The Weasel was within a few feet of his victim and ready for the final spring, when that Rabbit made a rush toward me, and took refuge under the sleigh near my feet – *came to me*, who had been trying to kill it a few minutes before.

The Weasel flashed about and under the snow, curling his nose a little; then realizing that he was probably running into danger, darted under brush and snow to vanish. The Rabbit cowered at my feet for a few minutes, but recovered and hopped away in another direction.

4th. In the October of 1898, I was riding across the Bighorn Basin (Wyoming) with Mrs. Seton and Mr. A. A. Anderson, when we noticed near the horizon some bright white specks. They were moving about, disappearing and showing again. Then two of them seemed to dart erratically over the plain, keeping always just so far apart Soon these left the others and careered about like twin meteors, this way and that, then our way; at first in changing line, but later directly toward us.

Their wonderful speed soon ate up the intervening mile or two, and we now saw clearly that they were Antelope, one in pursuit of the other. High over their heads a Golden Eagle was sailing.

On they came; the half-mile snrank to a couple of hundred yards, and we saw that they were bucks, the hinder one larger, dashing straight toward us still. As they yet neared we could see the smaller one making desperate efforts to avoid the savage lunges of the big one's horns, and barely maintaining the scant six feet that were between him and his foe.

We reined up to watch, for now it was clear that the smaller buck had been defeated in battle with an exceptionally vicious rival, and was trying to save his life by flight. But his heaving flanks and gaping, dribbling mouth showed that he could not hold out much longer. Straight on he came toward us, the deadliest foes of his race, the ones he fears the most

He was between two deaths – which should he choose? He seemed not to hesitate – the two hundred yards shrank to one hundred, the hundred to fifty – then the pursuer slacked his speed. It would be folly to come farther. The fugitive kept on until he dashed right in among our startled horses. The Eagle alighted on the rock two hundred yards away.

The victorious buck veered off, shaking his sharp black horns and circling at a safe distance around our cavalcade to intercept his victim when he should come out the other side. But the victim did not come out. He felt he was saved, and he stayed with us. The other buck seeing that he was balked, gave up the attempt, and turning back, sailed across the plain till he became again a white speck that joined the other specks, no doubt the does that had caused the duel.

The vanquished buck beside us stood panting, with his tongue out, and showing every sign of dire distress. It would have been easy to lasso him, but none of us had any desire to do him harm. In a very short time he regained his wind, and having seen his foe away to a safe distance, he left our company to go off in the opposite direction.

The Eagle realised now that he was mistaken in supposing that something was to be killed, and that there would be pickings for him. He rose in haste and soared to a safe distance.

5th. This I heard from George Crawford, the well-known guide of Mattawa; it was corroborated by others in camp:

In March, 1888, while out with his partner to catch Moose for Dr. S.

Webb, he came on a Moose-calf track in the deep snow. There was no sign of a cow, so they turned their Dog loose. Very soon they heard him barking, and came up to the calf It rushed toward them with bristling mane. His partner ran away, and he got behind a tree. The calf charged up to him and quickly wheeled to face the Dog. It paid no heed to the man then, but when he turned homeward it followed him for protection, crowding up close and watching the Dog. At home he put a halter on it, and it allowed him to lead it quietly into the stable. It was shipped to Dr. Webb, and is now roaming the Adirondacks.

6th. The following was related to me by Edouard Crête, of Deux Rivières:

In late September of 1893, a mail-carrier was starting from Bear Lake to Deux Rivières. Crête showed him the short cut over Brûlé Lake. Some hours later two men were out that way looking for axe-handles, and heard the mail-carrier shouting for help. Instead of going to him they ran back to camp in great fear. The foreman picked up a rifle and, accompanied by Crête, went as fast as possible to the place. They heard the shouting as soon as they came within a half-mile. When near enough, he called out: 'A Moose has got me up a tree.' They came close, and saw it was a cow Moose. She would neither go away nor charge. Indeed, she paid no attention to them. The foreman, Jean Basquin, walked up within twenty yards and shot her.

The mail-carrier, it seems, had come on the cow suddenly. She was alone, but came toward him squealing. Her mane was up, and she seemed to be threatening him. He had nothing but a hatchet, so ran for a tree, and happened to find one leaning so much that he could walk up. She ran behind him within touching distance all the way, but did not strike at him. The tree at the highest point was only ten feet up. Here the man sat, the Moose below. She could easily have struck him, but made no attempt to do so. There she stayed watching him; her mane bristled all the time.

When she heard the other men coming she merely turned her head, but during the three hours that she kept the man up that tree she did not leave the spot for a moment.

When examined after skinning, her left side was found in a dreadful condition. Evidently she had been attacked by a bull Moose some days before. The horns had pierced her flank in five places. The side was all inflamed and matter had formed in four places. She must have been suffering great pain, and would surely have died before long. They could not make out why she should go to the man, but it is quite certain she was not there to do him any harm, for she had every opportunity and did not strike at him once.

Why then the angry bristling of her mane? Perhaps it was not anger. It may have been any other intense feeling. It is not easy to discriminate so finely the expressions of animal emotion. We only know that she was greatly wrought up about something.

These are the incidents. They seem to have a common principle. Divested of externals, what is the cardinal thought in each? This, I take it – that when the animals are in terrible trouble, when they have done all that they can do, and are face to face with despair and death, there is then revealed in them an instinct, deep-laid – and deeper laid as the animal is higher –which prompts them in their dire extremity to throw themselves on the mercy of some other power, not knowing, indeed, whether it be friendly or not, but very sure that it is superior.

Here perhaps is the looked-for light. I was seeking in the animal nature for beginnings of the spiritual life in man, for something that might respond to the four higher ordinances. Maybe in this instinct of the brute in extremity, we have revealed the foundation of something which ultimately had its highest development in man, reaching, indeed, like the Heathen Thinker's Tree, from root in the earthy darkness to its fruit in the Realm of Light.